PUBLIC RELATIONS
RESEARCH ANNUAL
Volume 2

PUBLIC RELATIONS RESEARCH ANNUAL
Volume 2

A publication of the Public Relations Division, Association for Education in Journalism and Mass Communication.

EDITORS

Larissa A. Grunig
James E. Grunig
University of Maryland at College Park

EDITORIAL BOARD

PUBLIC RELATIONS RESEARCH ANNUAL
Volume 2

Edited by
Larissa A. Grunig
James E. Grunig

 LAWRENCE ERLBAUM ASSOCIATES, PUBLISHERS
1990   **Hillsdale, New Jersey**   **Hove and London**

Lawrence Erlbaum Associates, Inc., Publishers
365 Broadway
Hillsdale, New Jersey 07642

Library of Congress Cataloging-in-Publication Data
ISBN 0–8058–0678–4
ISSN 1042–1408

Printed in the United States of America
10 9 8 7 6 5 4 3 2 1

Contents

_____ **PART I**

RESEARCH REVIEWS

_____ **PART II**

REPORTS OF ORIGINAL RESEARCH

Preface

Our purpose in this second volume of a fledgling series is to challenge and extend the field of research in public relations. It is not enough to serve the existing interests of our contributors and our readers. As editors, we assume what our students would call an "awesome" burden: helping to develop the character of our discipline by determining what becomes legitimate knowledge.

Gatekeeper takes on new meaning when one understands that the contents of a volume result in setting the parameters of its field. We have become members of what Philip G. Altbach, editor of the *Comparative Education Review*, called "the small, largely invisible tribe of editors of scholarly journals. . . [who] have a great deal of power." Unremunerated, of course, but we will take what we can get. As David Sloan, who edits *American Journalism*, asked in a recent *CLIO*, "Does the world know anyone with more power over the lives of scholars than a journal editor?"

The more relevant concern, to us, is the power the *Public Relations Research Annual* may have over the life of the discipline. So, we have tried to publicize the existence of the *Annual* to disparate groups of scholars. We have, in some cases, solicited chapters directly from those whose work has excited and intrigued us. The tension in creating an annual that is stable yet not stagnant dictates this active stance.

At the same time, we assume much about the prior knowledge, interests, and commitment of our readers. Still, we hope that each chapter reporting on original research provides enough context for understanding even if the area of inquiry is a new one for the reader. We balanced this need for making sense out of novel information against the length inherent in contextualization. We hope these articles avoid the problem publishers call "mentioning," or being long on results without adequate conceptualization and explanation. This means, however, that in some cases the articles fail to provide the "quick read" that the busy educator, practitioner, or researcher may want. In other words, we do not impose length limits on manuscript submissions.

As we prepared for this second volume of the _Annual,_ we did develop explicit criteria for reviewing manuscripts. Like Scott Armstrong of the Wharton School, we consider the review process as one key discriminator between scientific and fiction journals. Writing on "Research on Scientific Journals: Implications for Editors and Authors" in the _Journal of Forecasting 1_(1), Armstrong described the six standards of objectivity, replicability, importance, competence, intelligibility, and efficiency. Thus, we ask our referees in the blind reviewing process to consider whether the chapter contains original research or observations (rather than literature reviews alone), makes a significant contribution to theory, relies on appropriate methodology, and is well organized and stylistically correct.

We are trying to avoid O'Brien's law: If an editor can reject your paper, he or she will. (O'Brien, of course, is a first cousin to Murphy.) The corollary? If you submit the paper to a second editor, that journal invariably demands an entirely different reference system. No small problem, when you consider that Maeve O'Connor of the _British Medical Journal_ has discovered at least 2,632 possibilities for reference style in scientific journals. The message for potential contributors? We use Lawrence Erlbaum guidelines, which are similar to APA style.

Attempts to write and edit intelligibly and to standardize style aside, we understand from postmodernist literary theory that objective, unambiguous communication may well be unattainable. We are hoping, rather, that each chapter contributes to our understanding of public relations—its history, its legal implications, its process and its effects, its relationship to other organizational functions, the gender gap therein, and so forth. We hope each reader learns something that will cause him or her to teach with a new perspective, to practice more effectively, or to conduct his or her own program of research with added vigor and insight.

Now a word of thanks for the members of our editorial board who served as referees for the chapters in this volume. The quality of their reviews and their commitment to meeting our deadlines should be rewarded. As Steve Chaffee, former editor of _Communication Research,_ said at a recent panel on academic journals, editors should be able to contribute letters for the tenure files of such superior commentators. The collegial review process is essential.

The final judgments about what chapters appear here, however, must lie with the _Annual's_ co-editors. So we end this preface as we began, talking about the role of the editors. In making hard decisions, we considered all relevant "publics" in the process: reviewers, authors, and readers alike. We are reminded here of Virginia Woolf, who argued that although each critic—or reviewer—may be correct in his or her assessment of a piece of writing, this "truth" never will be the same for any two people. Thus, we leave it to you, the reader, to decide in the end whether we have honored this second edition of the *Annual* with what we consider to be the best of the research in public relations available for publication this year.

Larissa A. Grunig
James E. Grunig

PART I

RESEARCH REVIEWS

The Innovation of Research in Public Relations Practice: Review of a Program of Studies

David M. Dozier
San Diego State University

This chapter reviews a stream of research on the diffusion of program research as an innovation in the practice of public relations. *Program research* is the use of social scientific research techniques—both quantitative and qualitative—to plan public relations programs, monitor their implementation, and evaluate their impact.

Ten separate empirical studies are reviewed, sketching a picture of the emergence of research in the practice of public relations and communication management. Empirical linkage is made among program research, the model of public relations practice, the roles practitioners play, the degree practitioners participate in management decision making, the organizational philosophy of the dominant coalition, and the role gender plays in these processes.

This chapter provides a partial explanation for why the innovation of research has diffused through the practice of public relations. This can be understood usefully at the individual level of analysis from a diffusion of innovations perspective. To understand program research at the organizational level of analysis, diffusion theory is supplemented with concepts from open systems theory as applied to organizations.

PUBLIC RELATIONS RESEARCH AS AN INNOVATION

An *innovation* is an "idea, practice or object that is perceived as new" (Rogers, 1983, p. 11). Program research in public relations fits this definition. Resistance exists among contemporary practitioners, trained as writers rather than social scientists, neither predisposed nor competent to conduct or use public relations research (Pennington, 1980; Wright, 1979). Diffusion of innovation concepts help explain why research is used by some practitioners in some organizations—and not by others.

At the individual level of analysis, public relations research is usefully analyzed as clusters of research activities, each cluster having attributes that speed or impede diffusion. These attributes interact with practitioner characteristics, affecting types of research adopted and rates of adoption.

Some practitioners do not engage in any program research; others conduct extensive research. Practitioners vary in the kinds of research methods they use, from intuitive, informal "seat-of-the-pants" research to rigorous scientific studies. Although little longitudinal scholarly research is available, the best evidence is that—over time—more practitioners are doing research and are doing research more frequently (Dozier, 1984b).

The Process of Innovation Diffusion

Prior diffusion research suggests that public relations program research is evaluated by individual practitioners in five stages: (a) knowledge, (b) persuasion, (c) decision, (d) implementation, and (e) confirmation. At any point, some practitioners are at the knowledge state, becoming aware of public relations research and learning something of how it works (Rogers, 1983). Others develop opinions about program research, either positive or negative (Rogers, 1983). Still others decide either to adopt or reject the innovation (Rogers, 1983). Some put program research to use to plan, monitor, and evaluate public relations programs. Of those, some continue to use research during the confirmation stage, whereas others discontinue research practices.

Technology Cluster

Program research is usefully regarded as a set of discrete innovations. Social scientific research uses multiple methodological approaches and techniques, each of which may be perceived by potential adopters as separate innovations. Thus, program research is a *technology cluster*, a set of distinguishable elements of technology that are perceived as closely interrelated (Rogers, 1983).

Program Evaluation

Conceptually, one innovation subset of the technological cluster is *program evaluation*, research used to determine if public relations programs have achieved their goals and objectives among target publics. Program evaluation research answers the question: "What works?" Evaluation research utilization in public relations, however, indicates that evaluation may be a relatively sophisticated research application only infrequently used (Dozier, 1984b). Grunig (1983) thus described the status of evaluation research in public relations, lamenting:

> I have begun to feel more and more like the fundamentalist minister railing against sin; the difference being that I have railed *for* evaluation [in public relations practice]. Just as everyone is against sin, so most public relations people I talk to are for evaluation. People keep on sinning, however, and PR people continue not to do evaluation research. (p. 28)

Although considerable lip service is paid to the importance of program evaluation in public relations, the rhetorical line is much more enthusiastic than actual utilization.

A problem with evaluation research is that such studies are among the most sophisticated research activities that practitioners can undertake. In program evaluation, clearly defined, quantified objectives must be set in terms of change or maintenance of knowledge, predispositions, and behavior of publics. Longitudinal designs are required to measure impact variables before and after program implementation. Practitioners must employ experimental or quasi-experimental designs, using control groups and comparison groups respectively, to isolate program effects from confounding influences of various threats to internal validity. In short, as Reeves (1983) argued, the "bad news is that evaluation is hard to do well" (p. 17).

The relative complexity of evaluation research as an innovation led academic researchers to seek less complex applications of social science research methods to public relations practices. Kettering argued that research is a state of mind, an attitude. Kettering said that the research-oriented mind holds a "friendly, welcoming attitude toward change, going out to look for change, instead of waiting for it to come" (Cutlip & Center, 1978, pp. 143–144). This attitude in public relations is perhaps best manifested in activities that make up environmental monitoring or environmental scanning.

Environmental Scanning

This innovation subset includes formal and informal activities that public relations practitioners use to learn what is going on in the organization's environment. In systems language, *environmental scanning* is the detection of environmental turbulence or change likely to affect the homeostasis of the system. On a practical level, environmental scanning is fact finding, a sensitivity to "what is going on out there."

Conceptually, program research can be divided into two separate innovation subsets: environmental scanning and program evaluation. Arguably, scientific scanning is easier to understand and easier to implement than scientific evaluations of program impact. Both scanning and evaluation can be conducted according to

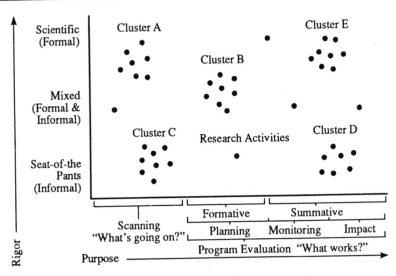

FIG. 1.1.   The rigor and purpose of program research.

stringent standards of the social sciences. However, scholarly study of public relations research must also consider less formal approaches to research. Robinson (1969) described public relations research techniques as ranging on a continuum from the rigorously scientific to informal, "seat-of-the-pants" research. Not only does program research vary in focus or purpose (scanning vs. evaluation), it also varies in scientific rigor.

Rigor and Purpose

Figure 1.1 displays the dimensions of rigor and purpose in program research activities. *Rigor* is the level of confidence practitioners can have in research findings. Rigor ranges from subjective, informal "gut" feelings about "what is going on" and "what works" (seat-of-the-pants) to mixed activities combining both formal and informal research to rigorous scientific studies.

Purpose is the use to which research findings are put. Scanning research serves the purpose of answering the question: "What is going on in the organizational environment?" Program evaluation serves the purpose of determining which program activities are effective, which ones "work." Evaluation research may be divided into formative and summative evaluation. Formative evaluation helps practitioners plan programs and design communication strategies. Summative evaluation research measures the public relations program, both to monitor its implementation (permitting "mid-course" correction) and determine its impact. Figure 1.1 shows illustrative groupings of research activities in the rigor–purpose matrix, as they might be determined by the patterns of practitioner usage.

Attributes of Innovation Subsets

If different research activities form distinct clusters according to how they are used, then each cluster may be conceptualized as an innovation subset. Each innovation subset is posited to have distinct attributes that affect the rate of adoption of that subset. Drawing from diffusion theory, the innovation attributes most relevant to public relations research are perceived complexity and compatibility.

Complexity is the "degree to which an innovation is perceived as difficult to understand and use" (Rogers, 1983, p. 15). *Compatibility* is the "degree to which an innovation is perceived as being consistent with existing values, past experiences, and needs of potential adopters" (Rogers, 1983, p. 15). Rogers said that relative advantage is the "degree to which an innovation is perceived as being better than the idea it supercedes" (p. 213).

Perceptions of compatibility, complexity, and relative advantage are likely affected by practitioners' prior experiences. Particularly relevant to such perceptions are practitioners' formal training in social science research methods. In studies reported here, innovation attributes are not measured directly. However, objective attributes of innovation clusters can be used to posit how they are likely to be perceived by practitioners trained in journalism, English, and speech communication rather than the formal social sciences, mathematics, statistics, and computers.

Prior diffusion research suggests the following propositions:

P1: The more scientific an innovation subset, the more complex and the less compatible practitioners will perceive that innovation subset to be.

P2: The more complex and the less compatible an innovation is perceived to be, the less frequently such a subset is used.

P3: Practitioners with training in social science research methods and techniques will perceive scientific program research as less complex and more compatible than will practitioners without such training.

P4: Practitioners with training in social science research methods and techniques will use scientific program research more frequently than practitioners without such training.

PROGRAM RESEARCH AND THEORIES OF ORGANIZATIONS

Individual practitioners do not make adoption decisions about program research in a vacuum. Rather, program research requires organizational resources and affects the planning, monitoring, and evaluation of public relations programs. Understanding diffusion of public relations program research requires an understanding of how public relations functions in organizations and how program research affects that function.

Program Research From a Systems Perspective

Viewed from an open-systems perspective, public relations is part of the *adaptive subsystem* of the organization (Cutlip, Center, & Broom, 1985; Glaser & Halliday, 1980). This subsystem engages in boundary-spanning activities, gathering information from outside the organization's boundaries to help the organization adapt to its environment.

Public relations has traditionally functioned as if organizations were closed systems. Practitioners who treat their organizations as closed systems, according to Cutlip, Center, and Broom, are like the cuttlefish. A simple-minded squidlike mollusk, the cuttlefish squirts ink indiscrimately when threatened by environmental turbulence, regardless of the nature of the threat. Bell and Bell (1976) described such public relations practitioners as *functionaries* who "attempt to preserve and promote a favorable image of the organization" without regard to the dynamics of changing organizational environments. They noted that such a practitioner "does not function in decision making or even in advisory roles in relation to environmental concerns" (pp. 51–52).

The Importance of Program Research. Systems theory encourages both researchers and practitioners to look at the public relations function from a new perspective. Instead of maintaining a one-way flow of messages outward from the organization, practitioners are encouraged to look at their role as information gatherers, as part of the organization's adaptive subsystem. Program research is essential to the public relations function, when that function is defined in open-systems terms.

Inherent in adaption is the view that the organization itself must change in order to maintain its goal states or *homeostasis.* Paradoxically, organizations as open systems must change themselves in order to endure. When an organization alters its structure and function, systems theorists call the process *morphogenesis.* Applied to public relations, elements of morphogenesis appear in Cutlip et al.'s (1985) *action strategies.* Action strategies make up one part of the planning process. These strategies are steps taken by practitioners and others in the organization to "change the organization's policies, procedures, products, services and behavior to better serve the mutual interests of the organization and its publics" (p. 258). To perform this function, practitioners must use program research to scan the environment and to evaluate programs.

Grunig and Hunt (1984) labeled such morphogenesis within organizations initiated by public relations practitioners as the *two-way symmetrical* public relations model. Unlike the two-way asymmetrical model, where organizations attempt to dominate and control their environments, the two-way symmetrical model presumes that organizations cooperate with and adapt to interpenetrating publics that affect the organization's survival and growth. Program research is essential to both two-way models of public relations.

The two-way models differ from traditional press agentry and public information practices. Information is collected by the practitioner from the environment to contribute to management decision making. Two-way symmetrical public relations practices, as typified by action strategies in the planning process, require practitioner participation in the dominant coalition.

The Dominant Coalition. The *dominant coalition* is made up of constituents within organizations with the power to influence decisions, set organizational goals, and decide how those goals will be met (Robbins, 1987). Membership in the dominant coalition involves more than personal or professional status. Indeed, the very definition of the function depends on the vertical location of public relations in the organizational structure (Dozier, 1988a). When the top practitioner in an organization is excluded from the dominant coalition, strategic decisions are made without benefit of information about the probable reactions of key publics. The function is not part of the organization's adaptive subsystem; public relations programs become reactive and one-way.

When the public relations function is included in the dominant coalition, practitioners can guide strategic decisions to avoid threats in a turbulent environment. Public relations programs are implemented proactively to avoid conflicts that reduce autonomy. Publics are defined dynamically. The horizontal structure of the public relations unit is ad hoc, typified by "tasks forces" and "special committees" assigned to publics and programs to solve problems and move on to new challenges (Dozier & Grunig, 1989).

Roles and Program Research. Practitioners play different roles in organizations. Generally, practitioners play either the manager or the technician role predominantly. Public relations *managers* make communication policy decisions and are held accountable for the success or failure of public relations programs (Dozier, 1983). They regard themselves, and are regarded by others, as public relations experts. Playing the manager role predominantly is posited to correlate with research utilization, because scanning information is essential for program planning and impact evaluation is essential for program accountability. Because planning and accountability are attributes of the manager role, managers are posited to do more research than practitioners who do not manage (Broom & Dozier, 1986).

Public relations *technicians*, on the other hand, implement communication programs planned by others. Removed from the dominant coalition, such practitioners crank out communications about the organization in isolation from management decision making, a low-level output function (Broom, 1982; Center & Broom, 1983). Playing the technician role predominantly is posited to be unrelated to the use of scientific or informal research (Broom & Dozier, 1986).

John A. Koten, then vice president for corporate communications at Illinois Bell, summed up the relation between program research, practitioner role, and participation in management decision making:

to be influential, you have to be at the decision table and be part of corporate governance. You can be there if the things you are doing are supported by *facts*. That is where the public relations person has generally been weak and why, in most organizations, public relations functions at a lower level. The idea is to be where decisions are made in order to impact the future of the company. To do so, you have to be like the lawyer or financial officer, the personnel officer or operations person. You have to have *hard data*. All of these guys are operating with information. If public relations people want to be there and participate, then they need to have some hard data to work with. Since most of them don't have hard information, they're never part of decision making. (Dozier, 1986, p. 2)

The Environmental Imperative.   Open-systems theory—as applied to the public relations function in organizations—suggests that the organization's environment should have a lot to do with the structure and function of public relations. Some organizations operate in organizational environments fraught with turbulence and threats to autonomy. The more turbulent and threatening the environment, the more important the public relations function should be to the organization (McElreath, 1977).

Some research indicates that the manager role is positively related to environmental uncertainty (Acharya, 1981, 1983). However, empirical linkage is weak between the way public relations functions and the way environments change and threaten organizational autonomy. L. Grunig, J. Grunig, and others have conducted a number of studies linking environmental niche, organizational type, and the model of public relations practiced in organizations. They conclude that such linkage is weak, and that the application of open systems theory was more normative than positive (Grunig & Grunig, 1986).

Scholarly research of public relations practices has found only weak links between what goes on outside organizations and how public relations is practiced inside organizations. This finding is not unique to public relations. Organizational theorists have generally found that organizational structures poorly match environmental conditions (Child, 1972; Pfeffer, 1978, 1979, 1981; Simon, 1976).

Impermeable Boundaries and Historicist Models.   The concept of impermeability of organizational boundaries permits open-systems theory to accommodate weak relations between environmental conditions and internal structures. Organizations with *impermeable* system boundaries are insensitive to environmental conditions; internal structures have little or no relation to environments. In such organizations, the public relations function is unresponsive to environmental pressures and program research is nonexistent. That is because the organization does not factor environmental inputs into organizational decision making.

Systems theorists argue that structures that are not responsive to environmental conditions are products of an historicist causal model (Stinchcombe, 1968). Organizations—acting as *closed* systems—structure or "define" the public relations function at one point in time, as a preference of those with decision-making power.

Thereafter, the structure, plans, and programs of public relations are institu-tionalized, replicated each planning cycle as appropriate because "that's what we've always done." The horizontal structure and vertical position of the public relations unit is not a response to the organization's environment. Rather, the horizontal and vertical attributes of the unit reflect "historical, routine, and institu-tionalized behaviors" (Broom, 1986, p. 7). Further, the costs of the public relations unit are sunk. Changing the function involves redesign and replacement costs, whereas institutionalized replication need not reconsider sunk costs (Broom, 1986).

Broom's use of the concepts of impermeable system boundaries and the histor-icist causal model led public relations scholars to look further for theory that would explain weak linkage between organizational environments and the structure and function of public relations within organizations (Dozier & Grunig, 1989). Such concepts are found in the power-control perspective in organizational theory.

Power-Control Perspective and Program Research

Weak relationships between environments and organizational structure have forced organizational theorists to rethink ways organizations are structured. The power-control perspective suggests that dominant coalitions do not seek structures that match environmental conditions to optimize organizational goals. Because overall organizational goals and the goals of individual members of the dominant coalition are infrequently the same, decisions are inherently nonrational and are sensitive to the size and domain of internal subunits. Decisions are outcomes of power struggles among competing interests in the coalition. Decision making does not optimize but "satisfices" organizational effectiveness. Outcomes are not op-timal, only "good enough" (Robbins, 1987, p. 178).

How Public Relations is Defined.   Public relations units do not reflect rational optimization of the goodness of fit between internal structure and external environ-ment. According to the power-control perspective, the function is defined politi-cally, as the outcome of a power struggle within the dominant coalition. Once set, according to this perspective, organizational structure is difficult to change. Chang-ing the structure of the public relations unit, such as including practitioners in the dominant coalition, borders on quasi-revolutions (Pfeffer, 1978).

Research and Optimization of Response.   What role does public relations re-search play in the power-control perspective of the function? Both open-systems theory and the power-control perspective suggest the importance of research—but for different reasons. Open-systems theory (and its application to organization theory as the environmental imperative) suggests that organizations value environ-mental scanning and public relations program evaluation because organizations seek to *optimize* responses to environments. The value of program research in decision making is a function of the "openness" of the dominant coalition to its environment, the degree to which the dominant coalition runs the organization like an open system.

The power-control perspective suggests that dominant coalitions tend toward mechanization and bureaucracy (Robbins, 1987). Organic structures, which resist mechanization and bureaucracy, are arguably products of failures by dominant coalitions to resolve conflicting size and domain struggles among constituents. Organic structure is not necessarily an optimizing structure, a rational response to perceived environmental turbulence and threat as the environmental imperative implies. Rather, organic structure is what organizations get when differing goals of members of the dominant coalition cannot be reconciled in a more mechanistic, bureaucratic structure.

Program Research as a Scarce Resource.   Research, from a power-control perspective, is a scarce and valued resource. Research is used to determine which policies, procedures, and actions will "satisfice" environmental imperatives while accommodating the divergent interests of coalition members. Research may be used to delay decisions, to justify politically expedient decisions, to torpedo decisions that run counter to vested interests of coalition members, and to legitimize a covertly political decision-making process as objective optimization of organizational responses to environmental pressures (Suchman, 1967).

The Politics of Program Research.   Studies by Weiss (1975) and others of utilization of evaluation research point to the political nature of research in organizations. This is consistent with the power-control perspective. Those who do research can use that information to influence highly politicized decisions of dominant coalitions. The power-control perspective suggests that public relations program research is a tool—a weapon perhaps—in the political struggle to demonstrate the impact of public relations programs and to contribute to decision making by knowing "what is going on out there." Success in this struggle means greater financial and personnel resources for the public relations unit and greater power over decisions of the dominant coalition.

The power-control perspective suggests that practitioners doing research should understand the political nature of its role in decision making. Broom and Dozier (1990) suggested several steps that practitioners take to insure that program research is actually used. These include:

1. Show how research findings relate to current concerns, policies, procedures, and practices of the organization before discussing long-term relevance.

2. Maintain frequent and direct participation of members of the dominant coalition throughout the research project.

3. Avoid the appearance of a vested interest in research outcomes among research service providers.

4. Use research designs and methods that cannot be discounted by the dominant coalition members on scientific or technical grounds.

5. Emphasize those research findings that corroborate rather than contradict the reference frame and expectations of the dominant coalition.

6. Avoid negative surprises from research findings and provide wiggle room for compromise when recommendations are politically sensitive.

These recommendations recognize that there is nothing neutral about program research. Environmental scanning and program evaluation affect a wide range of organizational decisions. Research findings can threaten assumptions of the dominant coalition, upset delicate political compromises, and introduce new members to the dominant coalition. Seeking rational and apolitical optimization of organizational responses to environmental pressures, as suggested by systems theory, is naive and ineffective.

A Synthesis of Theories

The diffusion of program research in public relations practices is usefully understood at both the micro (practitioner) and meso (organization) levels of analysis. At the practitioner level, program research is perceived as a technology cluster, a set of interrelated technologies with differing perceived attributes. Key perceived attributes are the compatibility of program research with existing values and past experience, the complexity of each cluster, and the relative advantage of program research over traditional approaches to planning, implementing, and evaluating public relations programs. When program research is perceived as complex, as lacking relative advantage, and as incompatible with values and experience, adoption of program research is unlikely.

Adoption decisions are stimulated or impeded by organizational factors as well. When practitioners perform technician roles predominantly at lower hierarchical levels in organizations, adoption of program research is impeded. Excluded from the dominant coalition, such practitioners implement program decisions made by others. Such practitioners are unlikely to need program research (low relative advantage). Trained largely in the communication arts and ill-equipped by training or experience to understand and use social science research methods, such practitioners are likely to view program research as complex and incompatible. Organizational factors reinforce these predispositions of practitioners. Routinized public relations programs are replicated year after year by dominant coalitions. Innovative practitioners who perceive program research as relatively advantageous, compatible, and simple may well experience frustration with the role expectations sent by the dominant coalition and leave the organization.

Adoption of program research is stimulated by quasi-revolutions in dominant coalitions. Dominant coalitions—typified by mechanistic, bureaucratic decision making—yield to more organic structures. Routinized public relations programs, as well as other forms of organizational behavior, no longer satisfice. Public relations units may be asked to account for their effectiveness. Opportunities exist for practitioners to use program research as a scarce resource, as a passport to management decision making. Practitioners who perceive program research as relatively complex, incompatible, and disadvantageous are likely to be threatened by new role expectations sent by the dominant coalition. Such practitioners may leave the organization, either voluntarily or involuntarily.

Individual and organizational factors interact in complex and dynamic ways to either impede or stimulate program research adoption. Program research adoption is optimized when two conditions simultaneously occur:

1. The practitioner is predisposed by training and experience to perceive program research as simple, compatible, and relatively advantageous.
2. The organization's structure is organic and the dominant coalition includes public relations practitioners in decision making.

Adoption is impeded whenever either condition does not prevail. Theory suggests that adoption of program research occurs only infrequently at the intersect of optimal practitioner and organizational conditions.

FINDINGS FROM PRACTITIONER STUDIES

The synthesis of theories provides a framework for interpreting findings of several scholarly studies of practitioners and program research utilization. A 1981 study of professionally affiliated practitioners in San Diego, California, provided an empirical basis for clustering a variety of program evaluation activities into distinct innovation subsets. A 12-item set was developed, asking practitioners how often they engaged in different types of evaluation activities. Items measure frequency of formative evaluation, dissemination evaluation, and impact evaluation. For each type, items measured both rigorous scientific evaluation activities and more informal "seat-of-the-pants" evaluation activities (Dozier, 1981, 1984a).

Three Approaches to Evaluation Research

Factor analysis of the item set yielded three approaches to program evaluation.[1] One approach uses scientific cross-sectional studies, focus group studies, public opinion surveys, and quantitative studies of complaints by phone and letter to

---

[1]Factors were extracted using principal factoring with iterations. Three factors with eigenvalues greater than 1 were rotated to a varimax solution. Factor indices, using the computed means of items with strong loadings on each factor, were created for each factor. All relationships were tested using these indices. The extraction strategy was selected for the pragmatic reason that this is the method of extraction most frequently utilized and most familiar to the largest number of readers. Alternate extraction strategies were used on these and other data reported in this chapter. The extraction strategy had little substantive impact on the emergent factor structure. The rotation strategy was selected to maximize item loadings on a single factor, expediting interpretation.

measure public relations program impact. A second approach uses informal information-gathering techniques. This style includes monitoring placements through close media contacts, attending meetings and hearings, reviewing communication strategies with other professional communicators, and "keeping my eyes and ears open" for public reactions to the organization. A third approach involves measures of media placements, including a comprehensive clip file, inches placed, reach, and other vital statistics, as well as formal, ongoing content analysis of placements (Dozier, 1984a).

These findings suggest that program evaluation research in public relations is not unidimensional. Rather, program evaluation is a cluster of technologies, each approach with its own distinct attributes as an innovation. Scientific evaluation requires understanding of social scientific methodologies. Seat-of-pants evaluation, on the other hand, is a simple extension of informal newsgathering techniques more familiar to practitioners. (Of the practitioners surveyed, 43% said they were reporters before becoming public relations practitioners, averaging 3.5 years of employment as journalists.) Evaluations of clip files fall in between, as they require some computational skills but involve counts of newspaper and magazine clips familiar to working journalists.

Compatibility and Complexity. Using diffusion theory, different rates of diffusion are posited, based on attributes of the different subsets of the technology cluster. The more compatible an evaluation style is perceived, the more rapidly that subset of the technology cluster will diffuse. The less complex an evaluation style is perceived, the more rapidly it will diffuse.

Academic Preparation. Respondents did not report their perceptions (complexity and compatibility) of each evaluation approach. Respondents were asked, however, to indicate college coursework they had taken. Theoretically, practitioners who have taken coursework related to social scientific research methods would find scientific impact evaluation more compatible and less complex than would practitioners without formal preparation in social scientific methods. This, in turn, would speed adoption of scientific evaluation methods among practitioners receiving such preparation.

Preparation and Research Activities. Frequency of scientific evaluation activities by practitioners correlate with coursework (number of courses) in the social sciences ($r = .20, N = 163, p = .006$), statistics ($r = .29, N = 163, p < .01$), and computers ($r = .15, N = 163, p = .03$). Social science and statistics coursework do not correlate with seat-of-pants evaluation and computer coursework posted a negative correlations ($r = -.16, N = 164, p = .02$). Whereas a majority of practitioners had taken at least one course in sociology, psychology, political science, and so forth, only 25% had ever completed a statistics course. Only 12% had ever completed a computer class.

Indeed, scientific evaluations of public relations programs (at the time of the

survey) was the least frequent evaluation strategy. Twenty-two percent of respondents reported "never" engaging in scientific impact evaluation (on a 7-point
"never" to "always" scale) and none reported "always" using such research. Median
practitioner scores on the scientific evaluation scale was 2.4. The most popular
evaluation technique is seat-of-pants evaluation, showing a median score of 5.0,
followed by clip file evaluation with a median of 4.4. According to theory, the more
scientific the evaluation style, the less compatible and the more complex practitioners are likely to perceive it. Findings show that the more scientific the style, the
less frequently it is used.

Two Approaches to Environmental Scanning

In 1985, a national survey was conducted of members of the Public Relations
Society of America (PRSA) and the International Association of Business Communicators (IABC; Dozier, 1986). As in prior studies of evaluation research, the survey
sought to determine if scanning research is unidimensional or if scanning activities
cluster empirically to form distinct innovation subsets.

Two approaches to scanning emerged from factor analysis of 40 items measuring
public relations scanning activities.[2] Items were drawn from the professional public
relations literature and from a focus group study of practitioners. One approach
consists of formal studies, surveys, subscription to public opinion surveys, public
relations audits, demographic data, and outside specialists to gather information on
publics and the organization's environment. A second approach consists of phoning
members of publics to keep in touch, talking with field personnel, depth interviews,
phoning participants after special events, reviewing complaints, tracking public
opinion through newspapers, and work-group meetings to gather information
(Dozier, 1986).

Combined Measures of Scanning and Evaluation

In 1987, a survey of IABC members in the United States, Canada, and the United
Kingdom measured the frequency of evaluation and scanning activities in a combined instrument (Dozier, 1988b). Three factors emerged from the item set,
constituting three empirically derived program research approaches combining
evaluation and scanning.[3]

---

[2]Factors were extracted using principal factoring with iterations. Ten factors with eigenvalues
greater than 1 were rotated to a varimax solution. Of the 10 factors, the first 2 factors accounted for 64%
of common variance and were used to construct indices of environmental scanning. All relationships
were tested using these indices. The large number of factors was due in part to the large number of
items in the item set. The 8 factors not included in subsequent analysis were excluded because they
accounted for little of the common variance, included few items (which reduced their interpretability),
and would likely prove unstable in subsequent studies employing the same item set.

[3]Factors were extracted using principal factoring with iterations. Four factors with values greater
than 1 were rotated to a final varimax solution. Indices were created for three factors, which accounted

TABLE 1.1
The Scientific Research Approach

	Factor Score	Item Type
I use formal research studies to track public reations to my organization.	.76	Scientific scanning
I have surveys conducted of key publics.	.72	Scientific scanning
I conduct public relations audits to find out about publics.	.69	Scientific scanning
I subscribe to or use the services of public opinion research agencies.	.59	Scientific scanning
I check PR impact through interviews with a scientifically selected cross-section of significant publics.	.56	Scientific impact evaluation
I use demographic data to help make decisions concerning my publics.	.55	Scientific scanning
I prepare communications by testing preliminary message strategies and formats on focus groups drawn from publics involved.	.50	Scientific formative evaluation
I prepare communications by first reviewing relevant published surveys (Gallup, Harris) on attitudes of publics involved.	.47	Scientific formative evaluation

Scientific Approach. This approach consists of scientific scanning methods, scientific impact evaluation methods, and scientific formative evaluation methods (see Table 1.1). Practitioners following the scientific research approach use formal research to survey publics and track reactions to the organization, conduct public relations audits, subscribe to public opinion research services, use demographic data for decision making, conduct focus group message tests, and review published public opinion surveys. These research activities are all rooted in the social sciences.

Mixed Approach. This approach consists of some scientific research techniques focused on the content of media and of mediated (phone and letters) feedback from publics (see Table 1.2). Scientific activities such as clip file content analysis and quantitative measures of complaints by mail and phone are mixed with seat-of-the-pants techniques such as attending meetings, conferences, and monitoring placements through close media contacts. Less formal than the scientific research approach, this approach combines both scientific and seat-of-the-pants research activities.

Informal Approach. A third approach emphasizes scanning activities that involve oral communication (face-to-face or phone) between practitioners and publics (see Table 1.3). The only "scientific" item in this factor involves frequency of

---

for 94% of the common variance. The fourth factor included only two items with high loadings, one of which was cross-loaded with the mixed factor. For these reasons, the factor was not interpretable and was not used in subsequent analysis.

TABLE 1.2
The Mixed Research Approch

	Factor Score	Item Type
I monitor dissemination of messages (news stories, editorials, letters to editors) through a formal ongoing content analysis of items in the clip file.	.63	Clip file evaluation
I check PR impact through ongoing counts tabulated of public complaints by phone or letter.	.63	Scientific impact evaluation
I check PR impact by attending meetings and hearings of groups representative of significant publics.	.57	Seat-of-the-pants evaluation
I review complaints via mail and private conferences to find out how publics feel about my organization.	.56	Informal scanning
I monitor dissemination of messages (news releases, etc.) through my close personal contacts among mass media professionals.	.48	Seat-of-the-pants evaluation
I monitor dissemination of messages (press releases, etc.) through a comprehensive clip file and a log of inches placed, reach, and other vital statistics.	.44	Clip file evaluation

practitioner depth interviews with publics. However, "depth interviews" may mean one thing to practitioners trained as journalists who filled out the questionnaire and social scientists who designate depth interviews as scientific. The informal oral approach emphasized direct communication between practitioners and publics for scanning purposes only. No program evaluation, even seat-of-the-pants evaluation, is involved in this approach.

The three approaches to program research range from rigorous scientific research to intermediate mixed research to casual, informal research. Diffusion theory suggests that, due to the greater perceived complexity and the lesser perceived compatibility of the more rigorous approaches, the informal approach is used most frequently, followed by content-based mixed research. Scientific research is posited to be used least frequently. The 1987 IABC survey supports these hypotheses. The most frequent approach to program research is informal ($M = 4.3$ on a 7-point

TABLE 1.3
The Informal Research Approach

	Factor Score	Item Type
I make phone calls to members of my target publics to keep in touch.	.72	Informal scanning
I call back people who attend a special event or presentation my organization has done to get their reactions.	.57	Informal scanning
I conduct depth interviews with members of the organization's publics.	.47	Scientific scanning
I talk with field personnel to find out about key publics.	.37	Informal scanning

"never" to "always" scale), followed by mixed ($M = 4.1$) and scientific ($M = 2.9$). Differences in means (one-tailed paired t tests) are statistically significant ($p < .05$). (See Table 1.4.)

Participation in Decision Making

A 1985 survey of PRSA and IABC practitioners in the United States and Canada showed that scanning research is positively associated with participation in management decision making and membership in the dominant coalition (Dozier, 1986, 1987). Scientific scanning activities are most strongly associated with participation in management decision making ($r = .46$, $N = 258$, $p < .001$) but informal scanning techniques are also positively correlated ($r = .36$, $N = 257$, $p < .001$).

In the 1987 IABC survey, scientific research, mixed research, and informal research are all positively correlated with participation in management decision making. The correlation between informal oral research and management decision making is much weaker than the correlation between scientific/mixed research and decision-making participation (see Table 1.5).

Practitioner Roles

In a 6-year panel study of PRSA members, Broom and Dozier (1985, 1986) found that practitioners who increased their manager role activities from 1979 to 1985 were more likely to evaluate their public relations activities than were practitioners who did not change or who decreased their manager role activities from 1979 to 1985. Changes in technician role activities over the same period of study were unrelated to program research activities.

In the 1985 survey of PRSA and IABC members, manager role playing is related to both scientific scanning activities and to informal scanning activities. Technician role playing is only weakly related to scientific scanning and unrelated to informal scanning activities.

The 1987 survey of IABC members provided the most comprehensive test of role playing and program research activities (Dozier, 1988b). Using combined scanning

TABLE 1.4
Tests of Differences in Frequencies of Scientific, Mixed, and Informal
Research Activities

	Mean	Differences in Means	t	df	One-Tail Probability
Informal approach	4.3	0.2	1.87	201	.031
Mixed approach	4.1	1.2	11.30	197	<.001
Scientific approach	2.9				

Note: Frequency of research activities was measured on a common 7-point "never" (1) to "always" (7) index.

TABLE 1.5
Pearson Correlation Tests of Scientific Research, Mixed Research,
and Informal Research
With Key Variables

	Scientific Research	Mixed Research	Informal Research
Participation in dominant coalition (management decision making)	$r = .40$ $N = 196$ $p = .001$	$r = .39$ $N = 197$ $p = .001$	$r = .23$ $N = 200$ $p = .001$
Public relations manager role playing	$r = .28$ $N = 198$ $p = .001$	$r = .42$ $N = 200$ $p = .001$	$r = .19$ $N = 202$ $p = .003$
Public relations technician role playing	$r = -.03$ $N = 201$ $p = .357$	$r = .12$ $N = 204$ $p = .041$	$r = .04$ $N = 205$ $p = .251$
Female gender (of practitioner)	$r = -.15$ $N = 198$ $p = .018$	$r = .03$ $N = 202$ $p = .349$	$r = .05$ $N = 203$ $p = .308$
Press agentry model of public relations practice	$r = -.13$ $N = 167$ $p = .050$	$r = .27$ $N = 170$ $p = .001$	$r = .05$ $N = 172$ $p = .264$
Public information model of public relations practice	$r = -.22$ $N = 167$ $p = .003$	$r = .05$ $N = 171$ $p = .264$	$r = -.05$ $N = 177$ $p = .245$
Two-way assymmetrical model of public relations practice	$r = .34$ $N = 172$ $p = .001$	$r = .34$ $N = 175$ $p = .001$	$r = .17$ $N = 177$ $p = .013$
Two-way symmetrical model of public relations practice	$r = .08$ $N = 170$ $p = .148$	$r = .16$ $N = 173$ $p = .020$	$r = .10$ $N = 175$ $p = .249$
Environmental sensitivity of the dominant coalition (mgmt. perception)	$r = .08$ $N = 133$ $p = .172$	$r = .21$ $N = 137$ $p = .008$	$r = .04$ $N = 137$ $p = .308$
Organic structure of decision making (mgmt. perception)	$r = .21$ $N = 133$ $p = .007$	$r = .13$ $N = 137$ $p = .069$	$r = .15$ $N = 137$ $p = .040$

and evaluation measures from the 1987 survey, manager role scores correlate positively with scientific, mixed, and informal research. Manager scores correlated strongest with mixed research, followed by scientific research and oral research (see Table 1.5). Technician role scores post weak correlations with mixed research but not at all with scientific research and informal research.

Decision Making, Roles, and Research

Doing research activities, especially scientific research activities, increases practitioner participation in management decision making, above and beyond the entree provided by manager role playing (Dozier, 1986). The partial correlation between decision making and scientific scanning remains positive and significant (partial r = .36, N = 241, p < .001), after controlling for the influence of manager role playing. Informal scanning is also related to participation in decision making, although the relationship is not as strong. The relationship remains significant (partial r = .28, N = 241, p < .001) even after the influence of manager role playing is controlled (Dozier, 1986).

Women, Research, and Decision Making

In the 1985 study of PRSA and IABC members, women practitioners were significantly less likely than men practitioners to conduct scientific scanning (Dozier, 1987). However, women who do conduct scientific scanning find that such activities are more important to their participation in management decision making than it is for men (Dozier, 1987).

The influence of manager role playing, gender, and research activities were used in a regression model to predict participation in management decision making. In the panel study of PRSA members, being male was shown to be a powerful predictor of participation in management decision making (Broom & Dozier, 1986). In the 1985 PRSA and IABC survey, however, being male was not as important as which role the practitioner played predominantly and how much scientific scanning the practitioner conducted. For all practitioners in the sample combined, the post powerful predictor in the stepwise model was doing scientific scanning activities (beta = .44) and playing the manager role predominantly (beta = .26), whereas being male was a weak predictor (beta = .03).

Different Models for Women and Men. Women and men practitioners were analyzed separately in a stepwise regression analysis. The relative importance of playing the manager role predominantly and doing scientific scanning differed. Among men in the sample, doing scientific scanning is the best predictor of participating in management decision making (beta = .41), as is playing the manager role predominantly (beta = .26). For women in the sample, doing scientific scanning is more important (beta = .46), whereas playing the manager role is roughly equivalent to that in the male regression model (beta = .25).

These findings were tested again in the 1987 IABC survey. The results were more dramatic. In the retest, the dominant role of the practitioner, practitioner gender, and the amount of scientific scanning and evaluation (combined score) were regressed on participation in management decision making. In this study, combined scientific scanning and impact evaluation activities are the most powerful predictors of management decision-making participation, with a beta coefficient of .35 in the regression model. Playing the manager role predominantly is the second most powerful predictor, with a beta weight of .19. Being male is the third most powerful predictor, with a .14 beta weight.

Breaking the "Glass Ceiling." When men and women were analyzed separately, the relative importance of playing the manager role and doing scientific
program research differed. Among men in the sample, doing scientific scanning and
evaluation was important (beta = .29) but so was playing the manager role
predominantly (beta = .21). Among women in the sample, doing scientific scanning
is more important in predicting management decision-making participation (beta =
.42), whereas playing the manager role predominantly is somewhat less important
(beta = .15).[4] Program research is posited as an important tool for women practitioners trying to break through the "glass ceiling" that blocks their entree into the
dominant coalition (Dozier, 1989).

The gender of the practitioner (where women were arbitrarily assigned a higher
score) correlates with scientific research in the 1987 IABC study.[5] Women are less
likely than men to do scientific program research. Women, however, are no less
likely than men to do mixed research or informal research (see Table 1.5).

Models of Public Relations Practice

Program research is related to the model of public relations practiced by the public
relations unit. The models, as conceptualized by Grunig (1984), involve four
distinct definitions or approaches to the public relations function. The *press agentry*
model of public relations involves placements and attraction of media attention using
publicity "stunts" and other vehicles. Media attention is the sole objective. The
public information model involves the distribution of information to the public,
following journalistic standards of news value. Practiced by "journalist-in-resi-
dence" practitioners, truthful information is disseminated but unfavorable information is often suppressed. These first two models, with historical roots in early
practices of P. T. Barnum and Ivy Lee, involve the one-way flow of information
outward from the organization to publics (Grunig & Hunt, 1984). Because the flow
of information is one way, such models are posited to have little need for environmental scanning or evaluation research.

The *two-way asymmetrical* model of public relations represents a significant
departure from earlier historical models. This is the "persuasion" model of public
relations. This model posits heavy dependence on program research to identify
strategies and messages to bring public knowledge, predispositions, and behavior
in line with interests of the organization. Scanning research is used to identify
problems and opportunities with publics. Persuasive public relations campaigns

---

[4]Comparisons of beta weights in this discussion are restricted to descriptions of path structures in
the sample itself. The conclusions are restricted to the sample and are not statistical inferences to the
population of practitioners studied.

[5]Certain liberties were taken in the treatment of respondent sex, a dichotomous variable, as a metric
appropriate for a parametric statistic (Pearson product-moment correlation coefficient). The logic here is
similar to the use of dummy variables in regression analysis. The findings are the same when non-
parametric statistics are used on the same data.

are designed, using formative evaluation techniques to make them more effective. Summative or impact evaluation research is used to determine if publics were persuaded according to plan. In the asymmetrical model, publics change—not organizations. Policies, procedures, and actions of organizations are not changed to accommodate interests of publics. Research is used to help the organization impose its will on publics.

However, the asymmetrical approach is not the only way research can be used. Another use of research, as dictated by the *two-way symmetrical* model, is to help organizations understand publics in order to negotiate or bargain mutually beneficial, reciprocal relationships. In this model, research is important to facilitate negotiation and conflict resolution. Both publics and organizations change when two-way symmetrical public relations is practiced.

Prior Studies.   Research at the University of Maryland indicates that scientific impact evaluations are conducted by organizations following both two-way models. Both two-way models were positively correlated with informal research before and after implementing programs. The press agentry and public information models posted weak, negative correlations with scientific impact evaluation and informal research before and after program implementation (Fabiszak, 1985; Grunig & Grunig, 1986; McMillan, 1984; Pollack, 1984; R. Pollack, 1986).

However, measures of program research used in the University of Maryland studies involved single-item indicators of unknown reliability. The 1987 survey of IABC members in the United States and Canada asked practitioners to name their organization's top priority public. Practitioners then indicated the degree to which each model of public relations applied to their program for that public.

Scientific Research and Two-Way Models.   Using combined scanning and evaluation measures of program research, the two-way asymmetric model of public relations is positively correlated with scientific research, mixed research, and informal research. However, the correlation with informal research is weaker than correlations for the other two research types. The two-way symmetrical model of public relations is positively correlated with mixed research but not with scientific research nor with informal research (see Table 1.5).

Research and One-Way Models.   The press agentry model and the public information model are both negatively correlated with scientific program research. The press agentry model is positively correlated with mixed research. None of the remaining correlations for these two models are significant (see Table 1.5).

Environmental Sensitivity

In the 1987 survey of IABC members, senior managers to whom top practitioners report were surveyed. These members of the dominant coalition were asked to indicate how sensitive the organization was to the organization's environment.

As posited by the environmental imperative and Broom's propositions about the *impermeability* of organizations' boundaries, environmental sensitivity of the organization is positively correlated with mixed research but—counter to theory—not with scientific research nor with informal research (see Table 1.5).

Importance of Organic Structure

Top managers were also asked how important they considered organic (decentralized decision making) to be. Both the environmental imperative and the power-control perspective posit a positive relationship between decentralized decision making and greater use of research. As posited, perceptions by senior mangers of the importance of organic organizational structure were positively correlated with scientific program research and informal research. Mixed research activities is not significantly correlated with decentralized decision making and organic structure. A strong trend, however, consistent in direction with the posited relationship, is present in the sample (see Table 1.5).

CONCLUSIONS AND IMPLICATIONS FOR FURTHER RESEARCH

Public relations program research is not unidimensional. Research activities cluster in distinct innovation subsets. When frequency measures of scanning and program impact research are combined, three distinct approaches to program research emerge, based on the ways practitioners actually use research. These approaches are scientific, mixed, and informal program research.

As posited by diffusion theory, scientific program research is less frequently used by practitioners than either content-based mixed or informal oral program research. By inference, the slower rate of diffusion (utilization) for scientific research is due to greater perceived complexity and lesser perceived compatibility, when compared to mixed and informal research. The rate of diffusion (level of utilization) increases when practitioners have formal training in social science, statistics, and computers.

The more a practitioner plays the manager role, the more he or she will do scientific, mixed, and informal program research. Scientific and informal program research are unrelated to playing the technician role. However, technicians do content-based mixed program research, principally clip file evaluation.

Practitioner participation in management decision making increases when the practitioner plays the manager role and conducts scientific, mixed, and informal program research. Such participation is not strictly a function of playing the manager role, wherein program research is simply something that public relations managers do. Rather, participation in management decision making is increased when the practitioner does research, independent of manager role playing.

Women practitioners do scientific program research less frequently than men. However, women who do conduct scientific program research find that such work is more important for their participation in management decision making than it is for men. Women are just as likely as men to conduct mixed and informal program research.

Practitioners who apply the two-way asymmetrical model to their practice use scientific, mixed, and informal research more frequently than to practitioners using other models of public relations practice. The two-way symmetrical model is correlated only with mixed program research, not scientific or informal research. Scientific program research is negatively correlated with the press agentry and public information models of public relations practice.

Organizations where the dominant coalition values decentralized decision making and organic structure are more likely to use scientific and informal research than organizations favoring bureaucracy and centralized decision making. The dominant coalition's sensitivity to the environment is only correlated with mixed program research, not with scientific or informal research.

Program research in public relations is core to modern practice. Theoretically, an open systems approach requires practitioners to scan the organization's environment and evaluate the impact of public relations programs. Empirically, practitioners who use scientific, mixed and informal program research are more likely to participate in management decision making.

Further Research.   Further studies of program research need to test more directly the perceived attributes of the different innovation subsets of program research. Rather than inferring differences in perceived complexity and perceived compatibility, these attributes should be measured directly.

A larger criticism of past studies is the use of cross-sectional designs. Public relations program research to date has been examined through a series of mailed, large-sample, cross-sectional studies. This research approach has provided useful insights and discoveries. However, the diffusion of innovations is a process, and processes are best understood over time.

Equally important is more extensive use of qualitative research techniques, including case studies of organizations that use and do not use program research. Such studies would sensitize researchers to concepts and issues not currently understood as relevant to the diffusion of program research.

Finally, linkages need to be posited and tested between the utilization of scientific, mixed, and informal program research and the effectiveness of decision making and programming. We know that doing program research is related to practitioner participation in management decision making. Core questions include: Do practitioners, armed with program research, *improve* the quality of management decision making when they participate? Are public relations programs based on sound program research *more effective* in achieving organizational objectives than programs that practitioners run by the seat of their pants?

REFERENCES

Acharya, L. (1981, August). *Effect of perceived environmental uncertainty on public relations roles.* Paper presented to the Public Relations Division, Association for Education in Journalism, East Lansing, MI.

Acharya, L. (1983, August). *Practitioner representations of environmental uncertainty: An application of discriminant analysis.* Paper presented to the Public Relations Division, Association for Education in Journalism and Mass Communication Conference, Corvallis, OR.

Bell, S. H., & Bell, E. C. (1976). Public relations: functional or functionary? *Public Relations Review, 2,* 51–52.

Broom, G. M. (1982). A comparison of sex roles in public relations. *Public Relations Review, 8,* 17–22.

Broom, G. M. (1986, May). *Public relations roles and systems theory: functional and historicist causal models.* Paper presented to the Public Relations Interest Group, International Communication Association Conference, Chicago, IL.

Broom, G. M., & Dozier, D. M. (1985, August). *Determinants and consequences of public relations roles.* Paper presented to the Public Relations Division, Association for Education in Journalism and Mass Communication Conference, Memphis, TN.

Broom, G. M., & Dozier, D. M. (1986). Advancement for public relations role models. *Public Relations Review, 12,* 37–56.

Broom, G. M., & Dozier, D. M. (1990). *Using research in public relations: Applications to program management.* Englewood Cliffs, NJ: Prentice-Hall.

Center, A. H., & Broom, G. M. (1983). Evaluation research. *Public Relations Quarterly, 28,* 2–3.

Child, J. (1972). Organizational structure, environment, and performance: the role of strategic choice. *Sociology, 6,* 1–22.

Cutlip, S. M., & Center, A. H. (1978). *Effective public relations* (5th ed.). Englewood Cliffs, NJ: Prentice-Hall.

Cutlip, S. M., Center, A. H., & Broom, G. M. (1985). *Effective public relations* (6th ed.). Englewood Cliffs, NJ: Prentice-Hall.

Dozier, D. M. (1981, August). *The diffusion of evaluation methods among public relations practitioners.* Paper presented to the Public Relations Division, Association for Education in Journalism Conference, East Lansing, MI.

Dozier, D. M. (1983, November). *Toward a reconciliation of 'role conflict' in public relations research.* Paper presented to the Western Communications Educators Conference, Fullerton, CA.

Dozier, D. M. (1984a). Program evaluation and the roles of practitioners. *Public Relations Review, 10,* 13–21.

Dozier, D. M. (1984b, May). *The evolution of evaluation methods among public relations practitioners.* Paper presented to the Educator Academy, International Association of Business Communicators Conference, Montreal, Canada.

Dozier, D. M. (1986, August). *The environmental scanning function of public relations practitioners and participation in management decision making.* Paper presented to the Public Relations Division, Association for Education in Journalism and Mass Communication, Norman, OK.

Dozier, D. M. (1987, May). *Gender, environmental scanning, and participation in management decision making.* Paper presented to the Public Relations Interest Group, International Communication Association Conference, Montreal, Canada.

Dozier, D. M. (1988a, May). *The vertical location of the public relations function in organizations.* Paper presented to the Public Relations Interest Group, International Communication Association Conference, New Orleans, LA.

Dozier, D. M. (1988b, July). *Organic structure and managerial environmental sensitivity as predictors of practitioner membership in the dominant coalition.* Paper presented to the Public Relations Division, Association for Education in Journalism and Mass Communication Conference, Portland, OR.

Dozier, D. M. (1989). Breaking the public relations glass ceiling. *Public Relations Review, 15,* 6–14.

Dozier, D. M., & Grunig, L. (1989). *The organization of the public relations/communication function.* Manuscript submitted for review.

Fabiszak, D. L. (1985). *Public relations in hospitals: Testing the Grunig theory of organizations, environments and models of public relations.* Unpublished masters' thesis, University of Maryland, College Park, MD.

Glaser, S., & M. I. Halliday (1980). Organizations as systems. *Human Relations, 34,* 917–28.

Grunig, J. E. (1983). Basic research provides knowledge that makes evaluation possible. *Public Relations Quarterly, 28,* 28–32.

Grunig, J. E. (1984). Organizations, environments, and models of public relations. *Public Relations Research & Education, 1,* 6–29.

Grunig, J. E., & Grunig, L. (1986, May). *Application of open systems theory to public relations: Review of a program of research.* Paper presented to the Public Relations Interest Group, International Communication Association Conference, Chicago, IL.

Grunig, J. E., & Hunt, T. (1984). *Managing public relations.* New York: Holt, Rinehart & Winston.

McElreath, M. P. (1977). Public relations evaluation research: summary statement. *Public Relations Review, 3,* 129.

McMillan, S. J. (1984). *Public relations in trade and professional associations: Location, model, structure, environment and values.* Unpublished masters' thesis, University of Maryland, College Park, MD.

Pennington, B. (1980). How public relations fits into the puzzle. *Public Relations Journal, 36,* 18–20.

Pfeffer, J. (1978). *Organizational design.* Arlington Heights, IL: AHM Publishing.

Pfeffer, J. (1979). Power and resource allocation in organizations. In B. M. Shaw & G. R. Salancik (Eds.), *New directions in organizational behavior* (pp. 240–248). Chicago: St. Clair Press.

Pfeffer, J. (1981). *Power in organizations.* Marshfield, MA: Pitman Publishing.

Pollack, E. J. (1984). *An organizational analysis of four public relations models in the federal government.* Unpublished master's thesis, University of Maryland, College Park, MD.

Pollack, R. A. (1986). *Testing the Grunig organizational theory in scientific organizations: Public relations and the values of the dominant coalition.* Unpublished master's thesis, University of Maryland, College Park, MD.

Reeves, B. (1983). Now you see them, now you don't: Demonstrating effects of communication programs. *Public Relations Quarterly, 28,* 17–27.

Robbins, S. P. (1987). *Organization theory: Structure, design and applications* (2nd ed.). Englewood Cliffs, NJ: Prentice-Hall.

Robinson, E. J. (1969). *Public relations and survey research.* New York: Appleton-Century-Crofts.

Rogers, E. M. (1983). *Diffusion of innovations* (3rd ed.). New York: The Free Press.

Simon, H. A. (1976). *Administrative behavior* (3rd ed.). New York: The Free Press.

Stinchcombe, A. L. (1968). *Constructing social theories.* New York: Harcourt, Brace & World.

Suchman, E. A. (1967). *Evaluation research.* New York: Russell Sage.

Weiss, C. H. (1975). Evaluation research in the political context. In E. Struening & M. Guttentag (Eds.), *Handbook of evaluation research* (pp. 13–26). Beverly Hills, CA: Sage.

Wright, D. K. (1979). Some ways to measure public relations. *Public Relations Journal, 36,* 17.

Chapter 2

Corporate Issues Management: Theoretical Underpinnings and Research Foundations

Robert L. Heath
University of Houston

Issues management became a buzzword after its coinage in the 1970s and continues to struggle for identity among traditional corporate management and staff departments such as public relations and strategic planning. "The concept, insofar as it is a new future oriented policy and planning tool, and insofar as it involves practice across many kinds of organizations, businesses, industries, and trade associations, is still evolving in terminology, technique, scope and organizational setting" (Coates, Coates, Jarratt, & Heinz, 1986, p. 17).

A communication bias often permeates the discussion of issues management, perhaps because it originated with leading public relations practitioners such as Raymond P. Ewing, who was at Allstate Insurance Companies, and W. Howard Chase, who earned a reputation with the American Can Company. Making issues management an adjunct of communication, Chase (1984) encouraged corporations to influence public policy and allay activist group pressure before it leads to regulation. He advised corporate leaders to aggressively counter public suspicion of the private sector by employing proactive as well as reactive issue communication tactics. Viewed narrowly as only a communication activity, issues management can appear to be old hat for communication professionals. But public relations practitioners often do not help their managements weigh public policies during strategic planning (Ehling & Hesse, 1983).

Looking at the prospect of issues management, Wartick and Rude (1986) prophesied a bright future if it "can positively affect corporate performance by enhancing the firm's responsiveness to environmental change" (p. 125). Issues management can help organizations spot and cope with sharp criticism and prevent unwarranted regulation. To do so, Littlejohn (1986) argued, requires "the careful linkage of issue priorities to corporate objectives and the development of action plans to make the firm more competitive" (p. 121). Viewed this way, issues management is not only a communication activity, but a management activity with a communication option.

To realize its potential, issues management needs a clear identity and a solid foundation of theory and research. This chapter endeavors to make advances in these directions. To do so, it undertakes two broad objectives: (a) To analyze major writings on issues management to identify key themes, and (b) to use theory and research to lay a foundation and plot directions.

WHAT IS ISSUES MANAGEMENT?

"Issues(s) management isn't quite public relations. Neither is it government rela-tions, nor public affairs, nor lobbying, nor crisis management, nor futurism, nor strategic planning. It embraces all of these disciplines, and maybe a few more" (Miller, 1987, p. 125). This observation highlights the diverse staff functions and perspectives unique to issues management. It emphasizes the tactics and values necessary to assist organizations of various kinds, but especially businesses, in their efforts to adjust to and influence public policy. Following this reasoning, one of the best definitions was provided in the report by the Public Relations Society of America Special Committee on Terminology (1987). That report defined *issues management* as the "systematic identification and action regarding public policy matters of concern to an organization" (p. 9). Issues management involves commu-nicating, issue monitoring, achieving responsibility, and strategic planning.

Communicating

This view of issues management acknowledges that organizations inform key external stakeholders such as the media, shareholders, government officials, reg-ulators, activist, general public, or consumers. This information can foster thor-ough and accurate understanding of corporate operations and policies as well as discuss advantages or disadvantages of public policy options. Through issues communication, pressures are routinely brought to bear upon public policymakers by direct contact, through grassroots coalitions, and public communication cam-paigns such as that which fostered the repeal of the 10% withholding tax provision of 1982 (Elmendorf, 1988). However, to think that companies can manage or dominate issues is as incorrect as is the belief that companies cannot manage issues. Issues management can manage a company's or industry's reaction to and influence on a public policy issue. Issues management is not only designed to protect a company against unwarranted public policy; it also seeks favorable public policy.

By using communication to reach targeted audiences, organizations in various ways and degrees can change perceptions, ideologies, coalitions, beliefs, attitudes, understanding, and policy standards or priorities. Influence is needed to create an atmosphere as hospitable as possible to an organization and its stakeholders, even its critics. No one wants ill-advised policies, and organizations can act responsibly albeit self-interestedly by demonstrating that fact. Part of their stewardship is to support reasonable public policies. An honest conflict between groups having different values and interests is part of each organization's environment. Each competing interest in the public policy arena is responsible to its own group of constituents. Issues managements makes organizations aware of competing interests, locates advantages and resistance, and seeks constructive reconciliation of interests even through legislation or regulation. Companies may seek unilateral support from individual stakeholders, as food corporations do when they invite activists to give nutrition advice.

Issue Monitoring

Fitting the trend to build public relations theory and research upon general systems theory (Pavlik, 1987), issues management meets organizations' needs to obtain accurate and timely information from their environment. This information can be used in a planning capacity to assess whether the organization's goals and operating standards are viable or should be altered. These data can be applied to understand what forces are at play in the environment.

Attempts are being made to systematize this effort. Toward this end, Chase (1984; Jones & Chase, 1979) offered the Issue Management Process Model as "a tool for predicting the effect of internal and external environmental changes on the performance of the overall corporate system. This tool assigns decision-making authority and performance responsibility, and makes possible an objective review and evaluation of issue management performance" (p. 34). Companies have more response options the earlier they spot trends that portend public policy changes (Crable & Vibbert, 1985). The goal is to understand public influence dynamics well enough to be able to obtain accurate and helpful data, calculate response options, and take corrective actions while a company or industry has more, rather than fewer, options.

Achieving Responsibility

In a system, all entities struggle and adjust with the potential outcome of achieving harmony of interests. Pressure from one part of a system is met with a complementary response from other parts. This perspective justifies companies' use of influence, but cautions that it is limited by the dynamics among competing and counterbalancing entities of the system. Because of the variety of players in the public policy arena, it is incorrect to assume that issues management is needed only to deal with angry activists or investigative reporters. It is necessary to help companies work in a public policy arena that contains these groups along with legislators, regulators, other companies, trade associations, unions, and such.

Organizations need standards of social responsibility that are translated into internal actions through strategic management. As well as attempting to make business plans based on changes in the public policy environment, issues management can sense changes in the prevailing ethical standards and see that the appropriate strategic management efforts are made to incorporate the standards into daily operations.

Issues management can help companies engage in public policy power struggles when groups—whether activists, governmental, or inter- or intraindustry—attempt to change public policies in ways thought to be harmful. And companies should have the ability to seek to change public policies to foster their interests. Both kinds of actions must be tempered by standards of corporate social responsibility that, as much as possible, stress the greater good of all stakeholders. This struggle conforms to the traditional conflict model whereby all interests cannot be satisfied mutually (Stanley, 1985). It assumes compromise and acknowledges the responsibility companies have to influence policy. But this stance does not justify arrogance, an attitude that can harm companies' well-being (Ewing, 1987).

Strategic Planning

To counter the tendency to believe that issues management is only another name for traditional corporate communication practices, Ewing (1987; cited in Heath & Nelson, 1986, p. 15) demonstrated that issues management evolved from public affairs and public relations to help organizations integrate public policy planning and strategic planning. This development helped strategic planning mature from budgeting to long-range planning.

Some companies have assigned public relations units the responsibility of coping with public policy, including considering its implications for strategic plans. But public relations is often only responsible for product/service publicity, press agentry, and monitoring to determine whether company messages are getting across. When public affairs became popular in the 1970s, governmental affairs was added to the public relations mission. Despite this advance, companies have only recently begun to implement issues management in the truest sense (Ewing, 1987).

Although issues management is operationalized in different matrices in most companies, it is usually the responsibility of public affairs, corporate planning, corporate communication, government affairs, or policy analysis (Wartick & Rude, 1986). But a company has not implemented an issues management program until it has created the staff structure, corporate climate, and policies needed to integrate public policy planning and strategic planning (Ewing, 1987; Sawaya & Arrington, 1988; Stroup, 1986, 1988).

The strategic plan of a corporation is designed to achieve the mission—what the business seeks to accomplish. In support of this, the business plan states how material and human resources should be applied to achieve the mission. A counter-part of the business plan is the public policy plan that proposes how the company should respond to public policy changes to achieve its strategic plan. The public policy plan can call for changes in planning assumptions, new operating pro-cedures, an improved sense of corporate social responsibility, or communication goals and tactics vis-à-vis the developing public policy changes. It may discuss how changes in certain public policies offer business opportunities (Heath, 1988b).

Thus, issues management requires the activities and values needed to support strategic planning, monitoring, communicating, and achieving responsibility. These activities can help organizations adjust to and influence public policy. Because of the breadth of activities it must embrace, issues management is an amalgam of many disciplines including communication (Chase, 1982, 1984; Sethi, 1977, 1987), political science (Alexander, 1983; Stanley, 1985), futurism (Coates, Coates et al., 1986), and management (Buchholz, 1985; Buchholz, Evans, & Wagley, 1985; Dickie, 1984; Post, 1979; Post, Murray, Dickie, & Mahon, 1983; Preston & Post, 1975). Writers are beginning to draw these disciplines together (Goodman, 1983).

PULLING THE DISCIPLINE UP BY ITS BOOTSTRAPS

Justification for featuring these aspects of issues management is based on a wide array of comments by persons from several disciplines who have been instrumental in its development. The following review is intended to show the themes that are being brought together to form a coherent understanding of issues management.

Engineering Consent

No matter what other organizations have begun to employ the techniques and philosophies of issues management, its emergence as a discipline began as corpora-tions reacted to the antibusiness sentiment of the 1960s. In the 1950s, corporate America was aglow with the belief that it had helped win World War II and produced widespread prosperity. All was going well for business. But during the next two decades more bills would be passed to regulate business activities than occurred previously in American history. The genesis of issues management in the 1970s was a sense by some corporate communication experts that American com-merce and industry were ill-prepared to deal with the dramatic challenges facing the private sector in a new age of reform. Communication practices designed only to foster positive company images or to create product and service publicity could not adequately respond to critics. Often tension resulted, not from misunderstand-ing, but from differences of opinions and standards.

As the discipline began to emerge, it tended to rely heavily on communication to solve public policy problems by engineering consent. Believing that *business was the business* of America, Edward Bernays (1955) encouraged corporate communicators to engineer consent for their companies' operations and philosophy. This paradigm seemed workable and guided the corporate communication profession and underpinned management attitudes for many years. Only astute observers spotted the seams that were opening in the fabric of consent that prevailed until the 1960s. The new ear of activist protest evidenced that if consent had existed, it was dissolving.

Responding to the new communication needs, Stridsberg (1977), in conjunction with the International Association of Advertisers, used survey data to define the scope and nomenclature of issue communication that he said serves three purposes: (a) to defend companies' social or economic points of view, (b) to aggressively promote a point of view, and (c) to establish "a platform of fact." Public affairs came to be thought of as "a management function concerned with the relationship between the organization and its external environment, and involving the key tasks of intelligence gathering and analysis, internal communication, and external action programs directed at government, communities, and the general public" (Nagelschmidt, 1982, p. 290). And Nowlan and Shayon (1984) offered a comprehensive model for planning and executing corporate communication.

Communication can be an important component in public policy efforts. For instance, Pincus (1980) lauded the American Forest Institute communication campaign that helped increase favorable opinion regarding the forest industry. In 1974, 34% of the public believed that forests were being managed in the public interest. As a result of the "forests—the renewable resource campaign," 55% of the public had come by 1980 to believe the forest industry was doing a good job of managing the resources.

Failure to Achieve Consent

This kind of opinion shift assumes that tensions between organizations and their environment are only a matter of agreement that can be achieved through communication. But as Pavlik (1987) concluded, "it may take more than communication to manage a relationship" (p. 119).

The dynamics of the power struggle during the 1960s and 1970s led Stanley (1985) to base his approach to issues management on a game theory paradigm. He demonstrated how companies can assess the pressures being applied by activist groups, legislators, and regulators and, on that basis, calculate the relative strength of the combatants. Critical of the consent model advocated by Bernays, Stanley noted how the consensus that seemed to exist in the 1950s failed to survive the 1960s and 1970s. The point: Corporations lack the power to engineer social consensus, but they can manage their response to the policy environment. Even within and between industries, consensus does not prevail regarding the best standards for operations and corporate ethics. In place of a consent model, Stanley advised issues managers to adopt a power resource management model that treats the regulatory battle ground as a tug-of-war where companies compete with activists and governmental regulators. The goal is to maximize gains and minimize losses. Public policy contests are based on competing self-interests couched in ideology.

Although communication is a part of what is needed to organizations to deal with public policy problems, the real issue is responsible performance, the standards of which are contestable. Corporations' problems cannot be solved by communication if they do not result from misunderstanding or misperception. S. Prakash Sethi (1974) raised many eyebrows when he exposed corporations' failure to achieve social responsibility. He challenged companies to be aware of the changing operating standards being advocated by the critics of large corporations. In *Advocacy Advertising and Large Corporations* (Sethi, 1977), he deplored the millions of corporate dollars spent on advocacy advertising that failed to lessen—and even increased—the gap between companies' performance and societal expectations. His most damning indictments were based on evidence that some companies most vehemently protesting regulation were the least responsible. Featuring the gap between businesses' performance and societal expectation, he offered two options: Companies could lessen the gap by becoming more responsible or by persuading critics that business practices were more responsible than popularly believed. Sethi saw advocacy advertising as the "new" corporate response, but doubted that it could solve the problem, especially when it was used to shift blame, misinform, employ scare tactics, and distort public policy discussions.

Sethi's (1987) decade-old scrutiny of advocacy, "issue-idea" advertising led him to conclude the following:

> Advocacy advertising, ultimately, is an educational tool and a political tool designed to play an active role in influencing a society's priorities. Therefore, its legitimacy and effectiveness will also be judged in political terms—by the public's perception that its practitioners are using it responsibly and, in addition to their self-interest, also serving some larger public purpose. (p. 4)

Because corporations are important citizens, Sethi championed their right to communicate on crucial issues. Concerned that the exercise of this right leads to distortion, domination, or deceit, he was unsure whether advocacy advertising is effective.

Although most books on public relations applaud the efforts of the founders of the practice of public relations, Olasky (1987) believed these efforts have stifled competition. He implored practitioners to engage in responsible and informative communication that helps people understand issues as the basis of wise public policy.

Writers such as Sethi and Olasky provide valuable critiques of corporate communication without going to the extreme other critics have. One critic, Meadow (1981) claimed that product and service advertising are "political communication." Pointing to the materialism inherent in product and service advertising, he con-tended that companies maintain a capitalistic stranglehold over the perspectives people use to view themselves, their needs, and the requirements for happiness. Gandy (1982) warned that corporate deep-pocket spending leads to distorted, one-sided analyses of public policy issues. As do others, he argued that corporate expenditures on issue communication should not be tax deductible because the Internal Revenue Service should not subsidize corporate public policy discussion. In a similar vein, Parenti (1986) alleged that companies have undue advantages over unions and activist groups during public policy debate. These treatises dem-onstrate by counterposition the importance of influencing the ideological environ-ment that surrounds and is used to evaluate corporate activities. These critics fear that corporations can control the political agenda, as well as lie and mislead.

Public contests of policy issues present the risk that the worse rather than the better policy will prevail. But this risk is offset by the belief that public contest produces better decisions. Toward this end, Cheney and Vibbert (1987) encour-aged corporations to help shape the values that will be used to forge their operating guidelines. Efforts are likely to be made to constrain company activities if the guidelines they follow differ drastically from those held by activists, legislators, regulators, journalists, and even other companies. Changes in public policy result from opinions that are subject to influence by many voices. Companies operate within the standards embedded in the "social reality" which permeates their environ-ment. Corporate operating environments produce uncertainty that stakeholders experience. One legitimate role for public policy communication is to shape mean-ing, define events, and establish value priorities. Thus, companies should communi-cate to give meaning to events, to "derandomize" them. If the symbols that form the ideological environment of businesses are favorable to a company's efforts, how it plans and operates will be different than if the symbols are hostile (Mitroff, 1983).

Being sensitive to the influence companies have over the ideological environ-ment, rhetorical critics have begun to scrutinize the evidence businesses use to support their claims and question the strategies they employ (Crable & Vibbert, 1983; Dionisopoulos, 1986a, 1986b; Simons, 1983). Critical efforts such as these can prompt responsible and candid discussion of public policy topics and the values related to them. Analysis of corporate efforts to influence public policy gives insight into the tactics businesses use to shape social reality.

Activism: The Contest Over Social Reality

The public policy environment—its standards and guidelines—results from defi-nitions that are formed through contests combining power and persuasion. Activ-ists have called for a new sense of corporate social responsibility that has revealed the dramatic need for methods to help companies survive and prosper. Along with "hostile" journalists reporting on topics such as pollution or unsafe products, a major feature of the era has been the formation of large, powerful, and well-funded special interest advocacy groups. In the past few years, they have become firmly institutionalized and are at times even supported by tax dollars (Bennett & Di-Lorenzo, 1985).

Such groups are not new, but only recently have they grown strong enough to counterbalance the public advocacy campaigns and power tactics of corporate lobbying. Several scholarly studies have examined the power dynamics of social movements (for instance, Gamson, 1968, 1975; Oberschall, 1973). Special interest activist Saul Alinsky (1971) wrote a how-to manual, *Rules for Radicals*, in which he outlined the tactics and ethics activists need to battle the power establishment.

Challenged by new policy constraints, the private sector has adopted three public policy communication responses. Some businesses take a low profile by being silent on issues in hopes that activism will wane. Some companies have changed their policies and have become honest and open, genuinely trying to listen to critics but willing to take a high profile by saying their piece and working for coalitions to achieve what they think to be responsible public policy. Others bluster, blame, and carp.

One proponent of the high profile is Herbert Schmertz, who made his reputation at Mobil Oil Corporation. Schmertz (1986) claimed that businesses must have political acumen to survive. He offered salty advice for dealing with the media, believing deeply that advocacy ads should be used to debate issues and to discredit those journalists who are not scrupulous in reporting facts, who espouse value positions that may harm the private sector by leading to unwise public policies, or who hide behind the First Amendment. Schmertz encouraged businesses to tell their story before someone else tells it for them. Another advocate of bold public affairs, Philip Lesly (1984) advised managers to arm against the tactics of special interest activists in the manner and tone Schmertz employed against the media.

Statements such as those by Schmertz and Lesly support an argumentation paradigm for issue communication that some may find unacceptable. But the point Schmertz and Lesly made is worth considering: Should companies be unfairly indicted, tried, and found guilty? Should any company or industry easily yield to the public policy pressures of some stakeholders? Public policy that is not founded on fact and reason can waste corporate and tax dollars. Thus, issues management should help companies influence social, economic, business, and political policies. But contrary to the impression created by Schmertz and Lesly, public policy does not only originate with activist groups or crusading journalists. It also comes about through the influence of key legislative and administrative officials. And it originates within industries and from other industries. Issues management should help companies argue their cases openly and factually seeking to build coalitions and foster policies that advance as many interests as possible. But it must acknowledge that public policy is a contest among competing interests, some of which are bound to lose in the public policy fray.

Early Warning

Whereas Lesly and Schmertz advocate taking critics on as they come, Chase (1984) argued that the best communication responses occur before the opinions held by key audiences galvanize. He advised companies to create early warning systems that instruct them on the means by which to become involved in the public policy process as early as possible. Issues managers need to be able to "tell the future," to know what issues are emerging and have not become widely discussed or deeply felt.

Telling the future is extremely difficult, but early warning systems can help companies forecast shifts in stakeholder opinion with sufficient validity and relia-bility that the information can be used for strategic planning and communication campaigns (Coates, Coates et al., 1986).

One of the first books to integrate monitoring, planning, and communication was the study James K. Brown (1979) prepared for The Conference Board. It outlines measures that companies can use to identify and solve public policy difficulties in ways that are reasonable and responsible. Planning and operations, he argued, will be best if sensitive to public policy issues. Issues management is not only aimed at survival but also offers market advantage. It can aid executives' efforts to chart their companies' future and seek business opportunities.

Responsible Strategic Planning and Management

Issues management should be inseparable from corporate strategic planning and operations. Preston and Post (1975; Post 1979) challenged business managers to consider public policies in their corporate planning and to foster a systematic and less traumatic adaptation to public policy constraints. Public policy influences play havoc with traditional business decision making (Buchholz, 1982, 1985). Buchholz et al. (1985) concluded, "The manager in today's world must consider many additional factors in decision-making beyond strictly commercial factors to run a successful business. A broad range of potential consequences must be considered before a decision can be made in almost all business situations" (p. 36). For this reason, they observed the following:

> To survive, the modern business organization must serve other constituencies besides those interested in profit. Managers at all operational levels must be aware of these important nonfinancial or nontraditional objectives, which can affect profits as much as more traditional concerns. They must develop the instincts and habits of mind to be aware of external influences that can affect the corporation. (p. 36)

One of the major contributions of issues management has been to help companies respond to changing notions of what constitutes corporate responsibility. But Arrington and Sawaya (1984a, 1984b; Sawaya & Arrington, 1988) contended that issues management is more than a means for implementing standards of corporate social responsibility. To be a vital, functional part of strategic planning, issues management must forecast and create planned adaptation to public policy changes.

Issues managers can conduct public policy monitoring and analysis to make strategic planning more effective, but Marx (1986) concluded:

> Corporate strategic planners focus their efforts on creating sustainable competitive advantages, while public issues management tries to anticipate and respond to a growing number of social problems with little appreciation for the firm's competitive position or comprehension of its long-term business plans. The result is that social issues are not adequately addressed at the operating level, and business plan objectives are often not realized at the corporate level because of regulation or other forms of social constraint. (p. 141)

His remedy for this division was to create effective linkages between public affairs experts and strategic planners.

This review suggests that issues mangers can choose from three tactical options: Adaptation or accommodation, domination, or harmonization. Adaptation or accommodation is a corporate response option that calls for a company to bow to outside pressures. Domination is an aggressive response option that assumes that a company has the tactical power resources to intimidate opponents and control public policy. The third option features an effort to balance the interests of relevant parties with the goal of achieving harmony. The proper balance allows a company to earn profits while fostering harmony between its interests and those of its diverse stakeholders (Freeman, 1984). The corrective mechanism in planning starts by identifying issues that are developing or changing and that can influence the accuracy of long-range planning. Supporting this view, Freeman argued that strategic management should fit as closely and harmoniously as possible each company's values with those of its stakeholders, any group that has an interest in its operations and can affect those operations. This goal is difficult but worthwhile. Freeman reasoned that even if public relations personnel believe that they have been working constructively with stakeholders for years, they have not done enough to help management realize the value of such efforts. Thus, Freeman challenged public relations: *"Managers must see external groups for the stake that they, in fact, have"* (p. 225). Those involved in external affairs must manage tradeoffs among stakeholders, identify new stakeholders, and identify and manage persistent and emerging issues.

The management of external issues should assume that a balance of interests drives public policy efforts. An axiom of general systems theory is that the parts of a system tend to achieve balance. This paradigm is important for understanding that issues management is more than corporate efforts to dominate the public policy arena. Issues management employs company image, public consent, and political victories as means (not ends) to create a harmonious partnership with a variety of stakeholders. An issues management approach that narrowly concentrates on gaining all that power can deliver, too selfishly applied, will bring out critics in full force. Issues management can bring equilibrium between competing interests only by sharing the resources and rewards of the environment.

Harmony between corporate and other interests cannot be achieved over the long term through guile or intimidation. It requires honest, candid assessments of the operating environment and willingness to balance interests. This process begins when executive management develops its business plan to use financial, material, and human resources to maximize each company's profits. To support the business plan, a public policy plan needs to state when and how to use communication and other adjustive tactics to meld company interests with those of key external and internal stakeholders. Any view of issues management that fails to address profit is inadequate because profit is a legitimate motive of business and is not antithetic to corporate responsibility (Aupperle, Carroll, & Hatfield, 1985).

This review is designed to stress the array of activities and attitudes issues managers must perform and possess. Their job requires many tasks, such as discovering emerging public policy issues, analyzing them, and integrating this analysis into strategic planning. Issues management involves implementing codes of corporate responsibility and developing strategic responses to the advocates of public policy change. It assumes that strategic plans and operating procedures can be made more successful by adapting them to public policy or by adapting public policy to them. Not only does issues management require an understanding of the dynamics of the public policy arena, it also demands that companies be able to plan, operate, and communicate effectively to help formulate and implement public policies that are best for all self-interested parties. Issues management is not just communication, strategic planning, monitoring, forecasting, or refining and implementing codes of conduct. It is all of these and more.

This literature stresses the theme that planning and supervision are more effective if issues management comes into play at each phase of the planning and management process (Pavlik, 1987). First, the strategic plan can be designed and reassessed based on data generated by forecasting the public policy environment and after careful consideration of the success or failure of the issues communication effort. Second, new tactical plans can be laid out for changing operations and communication strategies based on the success or failure of the public policy efforts. Third, a new strategic management philosophy can be created, especially in cases when public policy efforts ease or constrain operations. Finally, management tactics can be politically sensitive to an environment influenced by conflicting opinion, values, and policy as well as the accompanying power struggles. Issues management may proceed most effectively by infusing current standards of corporate responsibility into internal operating procedures.

This review of major contributors on issues management reveals that the key themes are interdisciplinary, drawing together forecasting, political maneuvering, communication, as well as planning and management based on standards of social responsibility.

SYSTEMS THEORY: THE MACROLEVEL

To advance, the practice of issues management requires theory and research that can be addressed at three focal points: (a) the *macrolevel*, focusing on the relations between organizations and their environments to explain the dynamics unique to public policy contests and adjustment; (b) *links* tying groups together, whereby each system receives and supplies information and exerts influence internally and externally; and (c) the *intraindividual level*, involving the cognitive processes by which people receive and react to information and influence. This section and the two that follow offer theoretical foundations and research findings that promote the growth of issues management.

Systems theory has provided much of the underpinning to explain how organizations relate to their environments (Pavlik, 1987). For instance, this theory has been used to explain how public relations helps companies increase the quality of their communication, a means for making them open and responsive to their environment (Dozier & Hellweg, 1985).

How the flow of communication is understood is crucial to explaining the relationship between an organization and its environment. The mission to be served by issues management requires a global view of the relationship between each organization and the people and groups that have a stake in its actions. This stake is the product of the self-interest of each organization cast against the collective interests of all other stakeholders.

To obtain this level of analysis requires an understanding of the characteristics systems exhibit during interaction. *Balance* refers to systems' ability to self-correct; the need to achieve balance motivates corrective behavior. If systems are *permeable*, information can flow into and out of them; similar to energy in biological systems, this information is the lifeblood that allows systems to adapt to one another and achieve their goals. Systems theory assumes that entities respond to information in a cybernetic pattern that allows them to monitor their efforts in order to achieve their goals. Through the exchange of information, systems *interchange* dynamically with one another. The systems perspective offers a set of guiding assumptions regarding the adjustments that must be made by any open system to survive by adapting to its environment. From the organization's point of view, monitoring and forecasting provide the input part of the interchange between systems, and issues communication constitutes part of each organization's output. The system approach defines and gives scope to the factors relevant to how organizations and their stakeholders function as separate but interdependent entities.

An information flow model of systems, however, can miss the dynamic adjustments organizations make in regard to one another. An even more encompassing issue relates to the goal setting and planning functions that set the criteria by which the cybernetic part of the systems model can operate. How organizations are viewed as seeking balance with their environment is crucial to this analysis. They must accommodate to other organizations' assertions of their own self-interests. For instance, only those oil companies that have large domestic reserves want an oil import tax to maintain high domestic prices; oil companies that have nondomestic reserves oppose the fee. And airlines oppose the fee as do most consumers, with the possible exception of residents of oil-producing locales. The issue made salient by this example is that issues management operates from a model that asserts planning into the systems equation.

A systems model that merely assumes a free and open exchange of information can miss the dynamics of goal setting, strategic planning, and managed adjustments. Cautioning against a static view of systems theory, Morgan (1982) argued that it should be treated as an epistemology. If not it can be mechanistic focusing on feedback as a means for correcting organizational efforts to achieve goals. This cybernetic view can imply that systems are designed and set into operation to satisfy a narrow range of goals that may ignore other goals perceived to be outside of the immediate realm (or worse not perceived at all). Morgan argued that systems theory should guide searches for better goals by which to steer an organization and reduce uncertainty about its environment. The point is this, Morgan reasoned: Cybernetics can be applied only to determine whether a company is in balance when it is at peace with the environment—a view that can be too narrow and that can lead the organization to fail. The search for information should include surveillance of the environment to see whether it is changing and why. To avoid becoming static, a systems view must include the possibilities of making dynamic adjustments, establishing new goals, developing new criteria for evaluating success, and being sensitive to change and turbulence.

Support for Morgan's view can be found in the complaisance U.S. business people showed until they had lost commercial advantage in the international marketplace. Exploring this issue, Weaver (1988) concluded, "On issue after issue, from toxic wastes to auto safety, the pattern is the same. Again and again, business has supported policies that hurt business and weaken the economy. Again and again, it has opposed policies that would help business and strengthen the economy. In recent decades, the corporation has truly been its own worst enemy" (p. 130). Why has this been the case? Weaver answered that public policy has been a friend, not a foe, to business. Corporations achieved a lot of favorable legislation, such as tariffs, subsidies, official monopolies, tax breaks, wage controls, defense spending, and government-sponsored research. Because of these advantages, the American economy reflects what corporations believe is in their best interest, but they failed to realize that the U.S. economy is international. The privileges enjoyed here by businesses have lulled executives into lethargy, which has weakened international competitiveness. A systems perspective can lead those in the system to believe that all is well if they are constantly getting confirming feedback. The challenge facing those responsible for corporate public policy adjustments is to accurately identify and fully understand the challenges facing them.

Additional insights into the problem of organizations failing to adapt properly to their environments has been provided by case studies such as Firestone's problems with its radial tires (Buchholz et al., 1985; Post, 1979) and the reluctance of the asbestos industry to recognize changes in values regarding product liability and the accumulation of data connecting asbestos with severe health problems (Heath, 1988a). Additional case studies are needed to determine how companies, such as was true during the 1950s, can be caught off guard by believing they are correctly obtaining and interpreting data to assess their relationship to their environment.

One systematic research effort has attempted to generate data to compare models organizations can use in adapting to their environments. Grunig and Hunt (1984) used systems principles and empirical research to compare two-way asymmetrical and two-way symmetrical models of public relations. They argued that the two-way asymmetrical model assumes that a company can use audience analysis/feedback and strategic communication to get key audiences to accept the company's views on key public policy issues. This option can promote deceit and manipulation. In contrast, the two-way symmetrical model, they argued, offers many advantages for formulating corporate ethics and developing communication strategies that build harmony among all groups with which a company is involved. This model is superior, they believed, because it is not manipulative and allows information and influence to flow freely between companies and their stakeholders.

To add value to the bottom line, issues management must do more than merely attempt to influence the external environment. For this reason, Nelson and Heath (1986) concluded that issues management is a means "to help organizations fit themselves to long-term shifts in the climate of public sensitivity, whether by changing corporate policy, shaping legislation, or influencing public opinion" (p. 21). Issues managers can assist their organizations' efforts to obtain information from their environment. This information is used for decision-making and adjustive purposes, including yielding to external forces or seeking to influence them as means for achieving harmony. As Sethi (1977) reasoned, organizations either must perform as they are expected to do or they must change the standards they are expected to meet or convince their critics that they meet those standards.

Helping a company to be open to its environment does not fully justify issues management or establish its operating guidelines. As Freeman (1984) reasoned, corporate management must understand the values its stakeholders hold and work to assure that business operations are in harmony with them. Upon this rationale, Freeman advised the strategic manager (including the issue manager) to understand the organization's values, as well as those of each stakeholder group. This information can guide planning, strategic management, and communication. Information that is sent outside of a company can correct false conclusions that a company's actions and policies do not conform to stakeholder values. This approach postulates that a company can either change its own or its stakeholders' values or actions with the goal of achieving harmony among all.

A systems approach that is sensitive to the turbulence created by forces competing for domination can help scholars and practitioners understand how stakeholders, such as activist groups, develop values and employ tactics to influence the public policy environment surrounding businesses. Grunig (1987b), as do Heath and Nelson (1986), postulated that active publics become special interest activists when private sector actions threaten their self-interests. A feeling of imbalance motivates people to seek information and to coalesce into pressure groups (Bergner 1986a, 1986b). Laying out this equation, Grunig concluded that "Publics with high problem recognition and level of involvement and weak constraint recognition are most likely to communicate actively about situational issues, to construct organized cognitions about those issues, and to engage in individual behaviors related to those issues" (p. 30). Grunig believed that active publics know more about an issue and are easier to reach with communication because they are seeking information, but are harder to persuade since they acquire information from many sources. But passive audiences do not seek information and are therefore difficult to communicate with; if they receive a message they are not likely to hold it with much conviction in contrast to their activist counterparts who are more likely to resist persuasion. Activists make the difference in an issues campaign because they are involved, but working with them is difficult because they have formulated opinions.

One goal of research should be to add insight into the variables that produce compatibility or friction between stakeholders. How can they be brought into balance? What measures can be used to determine when balance has been achieved? One way to answer these questions may be to apply the assumptions of coorientation (Broom, 1977). What is especially important about this model is its ability to give issues managers "breadth or perspective" which Culbertson (1984) said "entails accepting one view as one's own and recognizing a difference between that and other positions" (p. 31). The result of this analysis is a clearer understanding of the points at which stakeholders agree or disagree with an organization. Culbertson doubted that many representatives of organizations can accurately state the positions on issues held by those with whom they are involved.

According to coorientation, organizations and their stakeholders can either hold opinions of one another that are accurate or inaccurate; either side may or may not accurately understand the motives, values, and activities of the other. Or the relationship can be evaluated by the extent to which each side is satisfied or dissatisfied by the actions, values, or motives of the other. Effective relationships, according to this coorientation model, assume that the parties need to accurately understand each other and be satisfied. The model can guide estimates of the extent to which the company and its key publics agree on public policy issue stances, views of a company's image, ethics, or standards of corporate conduct. Broom (1977) argued that a public relations problem exists when a company and its key publics have conflicting views.

Coorientation allows practitioners to measure the extent to which any public sees a company as the company wants to be viewed. The model assumes that a discrepancy between sets of perceptions can be remedied by changing policies or informing the publics so that they hold a more accurate view of the company. Or the parties involved can influence and be influenced regarding which standards of behavior are most appropriate. For instance, publics can accurately see a company as being a polluter and be dissatisfied by its failure to meet standards of environmental protection. Or a public may be dissatisfied by some aspect of a company's activities and not realize that the view is inaccurate. Either the company may not be engaging in those activities or they may not be harmful. Coorientation gives a systems-based guideline for estimating where problems exist and how they can be remedied.

Another standard systems assumption is that an open system constantly interchanges with its environments (and subsystems interchange with one another). This principle underpins corporate efforts to take information and influence from the environment in the form of input. This information is analyzed and output as persuasive or informative communication to help adjust the organization to its environment (Long & Hazelton, 1987; Nelson & Heath, 1986). This topic is considered in the next section that discusses factors accounting for the success or failure of the people who serve as links between systems.

Systems theory offers taxonomies and general principles that prescribe relationships and characteristics that are essential to organizations. But much more research is needed to determine what dynamics produce harmony among stakeholders, especially when each holds conflicting, justifiable, and self-interested stake in specific public policy positions. Given this summary, it is likely that companies that allow two-way information flow are likely to understand public policy positions and to be understood by their various stakeholders. It is also likely that companies that actively seek a balance between exerting and yielding to public policy influence will be appreciated by other stakeholders and will thereby exert influence in the public policy arena. In public policy contests, positive efforts beget positive responses, whereas negative efforts produce negative reactions. And companies that are open to external standards of corporate social responsibility are likely to achieve harmony with their stakeholders. Some evidence for these generalizations can be obtained by viewing the ease with which Johnson & Johnson handled its Tylenol crisis in contrast to the protracted battles waged by the tobacco industry, asbestos industry, and A. H. Robbins (Dalkon Shield). Another success story is Dow Chemical's product stewardship program.

A pure systems orientation can assume that systems seek to balance with their environment by reading information about how well they are adapting. This informational approach is inadequate to explain the full range of efforts needed for effective issues management that also assumes that organizations can affect and be affected by other systems in their environment through power and persuasion. This model carries issues communication beyond reactivity (adjusting to feedback) and proactivity (early intervention) to interactivity (dynamic interchange with influence flowing from and into the organization).

Taking the organization and its environment as the focal point of analysis, a systems perspective serves to remind researchers that organizations have many requirements, constraints, and options as they adjust to their environment. At the level of public policy, issues management serves to assist organizations to adjust their self-interests to those of various stakeholders. Communication, issue monitoring, ethical responsibility, and strategic planning and management are key elements in this adjustment process.

SYSTEMS LINKS: STRATEGIC REDUCTION OF UNCERTAINTY

Systems theory allows for imagining grand public policy chess games played between organizations. But the reality is that the success of any organization depends on the quality of the structure, culture, and personnel involved in issues management. If organizations must take in, process, and output information and influence to adjust to their environments, then the specific variables of this process deserve to receive increased insight. To do so requires an understanding of the attitudes, structural arrangements, and capabilities of the individuals who serve as links between systems (Long & Hazelton, 1987).

Links are the positions in a system where members join one system to another. How well organizations deal with the turbulence of the public policy arena depends on their members' ability to reduce uncertainty and the organizational climate and culture that determine how information will be obtained and processed and how influence will be exerted internally and externally. One model of links places the responsibility for this activity in a specific department, such as public relations. But a different model assumes that all of the members of an organization are capable of and can participate in the issues management process—by monitoring as well as communicating. If all members of the organization assume the responsibility of being alert for issues, the organization is highly permeable. For instance, personnel engaged in customer relations can look upon customer complaints as potential policy issues. Similarly, technical and legal personnel can be alert for policy changes relevant to their expertise.

Turbulence

Turbulence is a key variable that relates to the competence of the links between an organization and its environment. Turbulence is the product of instability or the frequency at which change occurs in a company's environment and randomness or unpredictability of the frequency and kind of change. In times of turbulence, Huber and Daft (1987) reasoned, organizations tend to protect the basis of their business and increase their means for adapting to their environment. More resources are devoted to issues management. The greater the uncertainty, the more resources the organization is likely to commit to scanning for information that can be used to exploit opportunities and avoid problems (Markley, 1988). Such decisions are motivated by the desire to reduce uncertainty.

Applying an uncertainty reduction paradigm, Huber and Daft (1987) studied the variables that affect how companies monitor their environments and extract, process, and act upon information needed for corporate success. One variable, complexity, is an estimate of the number of variables a company needs to consider when processing information about its environment; complex situations require attention to many variables. Another variable is information load: amount of information needed or available and the difficulty of obtaining and processing it.

This load is affected by variables such as quantity, ambiguity, and variety. *Quantity* is the number of symbols or messages received per unit of time. *Ambiguity* means that symbols or messages can have multiple interpretations. *Variety* refers to the complexity and turbulence of the information stream. Complexity can be subdivided into three components: numerosity, diversity, and interdependence. *Numerosity* is the number of components in the environment. *Diversity* refers to the differences among variables. *Interdependence* refers to the relationship that exists when many organizations share the same environment and develop complex dependencies on one another.

Uncertainty Reduction

One of the challenges to issues managers is to know when they should be uncertain about the organization's relationship to its stakeholders. The process of reducing uncertainty requires that links acquire information that accurately interprets environmental conditions. This information is interpreted in light of the corporate culture and the circumstances unique to each public policy effort. The culture will influence what issues managers believe to be policy issues and will shape their interpretations of these messages. The culture will be affected by the extent to which the willingness to manage issues is felt throughout the organization. A company can utilize the information obtained to support strategic planning. These are the crucial conditions if links are to be useful to the issues management process.

The variables regarding turbulence relate to the extent to which an organization experiences and reduces uncertainty. Viewing the relationship between uncertainty and information, Krippendorff (1975) argued that the amount of "information conveyed by a message is the product of the amount of uncertainty *before* the message was received minus the uncertainty *after* the message was received" (p. 359). Research into the dynamics of issues management can profit by learning how individual and group information-seeking behavior is motivated by the desire and tactics to reduce uncertainty, especially when that information affects self-interest (Berger, 1975, 1987; Berger & Calabrese, 1975).

Organizations experience uncertainty in their dealings with various stakeholders.

Savvy issues managers want to know what key stakeholders believe are the standards of responsible corporate behavior. They want to be able to accurately attribute motives and values to their stakeholders. This is not always easy. Ungson, James, and Spicer (1985) discovered that companies that deal with new regulatory agencies often experience more uncertainty than do those that deal with established agencies. Companies in new industries experience more uncertainty while interacting with regulators than do companies in established industries. The degree of uncertainty relates to the clarity and sufficiency of detail in which regulatory agencies state policies.

The unique informational needs of each organization should be reflected in its information gathering and analysis process. Information does not come to organizations in packages. Issues managers need to collect data, define issues, and give meaning to them in the context of the prevailing corporate climate. To support effective issues management, a company's culture must contain opinions and values needed to accurately determine the meaning and value of the information obtained.

Along with accuracy, speed is a variable in information processing. A strategic information management system (SIM) is expected to be timely and accurate in its transmission of information to key decision makers inside and outside the company. Organizations can fail at issues management if they try to process too many or too few issues or do not recognize the issues that require attention.

How information is received, interpreted, and used is a product of the personalities and skills of the parties involved and of the climate in the company. According to Dutton and Ottensmeyer (1987), when information equivocality rises in a company, the demand for information richness will increase. Information richness is a measure of the kind and amount of information available and needed. As demands for information increase, the SIM system is likely to become more active. When the amount of uncertainty is high and when organizational structures are characterized by high levels of differentiation, decision makers will experience higher levels of information equivocality. Under these circumstances, SIM systems need to be active. A SIM can be symbolic (giving definition to issues) or functional (processing information that is already defined). It is more likely to be functional and involve accountability when it produces lots of information, experiences risk, and is involved in political situations. When environmental uncertainty is high and the system is held accountable, the SIM needs to be active and symbolic. SIM personnel have considerable power over corporate responses to public policies because they define, interpret, and make available the information used to make public policy decisions. If this influence is used instrumentally, it is a vital, proactive force.

Strategic issues management is characterized by three critical events: activation, assessment of urgency, and assessment of feasibility. How these three factors interrelate in the decision making of each company will influence its ability to create momentum for change. These variables relate to each company's belief system and resources. Effective strategic issue diagnosis is an iterative and cyclical process that involves two major events. When used effectively, it is activated when some type of strategic issue is recognized. The corporate response will be influenced by the perceived urgency of taking action on the issue and the perceived feasibility of dealing with the issue. During the early stages in issues analysis, decision makers are likely to attempt to understand and give meaning to each issue that appears to have strategic importance for the company. Part of the acuity of each company rests with its ability to be triggered by an issue—to begin the response process. Triggering can result when decision makers perceive a gap between actual and expected performance on an issue. Urgency is a measure of the cost or advantage of taking or not taking action on a issue. The variables that produce urgency are time pressures, the degree of visibility (the amount of exposure and publicity an issue is receiving), and perceptions of accountability. Response options depend on two variables: The extent to which a company believes that it understands an issue and the extent to which it believes that it can do something about it. If a company believes that it understands an issue and can affect it, it will exhibit greater momentum to change. Effective issues management assists companies in establishing effective links with the stakeholders in their environments and assessing the urgency of the needed response while also calculating the feasibility of making various responses to the situation. All of this is governed by the interpretative criteria present in the company's corporate culture that assigns meanings to events. Responses by the company are conditioned by beliefs about risk preference, self-sufficiency, and competence. Beliefs exhibit two distinct dimensions: complexity and level of consensus. Consensus is easier to achieve when beliefs are simple and unvaried. When beliefs are complex and varied, consensus is more difficult to achieve. Companies with differentiated beliefs (lower consensus and greater complexity) will have response mechanisms that are more frequently triggered. Companies with differentiated beliefs are more likely to perceive the feasibility of change and exhibit greater momentum for change. When companies have many coping resources, they are less likely to perceive urgency of change and exhibit less momentum to change. When the amount of resources and the perceived feasibility of achieving change are high, so will be the momentum of change (Dutton & Duncan, 1987). Thus, issues management depends on the amount of belief consensus, ability to achieve change, availability of resources needed for change, and degree of momentum for change.

The organizational structure of each company and the personal variables of employees influence the amount of environmental uncertainty experienced by links. Cognitive complexity, a personal variable, refers to the ability of personnel to handle complex cognitive tasks required to process information. To cope with complex problems, effective companies vary the membership of their decisionmaking teams during periods of high uncertainty. And effective organizations reduce uncertainty by acquiring and internally distributing information about the environment. Studies along these lines emphasize the factors involved in the pro

cess, the organizational structure, the characteristics of the personnel, the characteristics of the information to be discovered and processed, and the climate that
influences what information is important and when and how the information is
going to take on meaning.

So that companies can communicate more effectively with their stakeholders,
Grunig (1987a; Grunig & Hunt, 1984) suggested that they use formative research
to find out what stakeholders know and believe; this research is designed to
discover problems and plan to solve them. After communication campaigns have
been conducted, public relations specialists should use evaluative research to determine whether the plan designed after the formative research isolated needs was
successful. Formative research can be used to learn how well publics understand
an organization and how well management understands its publics, information
that helps in choosing specific communication objectives. Evaluative research
measures whether a communication effort has actually improved the understanding
publics have of the organization and that management has of its publics.

The information needed to deal with turbulence is not only derived by using
surveys. Much valuable data come from scanning reports whether technical, legal,
legislative, or regulative. Public relations personnel may not be sufficiently educated to understand the implications subtle technical, regulative, legislative, or
legal changes can have upon their organization. Links may be stronger if the
persons involved come from the key disciplines that make up the organization.

External monitoring may use tactics other than surveys; one alternative is the
news hole technique (Naisbitt, 1982). Joseph Coates and associates (Coates &
Jarratt, 1986; Coates, Jarratt, & Heinz, 1986; Heinz & Coates, 1986) have
employed this technique to diagram the development of public policy issues by
measuring the ratio of space devoted to each issue (in proportion to all issues
covered in the media). This monitoring technique has been used to describe public
policy trends regarding environmental issues from 1970 to 1985 (Heinz & Coates,
1986). This technique assumes that a positive relationship exists between the
amount and type of information disseminated by the media and the interest or
demand by the public to know. This equation suffers from a chicken–egg relationship that assumes synergism between publics' desire to know and media's
willingness and ability to report. It is insensitive to opinion differences held by
stakeholder groups as well as by individual stakeholders of each group.

A company must bring in information, and it must send information to key
stakeholders—which may be experiencing various levels of uncertainty. Stakeholders of an organization acquire information that allows them to make attributions
about the character, values, and behavior of persons and groups involved. People do
this to satisfy their need to interact with companies.

In times of low uncertainty in regard to the legislative or regulatory environment, companies may be successful with one-way communication. But in times of
high uncertainty, they are likely to be more successful by adopting a two-way
model. The need for a two-way relationship increases as does the amount of
constraint that can be created by activist groups (Grunig & Grunig, 1989).

Organizational Culture and Climate

One key aspect of organizational culture and climate is the way in which key issues management efforts are incorporated into the decision-making structure. Pursuing this line of reasoning, Grunig (1985) demonstrated how organizational structure can affect employees' morale and their feelings of professional involvement. He reinforced the commitment to a two-way symmetrical organizational structure when he found that an asymmetrical structure constrains communication and innovation thereby harming morale and professionalism.

Exploring this relationship, Dozier (1988) reasoned that public relations personnel should have access to managerial decision makers and be an integrated unit if they are to help an organization increase its openness. If they do not achieve this status, they are likely to be used only for supplying information to external audiences. If this analysis is correct, the kind of links that issues managers provide is crucial to their company's adaptive ability. To be effective, issues managers should obtain, characterize and interpret, information in ways that help the organization to make decisions needed to maximize harmony and minimize friction with their stakeholders. The effectiveness of issues managers depends on the extent to which they are integrated into the information acquisition, characterization, and decision-making process.

Because of their cultures, some companies are likely to yield to pressures exerted by external organizations whereas others are likely to be more combative. How each organization makes such decisions results from its culture. For instance, Stanley (1985) recommended that issues managers use a rewards/losses decision matrix to decide whether to oppose or accept regulatory change. The decision is predicated upon a determination of the likelihood of victory versus the costs of failure. The rewards in the decision matrix can include profits, image attributes, or public policy power resources. Stanley advised issues managers on ways to decide whether to accept legislative restrictions or regulatory punishments or to contest them. This game theory approach recognizes that power resources are used in pressure politics. Activist groups seek to exert power over corporations through legislators, regulators, and court battles. This point is appreciated by Crable and Vibbert (1985) who advised practitioners on means by which to intervene early in public policy struggles.

If they are to be effective links, public relations practitioners should be involved in creating and implementing corporate codes of conduct, but they are often not included. When deciding what the code should contain, those responsible for its creation are likely to be more sensitive to internal stakeholders (executives, employees, and shareholders) than to external ones (customers, general public, regulators, legislators, and such) (Heath & Ryan, 1989).

To understand the relationship between organizations and their stakeholders requires insight into the variables that account for the effectiveness of the personnel, information-analysis process, and structure of the links between organizations and stakeholders. Organizational culture will influence how the personnel who are links perceive which issues are in the corporate interest and know how best to manage them. The personnel who are links and the structure in which they operate should be capable of handling many issues and obtaining much information about the issues and the dynamics that surround them.

Links will be more successful when they can appreciate what information actually reduces the uncertainty of all parties involved with key public policies. If belief consensus is too high, a company can become arrogant and insensitive. If it is too low, links lack viable criteria by which to determine which information reduces uncertainty, or how much uncertainty is reduced by each piece of information. If feasibility is perceived to be high regarding a public policy, the links may move confidently knowing what their company's negotiating position is. If perceived feasibility is low, links may be tentative and too eager or too reluctant to negotiate public policy. Links are more capable when they can discover many public policy options and understand the prevailing constraints. Considerations such as these may advance the research regarding how organizations span boundaries and build good relationships with stakeholders.

INTRAINDIVIDUAL VARIABLES

No matter how much emphasis is placed on system and structure variables, analysis should not dismiss the variables related to individual judgment. This section discusses factors that help explain how and why people receive, process, and use information and influence. In discussions of this kind, research should consider cognitive-processing variables of people who are inside organizations, particularly members of management who need to understand and accept information and influence. It is possible that people within a company, especially members of management, receive and process information about public policy matters (such as complaints about company actions) in quite different ways than do members of stakeholder groups. Management may bolster and erect defenses, whereas supporters of activist groups eagerly receive negative information about companies. Whether inside or outside of an organization, people construct a social reality that guides their thoughts and actions—including their expectations for the performance of organizations in which they have stakes.

Refinement of intraindividual analysis begins with an understanding of the role the individual mind plays in public policy discussion. Issues management research should acknowledge that opinions held toward a company, industry, policy, or activity are individual—not group or what is loosely called "public opinion." Opinion is an individual matter even though it can be generalized as group opinion. For instance, if pollsters are interested in what ecologists think about a company or an industry, they ask individual ecologists and generalize the group's opinions.

Such generalizations blur differences unique to each person's opinions; group opinion is neither singular nor uniform. All persons in a group do not respond in the same ways to messages even though they are mutually interested in the issue. Opinion change requires that individuals be influenced *as individuals,* even though they hold opinions as a result of group memberships and belong to groups because of shared opinions. Issue communication influences individual viewers, listeners, and readers.

Issues managers may falsely assume that the opinions of stakeholders are uniform rather than diverse. On a given day, many people have no opinion on matters relating to companies or public policy. Some people have opinions on these matters but are unlikely to do anything to affect public policy or act in favor of or against any company's or industry's interests. Regardless of which group is important to a company at a given moment, only a small part of the membership is likely to exert influence upon the company, related stakeholders, or members of that group. The best conceptualization of collectivized opinion is that some stakeholders' opinions support a company's efforts and some opinions conflict with those efforts.

Lacking the proper perspective, organizational decision makers can make several false assumptions about widely held opinions. One, they may focus on public opinion, not opinion of individual stakeholders. Stakeholders attend to mediated information selectively and idiosyncratically. Two, they may not account for the impact that recall of a few select pieces of information has upon stakeholder interest and opinion. (Classic examples of the phenomenon include Three Mile Island and the consequences of one car accident on Ted Kennedy's political fortunes.) Three, they may not recognize individual differences in information reception, denial, inattention, and distortion. Four, lots of press on an issue may be distorted by company decision makers who may under or overreact. The point: Increased insight into individual cognitive processes is the only way to understand the opinion formation and activation processes.

To demonstrate the complexity of cognitive processes, McGuire (1981) used a 12-part linear model to describe the stages of the information acquisition and activation process. These stages start with being exposed to communication and move from there to attending to it, becoming interested in it, comprehending it, learning how to process it, yielding to it, storing it in memory, retrieving it from memory, using stored information, behaving upon it, reinforcing actions based on rewards and punishments, and consolidating (or abandoning) behavior. This complex process suggests that individual stakeholders are likely to be at various stages in the model at any moment on a given issue.

Individual Uncertainty

Choices create uncertainty as do actions that appear to be contrary to individual self-interests. For these reasons, uncertainty reduction is a useful concept for understanding intraindividual processes. As people make decisions and form opinions related to personal and public interests, they do so out of the desire to reduce uncertainty. They seek information from and attribute causes to the actions of companies, groups, and individuals who participate in the public policy arena. How organizations perform will determine whether positive or negative attributions are made about them.

Attribution is likely to be unique to the stake each person has with the company, whether consumer, neighbor, regulator, legislator, competitor, or employee. The more important the behavior of the company is to the interests of individuals the more likely they will make attributions and seek information. People need satisfactory explanations of those factors that relate to their self-interest. By this activity, people establish the subjective probability of the likelihood of the occurrences of events or attributes (Berger, 1987).

Persons who are outside an organization are likely to receive, even seek, information about its policies and actions in the desire to protect their self-interest. People are motivated to find or receive information if they believe that it can help them protect or promote their self-interests. Individuals turn to those sources that make the most and best information available. Each public policy situation requires that sufficient information be available to help interested people inform themselves to make the necessary decisions. Information seeking creates a market for journalists to sell their wares and for activists, legislators, companies, and regulators to tell their side of the story. If some information sources do not share information, stakeholders suspect their motives and fear a cover up. The greater the uncertainty and the need to reduce it, the more likely people will turn to whatever sources of information are available and appear capable of reducing uncertainty.

Conventional wisdom is that companies help themselves by putting out enough information so that they increase the likelihood that people can discover and use it to reduce uncertainty. Issues communicators should provide information for persons, who as individuals, make up the opinions of various stakeholder groups. This assumption must be sensitive to the likelihood that people only find, attend to, and utilize information that affects their uncertainty and involvement on issues related to their self-interest. Although a company or industry is not being scrutinized and is not affecting stakeholder interests, it is unlikely to find willing audiences. But when organizations attempt to address their stakeholders, the nature of the stakeholder relationship forms the basis for what the content of the messages should be.

Even when self-interest is present (or at least potentially so) some people receive and retain information more quickly than others. Not all opinion bases develop at the same rate. For instance, many years passed before most people accepted the presence and harm of air and other forms of pollution. It is interesting to speculate how persons who are potential critics of a company progress from certainty ("no problem exists") to uncertainty ("what is happening") back to certainty ("X is a viable solution" or "the original information was incorrect").

Potential critics are prone to grasp and remember the initial information they receive during the transition from certainty to uncertainty and back again. This information can have a primacy effect on subsequent information and arguments received. Audiences may be less easily informed but more easily influenced at initial stages of opinion formation because they lack information and have not received issue position confirmation from several sources. Slowness to grasp information may also be due to the lack of appropriate cognitive frameworks with which to appreciate its relevance.

Research can discover what variables lead people to receive or resist information and influence (including active information acquisition). Are people more likely to receive information and make attribution about companies that are perceived to have the greatest impact on their well-being? If so, what kind of questions do people ask? Do their standards of what constitutes source credibility change? What influences retention and recall of information related to standards of corporate responsibility? Do people receive and process information seeking to reinforce or change existing opinions? Are print media more important than other media in dealing with sensational information—such as crises? Are print media more important than other media when discussing complex policy issues or when attempting to reach specific kinds of audiences? What roles do interpersonal contacts play in policy contests? What factors lead persons to become involved with activist groups? What criteria do people use to attribute motives to companies and thereby characterize them? For instance, despite thousands of responsible actions by companies, opinions toward the private sector during times of crisis are likely to center around negative attributions. Are the standards of corporate responsibility universal or situational? Are those standards anything more than concepts that express personal well-being? What sorts of communication and performance strategies are necessary to allay fears of persons who are hostile (or potentially so) toward companies? Is the likelihood to view or read about incidents predicated on the need to find information and attribute characteristics to establish a view toward individual companies or the private sector? Do people oppose activities of some types of organizations more than others? If so, why do these differences occur? What sorts of misattribution and stereotyping occur? How do people verify the information they receive regarding public policy issues? How much verification is necessary to reduce uncertainty? These are a few of the questions likely to produce useful insight; all of them can be extrapolated from uncertainty reduction theory and research.

Some research projects have been conducted along these lines. Grunig (1987b) systematically studied the interaction between information-seeking behavior and factors leading to public policy activism. He proposed that "a public is motivated to communicate about specific issues by high problem recognition, low constraint recognition, and high level of involvement." Given this interaction, the more active people are "the better formed will be their cognitions about those issues and the more often they will engage in individual behaviors related to those issues" (p. 27).

This finding justifies using uncertainty reduction to explain why people respond to corporate activities that have consequences for their well-being and when no major constraints stand in the way of information seeking and active participation.

The other side of the uncertainty reduction coin is the need on the part of companies to seek information needed to understand and analyze the forces in public policy environments that can affect operations. Accurate attribution by the company of stakeholder actions is vital to the success of this process. Corporations may misunderstand the motives of activist and other stakeholder groups and thereby respond to them inappropriately. Krippendorff and Eleey (1986) stressed the relevance of the concept of uncertainty reduction to public relations practitioners by showing that companies can reduce uncertainty regarding their environment by setting up information acquisition and decision-making systems. But beyond understanding these links, research is needed to explain how corporate culture influences issues managers' sensitivity to public policy changes. Some persons internal to a company are likely to resort to defensive behavior and bolstering which makes them insensitive to the external environment. Others are likely to overreact to turbulence. How can people accurately and sensitively receive, characterize, process, and utilize information needed to understand their environmental pressures and options?

If internal users of information experience uncertainty, they may be interested and attentive. Matters related to the apparent well-being of an organization should increase attention, but this may not be the case for several reasons. Related are factors of self-perceived competence to handle environmental turbulence and make changes needed to foster harmony of interests. For Dutton and Ottensmeyer (1987), an effective strategic issue management system is one that legitimately ignores some issues and acts on others. The key problem is making sense of the barrage of information with which corporate planners and managers must deal. Information about public policy matters is often equivocal. Issue managers are not always certain they have good information. Even if they are confident the information is accurate, they may be uncertain regarding its implications for planning and operation.

Relationship Variables

Understanding the cognitive processes of stakeholders may be fostered by utilizing interpersonal communication research in regard to relational variables, such as liking. Extrapolated from source credibility and interpersonal relationship studies, one may assume if stakeholders like a company, it would be trusted. Johnson & Johnson's success in allaying fears about Tylenol may have resulted because it was liked—as well as being responsive and innocent. Contrast this case against those regarding asbestos, the Dalkon Shield, or cigarettes.

In times of uncertainty, do people turn to sources of information and influence that are similar, familiar, and liked? Questions such as this suggest that the relationship between stakeholders and companies may predict communication and information reception/processing behavior in times of uncertainty. The paradigmatic relationship is two people coming to an agreement about an object or entity (or in this sense an issue or policy). As Pavitt and Cappella (1979) noted, the amount of liking one person has toward another will affect the accuracy of the first person's judgment toward an object of mutual interest. If person A likes person B, A will tend to like the object if B does. The amount of liking or disliking can affect the accuracy of person A's view of the object. The extent to which A likes B will influence the willingness to communicate with B. Willingness may affect amount of time spent communicating and amount of communication. The accuracy of A's understanding of the object will be affected by liking B, and if the amount of time spent listening to B increases because of liking, A is more likely to accurately know B's opinion toward the object. If A does not like B, they will spend less time communicating, and A will be less likely to know accurately what B thinks of A. Claims such as these suggest that preliminary to communication about a company image, products, services, or operating policies, the company and its spokespersons should be liked by members of stakeholder groups. Subsequent communication and willingness to agree with a spokesperson's assessment may depend upon the amount of liking.

Information Integration/Expectancy Value

Fishbein and Ajzen's (Ajzen & Fishbein, 1980; Fishbein & Ajzen, 1975, 1981) work on information integration and expectancy value offers a comprehensive and systematic explanation of how persons hold many interacting, sometimes conflicting, and differentiated opinions toward an object, situation, or issue. Information integration divides cognition into two dominant processes, attitudes (evaluations) and beliefs (the degree of certainty regarding the evaluation). This model suggests that an attitude toward an object (such as a company, action, or policy) is a product of positive and negative evaluations each of which has different weight (strength) in the total equation. For instance, people like the comfort made possible by gasoline products but dislike the pollution they cause. Or they may believe that nuclear generation of electricity is safe but too expensive.

Fishbein and Ajzen demonstrated how opinions are differentiated, not just favorable or unfavorable. This differentiation gives persuaders a more complex model with which to work and suggests that part of an opinion can be changed while other parts are maintained or augmented. According to the model, opinions change through increases or decreases of certainty or by creating or lessening specific evaluations. The expectancy value component of this theory views actions as products of attitudes (the subjective expected values of the action) compared against compliance with significant others' norms regarding the action. The model demonstrates why attitudes do not always lead to actions.

Involvement

Petty and his research associates (Petty & Cacioppo, 1981; 1986; Petty, Cacioppo, & Schumann, 1983; Petty, Kasmer, Haugtvedt, & Cacioppo, 1987) claimed that the influence of messages is either peripheral or central to the cognitive system depending on the degree of personal involvement. For this reason, all opinions are not equally complex. Peripheral opinions require little more cognitive information and processing than mere positive or negative association and depend more on the source of the message than its content. Central opinions are more complex, entail more information, result from involvement—desire to know information. Because they are complex and better supported, central opinions are more difficult to change and are likely to influence behavior. Opinions shift from peripheral to central because of the degree of involvement, the desire to reduce uncertainty about a topic of self-interest or importance. The degree of involvement may correlate with the number of statements that can be generated about the object or issue of concern.

Culbertson (1984) cautioned that the degree to which a person is involved with an issue seems not to correlate with the number of opposing arguments that person is able to generate. Based on these findings, a company may be astute to attempt to have audiences hold favorable associations peripherally in the event that a public policy issue emerges; the reasoning is similar to that regarding liking just discussed. Second, organizations are advised to provide information that can be acquired and used by persons whose opinions are becoming central. How persons communicate (seek or receive information on issues) may be influenced by the amount of affective or cognitive involvement (Gibbs & Ferguson, 1988). The first dimension refers to their self-interests; the second relates to the amount of information they have on a topic. This research substantiates the assumption that within stakeholder populations some members have central opinions, whereas others' opinions are peripheral. Information reception and processing as well as action on a policy issue may result from the amount of cognitive involvement.

Examining how people respond to product and service advertising, Wright (1973, 1981) offered three cognitive processes to explain how people receive and process information and influence. When confronted with ad copy, people generate arguments to support or oppose claims made by advertisers. People also engage in source derogation by attributing and evaluating the motives behind the advertising campaign. The amount of refutation increases as involvement does, whereas low involvement subjects made more source derogation comments (Wright, 1974). This model is supported by research findings that people who initially favor a policy listen to or read ads differently than opponents do (Douglas, Heath, & Nelson, 1987). How people receive information may determine the extent to which they recall it (Heath & Douglas, 1986). This research offers insight into how people respond to issue communication.

Research along these lines may help issues management mature by shedding light onto how people receive and process information as well as exert and yield to influence in the contest to formulate and impose public policy.

TOWARD AN INTEGRATED THEORY

This literature review highlights four molar concepts: uncertainty, evaluation, influence (including power resource management), and involvement.

The first factor, uncertainty, assumes that the relationship between organizations and their stakeholders can deteriorate when vital information does not flow both ways. If information flows between them so each can reduce uncertainty about the other, the relationship is sound, and parties can negotiate differences and increase understanding. But an understanding paradigm alone cannot explain the dynamic public policy adjustments needed for issues management. That paradigm can miss variables needed to explain why friction can exist between companies and stakeholders.

Information can increase understanding, but understanding does not equate with approval. Stakeholders, for instance, may know about the organization and not approve of its policies, values, goals, or behavior. Understanding and satisfaction may be at odds, and the only way to achieve the latter is to change legislation, regulation, adjudication, opinion or behavior. For instance, once an operating standard for acceptable mercury emission levels is established at Z parts per million, it becomes law. If a company had advocated Y parts and an environmental group had proposed X parts, neither may be totally satisfied. Both parties understand the new guideline, but are not satisfied by it. Likewise, an organization may understand the points of view advocated by a stakeholder, but not agree. So, understanding, with the accompanying requirement for the free flow of information, is a major part of a workable issues management model, but by itself is insufficient.

The second molar concept, evaluation, is the result of attitudes or values that become embedded into the social realties (internal and external) that are held in regard to an organization's policies and actions. Stakeholders may understand a company's activities, but evaluate it by applying different standards. For instance, environmentalists may know that a timber company is removing rain forests, a practice they believe harms the aesthetics of earth and contributes to the hot house effect both of which can severely reduce quality of life. In contrast, investor stakeholders interested in financial performance of a publicly traded company may approve of the timber harvesting methods. The evaluation part of the paradigm assumes harmony is possible by changing the values and operations of the company to satisfy stakeholder expectations. Or the company needs to change evaluations of stakeholders which disapprove of its policies, values, or operations. Or it may change policies by yielding to environmentalists and then have to convince the investors that the new operations will produce an attractive profit.

The third molar concept is influence—the ability to exert pressures in the public policy arena even at the loss of some stakeholder. This factor emphasizes the need to understand conflict resolution (Grunig & Grunig, 1989; Stanley, 1985). As Ewing (1987) concluded, "issues management is about power" (p. 1). Issues management assumes that organizations engage in rewards/losses analysis regarding the expedience of opposing or yielding to power pressures from stakeholders who can impose sanctions. The equation works like this: Assuming accuracy of understanding but an unchangeable difference in evaluation (dissatisfaction) companies, regulators, or activist groups have the option of exerting influence or opposing the influence efforts of others.

Involvement, the last molar concept, is associated with the self-interest that stakeholders have in organizations' actions. The greater the involvement, the more likely uncertainty reduction and influence efforts will be employed.

Taking these factors into consideration, the prediction is this: Entities seek to understand and be satisfied by the relationship between them. Consonant with the general systems perspective, the parts of any system will interact and interchange in dynamic ways seeking balance. The sides joined in controversy will continue to seek information, make evaluation, and exert influence until understanding is achieved and they are satisfied that they have done what they can to reduce uncertainty and protect their self-interest.

CONCLUSION

Issues management requires insight into behavior at the system level, into the linkage between companies and stakeholders, and into the cognitive processes that lead to intraindividual opinion formation, choices, and actions. Concerns of this kind hold the keys for discovering what is required for organizations to manage issues to achieve harmony with their stakeholders.

REFERENCES

Ajzen, I., & Fishbein, M. (1980). *Understanding attitudes and predicting social behavior.* Englewood Cliffs, NJ: Prentice-Hall.

Alexander, H. E. (1983). *The case for PACS.* Washington, DC: Public Affairs Council.

Alinsky, S. (1971). *Rules for radicals—A practical primer for realistic radicals.* New York: Random House.

Arrington, C. B., Jr., & Sawaya, R. N. (1984a). Issues management in an uncertain environment. *Long Range Planning, 17*(6), 17–24.

Arrington, C. B., Jr., & Sawaya, R. N. (1984b). Managing public affairs: Issues management in an uncertain environment. *California Management Review, 26*(4), 148–160.

Aupperle, K. E., Carroll, A. B., & Hatfield, J. D. (1985). An empirical examination of the relationship between corporate social responsibility and profitability. *Academy of Management Journal, 28*(2), 446–463.

Bennett, J. T., & DiLorenzo, T. J. (1985). *Destroying democracy.* Washington, DC: Cato Institute.

Berger, C. R. (1975). Proactive and retroactive attribution processes in interpersonal communication. *Human Communication Research, 2,* 33–50.

Berger, C. R. (1987). Communicating under uncertainty. In M. E. Roloff & G. R. Miller (Eds.), *Interpersonal processes: New directions in communication research* (pp. 39–62). Newbury Park, CA: Sage.

Berger, C. R., & Calabrese, R. J. (1975). Some explorations in initial interaction and beyond: Toward a developmental theory of interpersonal communication. *Human Communication Research, 1,* 99–112.

Bergner, D. J. (1986a). The maturing of public interest groups. *Public Relations Quarterly, 31*(3), 14–16.

Bergner, D. J. (Ed.). (1986b). *Public interest profiles* (5th ed.). Washington, DC: Foundation for Public Affairs.

Bernays, E. L. (1955). *The engineering of consent.* Norman, OK: University of Oklahoma Press.

Broom, G. M. (1977). Coorientational measurement of public issues. *Public Relations Review, 3*(4), 110–119.

Brown, J. K. (1979). *This business of issues: Coping with the company's environments.* New York: The Conference Board.

Buchholz, R. A. (1982). *Business environment and public policy: Implications for management.* Englewood Cliffs, NJ: Prentice-Hall.

Buchholz, R. A. (1985). *The essentials of public policy for management.* Englewood Cliffs, NJ: Prentice-Hall.

Buchholz, R. A., Evans, W. D., & Wagley, R. A. (1985). *Management response to public issues: Concepts and cases in strategy formulation.* Englewood Cliffs, NJ: Prentice-Hall.

Chase, W. H. (1982). Issues management conference—A special report. *Corporate Public Issues and Their Management, 7,* 1–2.

Chase, W. H. (1984). *Issue management: Origins of the future.* Stamford, CT: Issue Action Publications.

Cheney, G., & Vibbert, S. L. (1987). Corporate discourse: Public relations and issue management. In F. M. Jablin, L. L. Putnam, K. H. Roberts, & L. W. Porter (Eds.), *Handbook of organizational communication: An interdisciplinary perspective* (pp. 165–194). Newbury Park, CA: Sage.

Coates, J. F., & Jarratt, J. (1986). Mapping the issues of an industry: An exercise in issues identification. *Futures Research Quarterly, 2*(1), 53–63.

Coates, J. F., Coates, V. T., Jarratt, J., & Heinz, L. (1986). *Issues management: How can you plan, organize, and manage for the future.* Mt. Airy, MD: Lomond Publications.

Coates, J. F., Jarratt, J., & Heinz, L. (1986). *Issues management: Do the models do the job?* (unpublished manuscript). Washington, DC: Joseph Coates, Inc.

Crable, R. E., & Vibbert, S. L. (1983). Mobil's epideictic advocacy: "Observations" of Prometheus-Bound. *Communication Monographs, 50,* 380–394.

Crable, R. E., & Vibbert, S. L. (1985). Managing issues and influencing public policy. *Public Relations Review, 11*(2), 3–16.

Culbertson, H. M. (1984, August). *Breadth of perspective—An important concept for public relations.* Paper presented at the Association for Education in Journalism and Mass Communication, Gainesville, FL.

Dickie, R. B. (1984). Influence of public affairs offices on corporate planning and of corporations on government policy. *Strategic Management Journal, 5,* 15–24.

Dionisopoulos, G. N. (1986a). Corporate advocacy advertising as political communication. In L. L. Kaid, D. Nimmo, & K. R. Sanders (Eds.), *New perspectives on political advertising* (pp. 82–106). Carbondale, IL: Southern Illinois University Press.

Dionisopoulos, G. N. (1986b, November). *The atom and Eve: The atomic power industry's public relations campaign and the N.E. W. women.* Paper presented at the Speech Communication Association Convention, Chicago, IL.

Douglas, W., Heath, R. L., & Nelson, R. A. (1987, November). *Toward an information integration approach to issue advertising.* Paper presented at the Speech Communication Association Convention, Boston, MA.

Dozier, D. M. (1988, May). *The vertical location of the public relations function in organizations.* Paper presented at the International Communication Association Convention, New Orleans, LA.

Dozier, D. M., & Hellweg, S. A. (1985, May). *State of the art: A comparative analysis of internal communication and public relations audits.* Paper presented to the International Communication Association, Honolulu, HI.

Dutton, J. E., & Duncan, R. B. (1987). The creation of momentum for change through the process of strategic issue diagnosis. *Strategic Management Journal, 8,* 279–295.

Dutton, J. E., & Ottensmeyer, E. (1987). Strategic issue management systems: Forms, functions, and contexts. *Academy of Management Review, 12*(2), 355–365.

Ehling, W. P., & Hesse, M. B. (1983). Use of 'issue management' in public relations. *Public Relations Review, 9* (2), 18–35.

Elmendorf, F. M. (1988). Generating grass-roots campaigns and public involvement. In R. L. Heath (Ed.), *Strategic issues management: How organizations influence and respond to public interests and policies* (pp. 305–320). San Francisco: Jossey-Bass.

Ewing, R. P. (1987). *Managing the new bottom line: Issues management for senior executives.* Homewood, IL: Dow Jones-Irwin.

Fishbein, M., & Ajzen, I. (1975). *Belief, attitude, intention, and behavior.* Reading: Addison-Wesley.

Fishbein, M., & Ajzen, I. (1981). Acceptance, yielding and impact: Cognitive processes in persuasion. In R. E. Petty, T. M. Ostrom, & T. C. Brock (Eds.), *Cognitive responses in persuasion* (pp. 339–359). Hillsdale, NJ: Lawrence Erlbaum Associates.

Freeman, R. E. (1984). *Strategic management: A stakeholder approach.* Boston: Pitman.

Gamson, W. A. (1968). *Power and discontent.* Homewood, IL: Dorsey Press.

Gamson, W. A. (1975). *The strategy of social protest.* Homewood, IL: Dorsey Press.

Gandy, O. H., Jr. (1982). *Beyond agenda setting: Information subsidies and public policy.* Norwood, NJ: Ablex.

Gibbs, J. D., & Ferguson, M. A. (1988, May). *Grunig's decision-situation theory: A replication of research.* Paper presented at the International Communication Association, New Orleans, LA.

Goodman, S. E. (1983). Why few corporations monitor social issues. *Public Relations Journal, 39*(4), 20.

Grunig, J. E. (1985, May). *A structural reconceptualization of the organizational commu-*

nication audit, with application to a State Department of Education. Paper presented at the International Communication Association, Honolulu, HI.

Grunig, J. E. (1987a). Research in the strategic management of public relations. *International Public Relations Review, 11*(2), 28–32.

Grunig, J. E. (1987b, May). *When active publics become activists: Extending a situational theory of publics.* Paper presented at International Communication Association, Montreal, Canada.

Grunig, J. E., & Grunig, L. S. (1989). *Toward a theory of the public relations behavior of organizations: Review of a program of research.* In J. E. Grunig & L. A. Grunig (Eds.), *Public relations research annual* (Vol. 1, pp. 27–63). Hillsdale, NJ: Lawrence Erlbaum Associates.

Grunig, J. E., & Hunt, T. (1984). *Managing public relations.* New York: Holt, Rinehart & Winston.

Heath, R. L. (1988a, November). *Issues Management and The Asbestos Industry: A Case Study of a Corporate Culture that Failed.* Paper presented at the Speech Communication Association, New Orleans, LA.

Heath, R. L. (Ed.). (1988b). *Strategic issues management: How organizations influence and respond to public interests and policies.* San Francisco: Jossey-Bass.

Heath, R. L., & Douglas, W. (1986). Issues advertising and its effect on public opinion recall. *Public Relations Review, 12*(2), 47–56.

Heath, R. L., & Nelson, R. A. (1986). *Issues management: Corporate public policymaking in an information society.* Beverly Hills, CA: Sage.

Heath, R. L., & Ryan, M. (1989). Public relations' role in defining corporate social responsibility. *Journal of Media Ethics, 4.*

Heinz, L., & Coates, J. F. (1986). *Models for issues management: Superfund and RCRA as test cases.* Paper prepared for Environmental Emerging Issues Team, Edison Electric Institute, Washington, DC.

Huber, G. P., & Daft, R. L. (1987). The information environments of organizations. In F. M. Jablin, L. L. Putnam, K. H. Roberts, & L. W. Porter (Eds.), *Handbook of organizational communication: An interdisciplinary perspective* (pp. 130–164). Newbury Park, CA: Sage.

Jones, B. L., & Chase, W. H. (1979). Managing public policy issues. *Public Relations Review, 5*(2), 3–23.

Krippendorff, K. (1975). Information theory. In G. J. Hanneman & W. J. McEwen (Eds.), *Communication and behavior* (pp. 351–389). Reading: Addison-Wesley.

Krippendorff, K., & Eleey, M. L. (1986). Monitoring a group's symbolic environment. *Public Relations Review, 12*(1), 13–36.

Lesly, P. (1984). *Overcoming opposition: A survival manual for executives.* Englewood Cliffs, NJ: Prentice-Hall.

Littlejohn, S. E. (1986). Competition and cooperation: New trends in corporate public issue identification and resolution. *California Management Review, 19*(1), 109–123.

Long, L. W., & Hazelton, V., Jr. (1987). Public relations: A theoretical and practical response. *Public Relations Review, 13*(2), 3–13.

Markley, O. W. (1988). Conducting a situation audit: A case study. In R. L. Heath (Ed.), *Strategic issues management: How organizations influence and respond to public interests and policies* (pp. 137–154). San Francisco: Jossey-Bass.

Marx, T. G. (1986). Integrating public affairs and strategic planning. *California Management Review, 29*(1), 141–147.

McGuire, W. J. (1981). Theoretical foundations of campaigns. In R. E. Rice & W. J. Paisley (Eds.), *Public communication campaigns* (pp. 41–70). Newbury Park, CA: Sage.

Meadow, R. G. (1981). The political dimensions of nonproduct advertising. *Journal of Communication, 31*(3), 69–82.

Miller, W. H. (1987). Issue management: "No longer a sideshow." *Industry Week, 235,* 125–129.

Mitroff, I. I. (1983). *Stakeholders of the organizational mind.* San Francisco: Jossey-Bass.

Morgan, G. (1982). Cybernetics and organization theory: Epistemology or technique? *Human Relations, 35,* 521–537.

Nagelschmidt, J. S. (Ed.). (1982). *The public affairs handbook.* New York: AMACOM.

Naisbitt, J. (1982). *Megatrends: Ten new directions transforming our lives.* New York: Warner Books.

Nelson, R. A., & Heath, R. L. (1986). A systems model for corporate issues management. *Public Relations Quarterly, 31*(3), 20–25.

Nowlan, S. E., & Shayon, D. R. (1984). *Leveraging the impact of public affairs: A guidebook based on practical experience for corporate public affairs executives.* Philadelphia: HRN.

Oberschall, A. (1973). *Social conflict and social movements.* Englewood Cliffs, NJ: Prentice-Hall.

Olasky, M. (1987). *Corporate public relations: A new historical perspective.* Hillsdale, NJ: Lawrence Erlbaum Associates.

Parenti, J. D. (1986). *Inventing reality: The politics of the mass media.* New York: St. Martin's Press.

Pavitt, C., & Cappella, J. N. (1979). Coorientational accuracy in interpersonal and small group discussions: A literature review, model, and simulation. In D. Nimmo (Ed.), *Communication yearbook 3* (pp. 123–156). New Brunswick, NJ: Transaction Books.

Pavlik, J. V. (1987). *Public relations: What research tells us.* Newbury Park, CA: Sage.

Petty, R. E., & Cacioppo, J. T. (1981). *Attitudes and persuasion: Classic and contemporary approaches.* Dubuque, IA: Wm C. Brown.

Petty, R. E., & Cacioppo, J. T. (1986). *Communication and persuasion: Central and peripheral routes to attitude change.* New York: Springer-Verlag.

Petty, R. E., Cacioppo, J. T., & Schumann, D. (1983). Central and peripheral routes to advertising: The moderating role of involvement. *Journal of Consumer Research, 10,* 135–148.

Petty, R. E., Kasmer, J. A., Haugtvedt, C. P., & Cacioppo, J. T. (1987). Source and message factors in persuasion: A reply to Stiff's critique of the Elaboration Likelihood Model. *Communication Monographs, 54,* 233–249.

Pincus, J. D. (1980). Taking a stand on the issues through advertising. *Association Management, 32*(12), 58–63.

Post, J. E. (1979). *Corporate behavior and social change.* Reston, VA.: Reston Publishing.

Post, J. E., Murray, E. A., Jr., Dickie, R. B., & Mahon, J. F. (1983). Managing public affairs: The public affairs function. *California Management Review, 26*(1), 135–150.

Preston, L. E., & Post, J. E. (1975). *Private management and public policy: The principle of public responsibility.* Englewood Cliffs, NJ: Prentice-Hall.

Public Relations Society of America. (1987). Report of Special Committee on Terminology. *International Public Relations Review,* 11(2), 6–11.

Sawaya, R. N., & Arrington, C. B., Jr. (1988). Linking corporate planning with strategic issues. In R. L. Heath (Ed.), *Strategic issues management: How organizations influence and respond to public interests and policies* (pp. 73–86). San Francisco: Jossey-Bass.

Schmertz, H. (1986). *Good-bye to the low profile: The art of creative confrontation.* Boston: Little, Brown.

Sethi, S. P. (Ed.). (1974). *The unstable ground: Corporate social policy in a dynamic society.* Los Angeles: Melville.

Sethi, S. P. (1977). *Advocacy advertising and large corporations: Social conflict, big business image, the news media and public policy.* Lexington, MA: D. C. Heath.

Sethi, S. P. (1987). *Handbook of advocacy advertising: Concepts, strategies, and applications.* Cambridge, MA: Ballinger.

Simons, H. W. (1983). Mobil's system-oriented conflict rhetoric: A generic analysis. *Southern Speech Communication Journal, 48,* 243–254.

Stanley, G. D. D. (1985). *Managing external issues: Theory and practice.* Greenwich, CT: JAI Press.

Stridsberg, A. B. (1977). *Controversy advertising: How advertisers present points of view in public affairs.* New York: Hastings House.

Stroup, M. A. (1986). Questioning assumptions: One company's answer to the planner's nemesis. *Planning Review, 14*(5), 10–16.

Stroup, M. A. (1988). Identifying critical issues for better corporate planning. In R. L. Heath (Ed.), *Strategic issues management: How organizations influence and respond to public interests and policies* (pp. 87–97). San Francisco: Jossey-Bass.

Ungson, G. R., James, C., & Spicer, B. H. (1985). The effects of regulatory agencies on organizations in wood products and high technology/electronic industries. *Academy of Management Journal, 28,* 426–445.

Wartick, S. L., & Rude, R. E. (1986). Issues management: Corporate fad or corporate function? *California Management Review, 29*(1), 124–140.

Weaver, P. H. (1988). The self-destructive corporation. *California Management Review, 30*(3), 128–143.

Wright, P. L. (1973). The cognitive processes mediating acceptance of advertising. *Journal of Marketing Research, 10,* 53–62.

Wright, P. L. (1974). Analyzing media effects on advertising responses. *Public Opinion Quarterly, 38,* 192–205.

Wright, P. L. (1981). Cognitive responses to mass media advocacy. In R. E. Petty, T. M. Ostrom, & T. C. Brock (Eds.), *Cognitive responses in persuasion* (pp. 263–282). Hillsdale, NJ: Lawrence Erlbaum Associates.

Chapter 3

The Uses and Effects of Public Service Advertising

Garrett J. O'Keefe
University of Wisconsin-Madison

Kathaleen Reid
Lee College

Public service advertising (PSA) has become a significant component of American mass media systems. The intent here is to examine the uses made of public service advertising, and its impact and effectiveness both alone and in concert with broader kinds of public information campaigns.

We begin with an overview of the advertisements themselves, their role in campaigns and in society, and audience responses to them. A review of earlier PSA-based campaigns follows. Several conclusions are then offered concerning factors that may increase their dissemination and impact, drawing from more contemporary campaigns as examples.

PUBLIC SERVICE ADVERTISING

Public service advertisements or announcements are promotional materials that address problems assumed to be of general concern to citizens at large. PSAs typically attempt to increase public awareness of such problems and their possible solutions, and in many instances also try to influence public beliefs, attitudes, and behaviors concerning them. Most PSAs emanate from not-for-profit or governmental organizations and receive *gratis* placement in broadcast and print media.

The Content of PSAs

PSAs reflect the individual concerns of their sponsors. Content analyses of tele-vised PSAs during the 1970s indicated that nearly half of them dealt with health or personal safety topics, including alcohol and drug abuse, preventive health care, traffic safety, nutrition, and the like (Hanneman, McEwen, & Coyne, 1973; Paletz, Pearson, & Willis, 1977). Other topics included environmental concerns, community services, educational and occupational opportunities, consumer issues, volunteer recruitment, and general humanitarian concerns. The vast majority of the ads offered informative and in some cases persuasive messages, with a smaller number being fundraising appeals. Governmental agencies were responsible for about one quarter of all PSAs.

A more recent study of television public service directors indicates that their main choices of PSA content areas included alcohol and drug abuse, drunk driv-ing, missing children, child abuse, and such health concerns as cancer and diabetes (Needham Porter Novelli, 1985). (These findings in part likely reflect a national campaign underway during that time by the National Association of Broadcasters aimed at public education on substance abuse, particularly as related to driving habits. Studies by the National Association of Broadcasters (NAB) have indicated that nearly 100% of television and radio stations carried alcohol-related PSAs during 1984–1985; NAB, 1984, 1985.)

PSA Placement

Those PSAs warranting free media placement are ordinarily relegated to status behind regular paid ads or commercials and are often apt to appear only as space or time become available. Televised PSAs, for example, have traditionally run during lesser watched dayparts (although in doing so, some may well reach their appropri-ate target audiences, e.g., children or teenagers). Hanneman et al. (1973) found that in the early 1970s nearly two-thirds of all televised PSAs ran between 7 a.m. and 6 p.m. on weekdays.

However, there are recent indications of a more favorable time distribution being allocated to at least certain kinds of PSAs. During 1985, for example, the ABC network carried over 1,000 PSAs related to alcohol and drug abuse, with 47% of those being shown during prime time (32% were shown during daytime, and 21% late at night) (ABC, 1986a).

Competition among PSA sponsors for media placement is heavy, and many of the ads fail to be effectively disseminated. The dissemination of any particular PSA is at the discretion of the network, station, or publication management, and content as well as stylistic and production factors can influence decisions on whether to present it and if so, when and where (cf. McGowan, 1980). Goodman's (1981) survey of over 700 television stations indicated that the most desired PSAs were those addressing local market concerns, and those disseminated by the most reputable sponsoring agencies (i.e., those without hidden commercial agendas). At the time, 30-second spots were the most preferred, and attractive production and packaging helped their getting aired. More PSAs were used from post-Christmas to early spring, and during the summer.

Most of the television public affairs directors surveyed by Needham Porter Novelli (1985) concurred that the local impact or relevance of the spot was a decisive factor, followed respectively by subject matter and technical quality. A local identification tag with the PSA was deemed a strong asset. Contact by a local organization promoting the PSA was likewise seen as a plus, as was having it in either 1- or 2-inch videotape format as opposed to 16-mm film.

Although comparable data on PSA placement on radio and in newspapers and magazines are unavailable, there is little reason to suspect sizable difference in their content, distribution, or sponsorship.

Societal Functions of PSAs

It also may be that given their pervasiveness, PSAs serve important functions for the social system. Paletz et al. (1977) suggested that the social and political import of televised PSAs goes beyond their explicit contents.

> The values they contain, the images they collectively propound of authority and American institutions, their portrayals of the nature and causes of societal problems, and the solutions they designate for those problems . . . public service advertising should be considered as one way in which the American public is imbued with the values and attitudes that contribute to the current functioning and stability of the American political system. (p. 74)

A content analysis of televised PSA themes by Paletz et al. revealed that most of them included depictions of cooperation among citizens as an overriding theme. Moreover, cooperation, including increased individual awareness and concern as well as collective action, was often shown as a basis for solving many societal problems.

Paletz et al. found little if any PSA content indicating social conflict as either a cause of or possible solution to the ills described. Controversy was generally avoided, as was mention of citizen participation through political channels as means of problem attack. The authors noted that the content also gave a consistently positive view of governmental agencies; health, charitable and religious organizations; and traditional American institutions overall. The authors also pointed to possible dangers in that PSAs could serve propagandistic functions that could simply reinforce status quo social and political relationships while at the same time giving the appearance of promoting action and change. In a partial test of some of these assertions, however, O'Keefe, Mendelsohn, and Liu (1980) found no rela-

tionship between audience attendance to PSAs and degree of trust in either government or other people.

Public Exposure and Reactions to PSAs

Mass media audiences appear fairly attentive to PSAs and have generally favorable
reactions to them. A 1980 national probability sample survey of 1,500 U.S. adults
by the authors found that 30% said they paid "a lot" of attention to televised PSAs,
and another 44% claimed to pay at least "some" attention to them. Personal health
and safety were the topic areas most attended to, followed closely by energy
conservation (a high salient issue at the time), crime prevention, consumer protection, fire prevention, drug abuse, and traffic safety.

Of the respondents, 81% said they found PSAs at least "fairly helpful" in
making people like themselves "aware of problems that may affect their well-
being," and 30% called them "very helpful." Moreover, 68% saw PSAs as at least
fairly helpful in helping people solve problems they may have, with 20% calling
them very helpful. Forty percent were able to describe a particular PSA they had
recently seen. In terms of behavioral impact, 21% said they had previously written
or phoned in to get more information about something they heard about in a PSA.

Generally, women, younger adults, and people with children were found somewhat more attentive to PSAs and more favorably disposed to them. More highly
educated and upper income persons have somewhat more of a tendency to attend
to them as well. More recent findings suggest a continuing pattern of younger and
more educated audiences more likely to recall PSAs, although gender differences
seem to have diminished (McLeod, Pan, & Rucinski, 1988). Importantly, the
same research found recognition of consumer advertising higher among the less
educated, as well as among the young and females. This implies an ability of PSAs
to reach audiences atypical of those for other forms of advertising. Moreover, PSA
recall was higher for those more attentive to certain public affairs contents, those
more knowledgeable about current events, and for those engaged in more reflective, interpretive news information processing.

Audience evaluations of televised PSAs in a limited number of experimental
laboratory situations have been found to be influenced to some extent by source,
message, and receiver characteristics. Spots with Advertising Council source identification, for example, tended to elicit more positive evaluations than those identified as emanating from other noncommercial or commercial groups (Lynn, Wyatt,
Gaines, Pearce, & Bergh, 1978). Furthermore, audiences appeared to base their
evaluations of PSAs more on the type of appeal or persuasive argument used than
on the issue or topic dealt with (Lynn, 1974). Evans (1978) found newspaper
PSAs using evaluative appeals (opinion laden) to be more effective than those
simply presenting facts in changing behavioral intentions. Although higher socioeconomic audiences tended to rate PSAs as a group more positively (Lynn et
al., 1978), older and less-educated persons were likelier to be aware of the spon-

sorship sources of PSAs, suggesting closer attention to them by such individuals (Lynn, 1973).

PSAs and Public Service Campaigns: Some Caveats

Our specific concern with the impact of public service advertising presents a problem in that many if not most promotional programs use PSAs as only one segment of more extensive media campaigns incorporating news releases, other broadcast and print materials, direct mailing, and the like. In many instances more community and interpersonally oriented efforts are also carried out using volunteer organizations, local civic groups, speakers' bureaus, and so forth. Thus, although our focus is on PSAs, we typically need to consider them in the context of other campaign techniques. Unfortunately, most evaluations of information campaigns make little if any effort to distinguish among the effects of particular media or their contents.

The tradition of public information campaigns in American culture goes back to colonial times. Broadly speaking it can include such historical movements and appeals as those for unified national development, elimination of slavery, equal citizenship rights for minorities and women, and support for national policies in two world wars (Paisley, 1981). The mass media of each historical period played integral roles in the dissemination and impact of campaigns. The structure of media in each era and their relative import and credibility doubtlessly affected the influence of campaigns on the public.

Mass media have undergone radical changes over the past few decades and will continue to do so. Our review considers that an important caveat. There is ample evidence that the media—and especially television—are significant influences in our everyday personal, social, and political lives (cf. McQuail, 1987; NIMH, 1982; Roberts & Maccoby, 1985). There are indications that media were not as influential earlier in this century (cf. Lazarsfeld, Berelson, & Gaudet, 1948), and one can only speculate as to their impact on into the next. The efficacy of media as disseminators of information campaigns is tied to the immediate cultural context in which media operate, and the ways in which their audiences use, believe, and rely on them.

Another caveat is that our concern will be almost exclusively with campaigns that have been empirically evaluated with some degree of scientific validity. Such evaluations have the most promise in telling us not only whether a campaign was successful or not, but more importantly in teaching us what factors accelerated or inhibited its success. There are many examples of publicly and professionally acclaimed efforts, for example "Smokey the Bear" (cf. McNamara, Kurth, & Hansen, 1981), which most likely have had strong impact but because of a lack of clear audience evaluation may leave us wondering precisely why or how.

Unfortunately, the scientific validity of many of the evaluations considered here is of generally low order. There are relatively few instances of more experimentally based controls being used. This is due in large part to their complexity and expense in naturalistic field research situations. Fortunately, however, their use is on the rise.

A related issue is that one of the difficulties in assessing even the most productive of the previous research is that the criteria for success are typically statistical tests of hypotheses, and little account is taken of the power of those tests in allowing generalizations concerning the "real world" impact of the messages. Although it is helpful to know that attitudes toward a topic changed "significantly" following exposure to a campaign, the unanswered question that too often remains is how many individuals were affected, and to what extent. Such data are important for credible estimates to be made of the cost effectiveness and efficiency of various campaign efforts.

There have been several studies of public information campaigns in other countries (cf. Hornik, in press). Although many of them are of theoretical interest, we do not deal with them here because of the often substantial differences in media systems and cultural perspectives.

PSAs AND CAMPAIGNS:
EARLY RESEARCH PERSPECTIVES

As Rogers and Storey (1987) noted, research on communication campaigns has gone through eras emphasizing minimal effects (largely during the 1940s and 1950s), and more "moderate" campaign impact during the 1960s and 1970s. Here we review some key studies and perspectives pertinent to PSAs during each of those periods, with an eye toward the relevance of the findings to contemporary campaigns.

The Early Studies

Three perspectives on campaigns involving PSAs (or their equivalents) during the 1940s are worth reviewing for their relevance to many of today's research issues. One argues against wrongly inferring that audience effects during a campaign are necessarily a consequence of media interventions. Another demonstrates that even massive advertising input on a public issue can fail to move citizens. A third sets the stage for a "minimalist" view of media effects that dominated the field for some years to come.

Cartwright and Mass Persuasion.   Many recent PSA-based campaigns draw at least implicitly from the work of Dorwin Cartwright, and in particular his 1949 analysis of World War II war bond drive campaigns. On the surface, the intensive campaigns with their multi-million dollar media advertising budgets appeared to have had substantial impact in convincing close to a majority of wage earners to invest in the bonds.

Cartwright, however, questioned the efficiency of the campaigns in terms of the immense cost and effort expended. He presented some limited evidence that the media campaigns had been successful only in forming the public about the bonds and perhaps influencing their opinions, and not in the sense of directly affecting their motivations or behaviors. Moreover, he suggested that interpersonal contacts and persuasion were more effective in bringing about actual purchases of the bonds.

He called for more attention to the psychological processes of target audience members in promotional campaigns, particularly in terms of developing methods of influencing in turn their cognitive, motivational, and behavioral structures to provide congruency among them. He viewed multiple sources of influence, and not media alone, as being necessary to effectively bring about behavioral change.

The Cincinnati UN Drive. The campaign likely most often quoted as an example of the failure of multi-media programs was carried out in post-WWII Cincinnati and aimed to inform the citizenry of the advantages of the United Nations (Star & Hughes, 1950). The campaign appears to have inundated local radio stations and newspapers with spot ads as well as specially prepared programming and articles.

The campaign's impact was evaluated by use of fairly well-designed pre- and post-campaign measures of samples of citizens' levels of information and interest regarding the UN, as well as some of their attitudes concerning it. The before and after changes were largely minimal, leading to a general conclusion that the campaign was ineffective. Star and Hughes hypothesized that selective exposure was a factor, with the messages primarily reaching those already more interested in the UN.

However, although Star and Hughes did not give detailed descriptions of the messages used, there is some indication they may have been highly repetitive as well as somewhat sterile. Quantity may have been emphasized over quality. In a later review of the project, Atkin (1981) suggested that "less stress was given to designing appeals relevant to the needs and interests of the ordinary citizen. The campaign did not emphasize how the United Nations related to the personal lives of people living in Cincinnati, who saw little reason to learn the material" (p. 268).

Some Reasons Why Information Campaigns Fail. Although not strictly a media campaign evaluation, Hyman and Sheatsley's (1947) review of anecdotal evidence and their own experiences in public opinion and persuasion was influential in casting considerable doubt on the power of mass media in information campaigns. They proposed a series of psychological barriers confronting information dissemination efforts.

These included:

1. The existence of "a hard core of chronic 'know-nothings'" in the populace, whose general lack of knowledge made them extremely resistant to new information;

2. That "interested people acquire the most information," reducing the chances of reaching the disinterested;

3. That "people seek information congenial to prior attitudes," or the selective exposure hypothesis that indicates that people are most exposed to persuasive messages with which they already agree;

4. That "people interpret the same information differently," or selectively perceive what they want out of particular messages; and

5. That "information does not necessarily change attitudes," suggesting that more than "facts" provided by media are necessary to effect persuasion.

Although the validity of some of these factors has been put to serious question in more recent years, it is important to consider them here because they helped reinforce a generally pessimistic attitude about campaign effectiveness during the 1950s and into the 1960s. Indeed, the power of the media in general was thought to be rather minimal, as detailed in Klapper's (1960) study, *The Effects of Mass Communication*. From today's perspective, it remains an open question as to whether: (a) mass media were less influential during that era; and/or (b) ineffective campaign strategies were being used; and/or (c) the research questions being asked and the methodologies being used were inadequate to identify greater effects.

The Resurgent Period

Such pessimism also appears to have translated into a dearth of productive research on the effects of media information campaigns through the 1960s. However, the 1970s opened up several new avenues of inquiry, some supportive of campaign influences and others less so. More importantly, attention began to turn to the situations and conditions under which successes would be more likely to occur. As summarized by Mendelsohn (1973), more effective campaign strategies would do well to include formative research in campaign design, and increased cooperation between social scientists and communications practitioners. Greater attention to audience segmentation and the setting of "middle-range" campaign objectives (akin to Merton's, 1957, recommendation for social research) could also be productive, rather than aiming for significant behavioral changes across a wide range of audiences.

More sophisticated uses of evaluative designs were also coming into play. One campaign on mental health combining many of the elements just mentioned into a moderately "successful" effort was also exceptionally well documented by use of an experimental-control community methodology that set the stage for more ambitious research (Douglas, Westley, & Chaffee, 1970). Although PSAs were a relatively small segment of it, it is worth considering from an overall design perspective, and for the challenges it presented to earlier thinking on campaign effects.

The project aimed to promote more accurate information about and more positive attitudes toward mental retardation. The 6-month campaign in an experimental treatment rural community of 4,300 was extensive. It featured over 20 news and feature stories in the local newspaper, numerous radio news items, community meetings, special speakers before local organizations, and related community events. Advertising was limited to a newspaper display ad, posters, and announcements of events related to the campaign over radio. Respondents in limited panel samples were interviewed before and after the campaign in the experimental community and in a comparable control community.

Post-campaign knowledge of mental retardation facts was greater in the experimental community than in the control, as was attitude change. Moreover, information gain correlated with attitude change, conflicting with Hyman and Sheatsley's final proposition previously discussed. And, the group likeliest to be perhaps inappropriately described as "chronic know-nothings"—those with the least education—scored the highest information gains. Selective exposure did not appear to be a factor. Although interpersonal sources of information were cited as the most used, media source mentions were substantial.

Although the Douglas et al. study challenges some of the previous hypotheses on psychological barriers to campaign effects, it should also be noted that the effort appears to have been highly intensive, run over a rather long period, and conducted in a rather small and likely high-cohesion community.

Another formally evaluated and effective campaign—also dealing with mental health—deserving note was a 1-year television and radio PSA campaign in an urban area that appeared to nearly double awareness of a community mental health agency, with television appearing to have by far the most impact (Schanie & Sundel, 1978). More positive attitudes toward mental health issues also were found, as well as increased service utilization. The messages included specific examples of situations in which individuals came to realize their behaviors may have been inappropriate. Evaluation included telephone interviews with independent samples of 500 respondents prior to the campaign and at three points during it, with no control group being used. The topic of mental health may be one that reasonable people are unlikely to disagree over once credible information is fed into the system.

Also, moderate success in increasing public awareness of and strengthening attitudes toward safe use of pesticides was found in a small city media campaign featuring television, radio, and newspaper PSAs as well as direct mailings (Salcedo, Read, Evans, & Kong, 1974). Before and after measures were compared with those in a control city, and significant change differences were found despite reports of relatively low direct exposure to the campaign materials.

The Special Case of Counteradvertising.   One of the more interesting as well as controversial uses of PSAs involved the mandated broadcast cigarette counteradvertising campaign of the late 1960s, in which broadcast media were required to air a certain number of anti-smoking commercials in proportion to the numbers of cigarette advertisements shown.

O'Keefe (1971) found some rather slight attitude and belief changes occurring in response to the counteradvertisements. However, his methodology relied on self-reports of survey respondents, not necessarily the most valid measure for such a complex issue. Warner (1977) presented somewhat more formidable, albeit correlational, evidence that a noteworthy drop in a cigarette consumption patterns occurs as predicted at the time of the 1968-1970 campaign. Unfortunately, the study leaves us with little understanding of the processes of mechanisms by which influence may have occurred.

Flay (1986), however, suggested some reasonable possibilities as to why that campaign, unlike more typical PSA-based ones, should have greater impact: (a) The spots were novel, and quite varied; (b) Dissemination was widespread as well as frequent, with one PSA aired for every three to five cigarette ads; (c) The campaign spanned 3 years, providing endurance that should help minimize selective exposure and increase retention. (Flay also pointed to successes of smoking cessation media campaigns in such countries as Norway and Austria, and notes media influences in more elaborate programs aimed at promoting specific cessation activities, e.g., "stopping for a day" and joining cessation clinics.)

PERSPECTIVES FROM CONTEMPORARY PSA CAMPAIGN RESEARCH

A variety of innovative PSA efforts has been carried out on a number of fronts in more recent years, in many cases grounded in the work just described. Despite the diverse and sometimes scattershot approaches used in some of them—as well as in some of the accompanying evaluations—generalizations of value for subsequent programs can be gained. Here several conclusions—or recommendations—for more effective PSA-based campaigns are offered, supported by examples drawn from some of the more rigorously studied projects.

1. *The more recent successful PSA campaigns have incorporated theoretical models of communication or persuasion in their development.* Centering a campaign around a theoretical approach not only allows a broad base of knowledge to be

brought to bear on the problem, but it also provides a guiding model or structure that can help the sometimes complex and disorganized components of contemporary campaigns.

A prototypical example of this approach is the Stanford Heart Disease Prevention Program (Farquhar et al., 1985; Flora, Roser, Chaffee, & Farquhar, 1988), which includes perhaps the most extensive and methodologically rigorous self-evaluation to date. In brief, the objective of the campaign is to reduce heart disease probability among certain normally high-risk target audiences by informing them via mass media and personal interventions of the precise nature of the risks and attempting to reduce their potentially harmful behaviors. The campaign is based extensively upon Bandura's (1977) model of social learning theory that holds that new actions are learned largely by the imitation or modeling of specific acts of others, and are solidified through selective interpersonal support and reinforcement. The approach further avers that new behaviors acquired from mediated sources are unlikely to be performed unless the environment is one in which they can be reinforced. Another approach incorporated into the campaign was Cartwright's (1949) suggestion that although media campaigns can inform and may alter attitudes, interpersonal communication and persuasion make behavioral change more likely to occur.

The most recently reported campaign and evaluation designs involved five California cities over a 6-year period. Broadcast PSAs were a major source of information dissemination, as were direct mailings of newsletters and other information, newspapers columns, and lectures and training sessions. Messages were available in both English and Spanish. The evaluation provided quite convincing evidence that the media campaign alone produced positive changes in the knowledge of risk-preventive methods as well as in desired behaviors. (Changes mainly occurred in dietary habits; less impressive were changes in smoking activity.) The media campaign combined with intensive interpersonal instruction proved significantly more effective than media used alone. There was no evidence of knowledge-gap increases. The panel-based evaluative design apparently had some effects of its own, however, at least in terms of the repeated measures increasing knowledge among respondents (Chaffee, Roser, & Flora, in press).

Another major benefit of integrating conceptual models into campaign design is that modification of the hypotheses or theory can happen as a consequence of the findings. Somewhat similar large-scale community-based campaigns in Minnesota have provided evidence of the impact of media messages on the cognitive complexity of belief structures of individuals on heart health topics (Pavlik, 1987). PSAs and targeted newspaper columns were also found effective in reducing a knowledge gap between the more and the less educated (Ettema, Brown, & Luepker, 1983). Moreover, the level of audience involvement in an issue has been identified as an important contingency affecting campaign influence (Chaffee & Roser, 1986; Salmon, 1986). In extended analyses of the Stanford program data, Roser,

Flora, Chaffee, and Farquhar (1988) found motivation to learn about health, as well as information-processing ability, to be significant predictors of learning from the heart health campaign.

More theoretically based campaign evaluations also allow for more efficient generalization to future topic areas. For example, PSAs directed at AIDS-related issues may well benefit from the social learning context-based findings of the Stanford project (Flora & Thoreson, 1988), and from strategic recommendations identifying AIDS-related audience groupings based on Grunig's situational theory of publics (Grunig & Childers, 1988).

2. *The more influential campaigns have made extensive use of basic commercial advertising planning principles in their design and execution.* These include such rudimentary design components as concept testing, focus group analysis, pretesting of materials, and tracking of the dissemination of campaign materials. These approaches have been employed in recent Advertising Council national media campaigns, including the rather extensively evaluated "Take a Bite Out of Crime" project (O'Keefe, 1985; O'Keefe & Reid, in press). Initiated in 1980 under the sponsorship of the National Crime Coalition, the campaign promotes getting citizens more involved in helping to prevent crime by carrying out such actions as securing their homes, keeping watch on their neighbors' homes, reporting suspicious incidents to police, and a range of other activities.

"Take a Bite Out of Crime" has gone through several stages, in each case building more community support through programs at the local level. Pretesting has been an integral part of all stages. The media components, resting on PSAs via broadcast and print media as well as posters, billboards, and public transit cards, provide a common focus for those efforts. Evaluations of the media campaign were carried out from 1980 to 1982, when public awareness of the allied community efforts was still low (less than 10%) and thus allowing an unusually uncontaminated examination of the influences of PSAs per se.

A national survey of public exposure and reactions to the campaign was carried out, in addition to a three-city panel survey in which the same respondents were interviewed just prior to the program's inception and again 2 years later. The national survey revealed that 52% of adults had been exposed to the PSAs, predominantly via television. Reactions were highly positive, and nearly 25% of the respondents indicated they had taken crime preventive actions as a consequence of having seen or heard the spots. Self-reports of information gain and attitude change were considerably higher. Analysis of pre- to post-measures in the panel indicated significant increases among those exposed over those not exposed in prevention knowledge, positive attitudes, expressions of personal competence in helping prevent crime, and behavioral change. These findings held even when controlling for exposure to news about crime, other prevention campaigns, and actual victimization.

PSA exposure and influences seemed quite evenly distributed over all population segments, and there were no indications that the campaign widened any "knowledge gap" between persons already more prevention competent and those less so, nor was there evidence that the spots had significantly increased public fear of crime (an outcome the messages were designed to avoid). Interestingly, the effects found did not always suggest a "linear" pattern leading from awareness to attitude change to behavioral change. Rather, the PSAs appeared to have greater attitudinal effects on some persons while not necessarily increasing their information, whereas for other individuals it stimulated behavioral changes without concurrent attitudinal ones. Variations in audience involvement may have been a key factor here, as in the Stanford campaign previously described.

Formative research appears to be an especially critical element. Roberts, Bachen, Christenson, and Gibson (1979) particularly credit the pretesting of PSAs directed at children as essential to their success. Flay (1983) regarded formative research on target audiences as an essential component if drug abuse campaigns are to be successful. A national formative research study to improve crime prevention campaigns directed at elderly persons has indicated not only diverse orientations toward crime among that age group, but an unsuspectedly high reliance on PSAs for information in general (O'Keefe & Reid-Nash, 1987). Atkin, Garramone, and Anderson (1986) have suggested extensive formative research procedures for anti-drinking and driving campaign planning. In perhaps a model formative research design, Bauman et al. (1988) carefully delineated objectives and message and channel factors in designing a largely radio-based PSA campaign aimed at limiting smoking initiation among young adolescents.

Inherent in all of these efforts is a realization that each kind of audience is going to have special characteristics and needs, and that those have to be taken into account in campaign design. Campaign effectiveness appears in large part closely tied to: (a) How narrowly individual target audiences can be defined; (b) How much information about each of those audiences can be gathered prior to the campaign; and (c) How well that information can be utilized in the design of the campaign.

3. An allied issue is that *PSAs are likely to be more successful if their design takes into account not only existing awareness, attitudes, and behaviors of the target audience with respect to the topic, but their media preferences and tastes as well.* Previous research on source, message, and channel factors provides a substantial resource for campaign planners intent upon matching messages to particular audiences (cf. Bogart, 1986; Percy & Rossiter, 1980). Such elements as source credibility, fear appeals, use of humor, and channel-information capacities might well be taken more into account in designing PSA messages, which because of their brevity need to be as efficiently tooled as possible (cf. Atkin, 1981; Solomon, 1981). The uses made of particular media by specific target audiences should also be delineated by formative research, with emphasis on the extent to which given individuals may depend on certain media or seek need gratifications from them (cf. Rosengren, Wenner, & Palmgren, 1985).

Campaigns dealing with such potentially change-resistant topics as alcohol and drug abuse may particularly benefit from such inputs. Several content analyses of anti-drug abuse messages in the early 1970s suggested that they relied heavily on use of fear appeals, as well as exhortations of social disapproval, and that when factual information was presented it could be construed as being exaggerated (Capalaces & Starr, 1973; Hanneman, 1973). There was little message targeting to specific audiences as well. In contrast, at least limited success was reported in a panel study of a PSA campaign aimed at older, more affluent males perceived as influential community gatekeepers (Schmeling & Wotring, 1980).

As Hochheimer (1981) suggested, a lack not only of evaluative but also of formative research concerning alcohol and drug abuse campaigns make productive inferences about campaign design and effects extremely difficult, and in some cases hazardous. Pre-campaign research more recently has been developed pertaining to adolescents and drug abuse (Black, 1987), but post-evaluation of anti-drug PSA effects appears to remain highly correlational and only quite loosely tied to PSA exposure (Black, 1988).

A perhaps even more important target audience is young children, and since the mid-1970s several organizations including broadcast companies have produced televised PSAs aimed at providing instruction on such topics as smoking and drug abuse, proper nutrition, and other health and safety issues.

Evaluations of these have largely been limited to controlled experimental laboratory situations. The findings, however, have generally been encouraging in revealing that previously researched and well-designed spots appear capable of achieving information gain in children as young as age 4, and that older children learn even more from them (Roberts et al., 1979). Televised PSAs were also found capable of increasing awareness of the intent of televised commercial advertising (Christenson, 1982), although younger children may not fully understand the intent of PSAs themselves (Blosser & Roberts, 1985). The degree to which child-oriented PSAs are successful in naturalistic situations is likely to depend on the competing stimuli, as well as on the frequency and appropriateness of placement of the spots. Televised PSAs were found to compete successfully with supermarket displays and school programs aimed at promoting more nutritious "snacking" behavior on the part of children (Smith, Nelson, & O'Hara, 1982).

4. As an extension of the previous points, *successful campaigns are also more likely to have a clearly delineated set of operationalized campaign goals.* Planners need to specify at a minimum what kind of impact goals are being set, including the possible options of awareness, information gain, attitude change, motivation, and behavior change. Criteria should be established at the outset to allow subsequent judgment of the "success" or "failure" of a PSA campaign.

As Kotler (1982) suggested in his "social marketing" approach to public service campaign programs, such a systems-oriented approach forces immediate concern during the planning stage with specific end products or goals to be achieved. The approach increases the probability of a more appealing and attractive "product" in the form of campaign themes and messages particularly tailored to the target audience.

Perhaps most important is the development of clear—but flexible—objectives for each component and stage of the campaign, and the translation of those objectives into message components. Care should be taken to assure that the goals are realistic. No one campaign is going to eliminate heart disease or child abuse, but messages can emphasize quite specific short-term steps that individuals can take to help alleviate the situation. Also, as Pasick and Wallack (1988) noted, the objectives need to be flexible enough to accommodate changes suggested by formative research and the ongoing pragmatics of the situation. Getting locked into a rigid set of requirements in a typically fluid communication process can be as damaging as having no plan at all.

It is indeed possible to include a great number of highly specific subgoals, each of which can be attended to some extent in the design of a campaign. McGuire (1981), for example, has suggested a progressive list including: exposure; attention; liking or interest; comprehension; skill acquisition; attitude change; memory storage; information search and retrieval; deciding on basis of information retrieval; behaving in accord with decision; reinforcement of desired acts; and post-behavioral consolidating. McGuire also provided a checklist linking these to source, message, channel, receiver, and destination characteristics of a campaign.

On a more applied level, an evaluation paradigm designed for the "Take a Bite Out of Crime" campaign might have applicability to other campaign studies. The campaign was presumed to aim at building greater crime prevention *competence* among citizens in terms of: (a) increasing their awareness and knowledge of preventive techniques; (b) generating more positive attitudes about the effectiveness of citizen-based prevention; (c) building a sense of capability in ability to help prevent crime; (d) motivating them to act; and (e) encouraging them to engage in preventive actions (O'Keefe, 1985). It seems likely that many other campaigns are essentially directed at such competence building, whether in health, safety, or other pursuits, and the same dimensions previously noted may be applicable to them.

Adoption of such paradigms also can help resolve the related problem of the lack of comparability of evaluation evidence across campaigns. There has been little standardization of conceptualizations or of research designs, making it quite difficult to offer generalizations from the results of one campaign to another.

It is equally important to consider what PSAs themselves can and cannot do as part of a campaign mix. As Rogers and Storey (1987) noted, mass media seem to be most effective in creating awareness and/or knowledge, stimulating interpersonal discussion, and in recruiting people to participate in campaign activities. Although the McGruff and Stanford media campaigns did appear to influence behavior per se, we have no way of knowing whether they accomplished that "on their own," or more indirectly as a consequence of stimulating discussion among audience members. In their synthesis of interviews with information campaign practitioners and scholars, Pasick and Wallack (1988) also identified the ability of media alone to demonstrate simple skills (e.g., testing a baby's hearing), to disseminate new technologies or recommendations, and to influence one-time behaviors (e.g., installing a smoke detector). PSAs also may be effective at encouraging active information seeking on the part of audience members, such as phoning a number for more information on a topic. Using PSAs to encourage the help of others as change facilitators is also growing in use (e.g., "Friends Don't Let Friends Drive Drunk").

5. *The greater the dissemination of PSAs by broadcast and print media, the more effective they are likely to be.* This seems inherently obvious, but the implications are varied and need to be carefully considered. The vast majority of citizens are most exposed to PSAs via television, so we emphasize that medium in this discussion. Nonetheless, the same concerns hold for radio and the print media.

The first implication has to do with reach of the message. Given that most PSAs likely are televised during daytime or late evening, there is simply less of a chance of their reaching many target audiences. The spots can also be highly inefficient in being shown several times over to inappropriate audiences before a logical target group is exposed to them. On the other hand, the recent emphases by the broadcast industry on topics such as substance abuse indicates that a commitment can be made to more effective dissemination in terms of reach.

Another implication has to do with the frequency of repetition. Chances are even less of target groups being exposed to the messages for any reasonable duration, which lessens their potential for impact. A related concern is time span of repetition. Most of the campaign successes just noted used PSAs over periods of several months or years, typically varying specific spots to maintain freshness and novelty. This is quite difficult to do without a fair amount of control over the long-term scheduling of the ads, but is possible with adequate cooperation from the disseminating media.

These problems can be overcome, but often not easily. Some factors that offer partial solutions are included here. Early televised drug abuse PSAs, for example, tended to be shown more during daytime hours and late at night (Hanneman, 1973). More recently, Feild, Deitrick, Hersey, Probst, and Theologus (1983) found that only 20% of the television PSAs constituting NIAAA's 1982 alcohol abuse campaign were shown between 5 p.m. and 11:30 p.m., with an almost minuscule percentage broadcast during actual prime time.

However, the recent increased concern among broadcasters with anti-alcohol and drug abuse promotional efforts noted earlier in this report provides greater optimism at least with respect to dissemination. For example, the ABC television network reported nearly half of its substance abuse spots being aired in prime time during 1985 (ABC, 1986a). This appeared to be a continuing trend in recent years among many broadcast organizations, and ratings-based estimates of audience reach show upward trends (ABC, 1986b).

6. *PSAs that are of high professional quality, as well as having some entertainment value, are more likely to: (a) be placed in media; and (b) have an impact on audiences.*

This may also seem an all-to-obvious point—until one views some of the arguably poor quality PSAs produced over the years, albeit under the best of intentions. Given the competition among PSA producers, attractive packages are likelier to be aired or published (Goodman, 1981; McGowan, 1980; Needham Porter Novelli, 1985). The McGruff and other Advertising Council campaigns receive numerous plaudits for their quality, and are consistently highly disseminated as well. However, more work needs to be done assessing what is meant by quality here. There has been scant if any research—either quantitative or qualitative—on the styles and content formats that may most attract audience attention.

7. *PSAs are generally more effective when tied to more extensive campaigns.* Media campaigns that augment PSAs with such activities as press coverage and pamphlet distribution appear to have a greater chance of success. The probability increases even more when interpersonal and community support systems are engaged, assuming adequate orchestration among the various components.

The interchange or supplementation of media with other sources (Flay & Sobel, 1983) optimally leads to mutual reinforcement of campaign goals through several channels. Benefits can include the presentation of a "unified" front to target audiences, as in Douglas et al. and in the Stanford program.

Using a multi-media mix to stimulate interpersonal interaction may have added impact as well. A multi-year federally sponsored campaign against drinking and driving included both targeted PSA materials as well as publications specifically tailored for law enforcement professionals and physicians (Swinehart, 1981). A major theme centered on interpersonal influence, attempting to persuade citizens to intervene in not letting other individuals drive under the influence. Annual surveys of public knowledge, attitudes, and behavior indicated a steady increase in such intervention behavior. An open question is the extent to which news coverage per se, as well as other campaigns may have been in part responsible for encouraging such behavior. Grunig and Ipes (1983) similarly recommend that interpersonal support can be an effective tool for activating audiences of drunk driving campaigns.

Evidence against perhaps trying to accomplish too much across too wide an audience with PSAs alone was also documented during the 1970s, particularly in the case of traffic safety. For example, several national and local programs were carried out to encourage citizens to "buckle up" with safety belts, with apparently minimal results (NHTSA, 1979; Swinehart, 1981). (One such campaign imaginatively used a dual-cable system to set up an experimental and control-group design in which PSAs advocating seat belt use were disseminated over one cable only. The impact of the PSAs was evaluated by observing seat belt use by motorists, recording their license numbers, and using those to determine home addresses and whether they were in the experimental or control cable group. However, no effects were found; Robertson, 1976; Robertson et al., 1974.)

8. *PSAs are more apt to be placed in local media when the spots are directly tied to local issues and concerns.* The research indicates a preference for locally oriented spots by media public affairs directors (Goodman, 1981; Needham Porter Novelli,

1985), as well as more willingness to use them when they are advocated by persons in the community. National spots are more favored when they include local tags or references, as was noted in the McGruff campaign (O'Keefe, 1986).

Feild at al. reported that PSAs in an NIAAA alcohol abuse campaign were shown on local stations with a total reach of 74 million households, with $3.8 million in broadcast time donated by the stations. Feild et al. credit the relatively high station usage of the PSAs in part to local campaign sponsors who made special efforts to approach station public affairs directors about airing the spots.

9. *PSAs have more impact when they ride on a wave of ongoing public opinion or concern.* While the McGruff PSAs had impact prior to the development of adequate supplemental support systems, they also had the advantage of being disseminated during the highly "crime conscious" early 1980s. They were there-fore supplemented by extensive news media coverage about crime in general, as well as a number of more localized prevention campaign efforts. Part of the cam-paign's impact may have resulted from its "fitting in" with the social environment of the times, and perhaps in its own way accelerating public awareness that citizens could responsibly contribute to crime reduction. The influence of the PSAs might well have been less had they appeared in a vacuum with little or no media or public concern. The current national concern with substance abuse may well work in concert with the rise in PSAs on that topic to increase their influence.

However, the separating out of the effects of PSAs, or an entire campaign for that matter, can be difficult. For example, the National Committee for Prevention of Child Abuse, in cooperation with the Advertising Council, has run spots for several years in all major media (Cohn, 1985). While tracking of public awareness of child abuse in a series of national polls by Louis Harris has indicated steady increases, there is no way to relate such change directly to the campaign, especially given news media attention to the issue.

10. *PSAs are more effective when they provide information about topics people already generally agree on.* Most of the campaigns discussed have dealt with issues already having a high degree of public consensus (e.g., mental health, drug abuse, drinking and driving, crime, etc.). Part of their success likely involved building off of that consensus and providing additional information or argumentation to devel-op or intensify specific kinds of attitudes or behaviors.

PSAs attempting to generate social change on more controversial issues (e.g., abortion, welfare reform, farm policy) may meet with less success. For example, an investigation of a 6-month four-city PSA information campaign on contraceptive use indicated minimal impact (Udry, 1974; Udry, Clark, Chase, & Levy, 1972). (Udry et al. delineated several problems with both the campaign per se and evaluation procedures. The campaign spots were quite nonspecific, and likely necessarily so to increase their possibility of being aired. Several difficulties also surfaced in adequately controlling for campaign effects per se.) In an extensive review of campaigns related to sexual behavior, Brown, Waszak, and Childers (in press) noted that such efforts meet with informal and often formal resistance, and may often work to disproportionately affect less powerful segments of society. The current debate over the content and explicitness of AIDS-related PSAs exemplifies the difficulties involved in producing effective material while refraining from offending social, political and religious arbiters of morality as well as taste.

PSAs are also apt to be less successful at getting people to stop performing either habitual and/or enjoyable behaviors. This is particularly true when there is no immediate reward for curtailing such behaviors (Rogers & Storey, 1987). The folk wisdom that the "only way to end bad habits is to begin good ones" appears to have some utility here.

There may also be risks in tampering with audiences already holding the dispositions being sought. Feingold and Knapp (1977) reported indications of a "boomerang" effect in an experimental setting using radio drug abuse PSAs: High school students' negative attitudes toward drug abuse decreased rather than increased. There may also be a tendency for older adolescents to counter-argue against such messages in televised PSAs (Ray & Ward, 1976). This possibility increases in importance given some evidence of adolescent reliance on media for general information about drugs and alcohol (Atkin, Hocking, & Block, 1984; Kline, Miller, & Morrison, 1976; Kline & Pavlik, 1981). The greater availability of such messages in recent years might well be expected to increase their potential for impact.

SUMMARY AND FUTURE DIRECTIONS

Public service advertising can be a significant factor in the dissemination of information and influence in contemporary society. The public-at-large is fairly attentive to PSAs, especially over television, and people have generally favorable reactions to them. Evaluations carried out during the 1940s and 1950s suggested that PSA-based public information campaigns—as well as mass media in general—had minimal effects on public beliefs, attitudes, and especially behaviors. By the early 1970s, however, some evidence began to indicate otherwise. More importantly, increasingly sophisticated research methods allowed closer examination of the situations and conditions under which successful campaigns would be more likely to occur.

Some recent campaign successes involving PSAs have been found in such areas as mental health, highway safety, smoking cessation, crime prevention, and heart disease risk prevention. There are also indications that children can learn information from certain types of PSAs.

Campaigns in general appear more likely to succeed if they incorporate theoretical models of communication or persuasion into their development. The more influential campaigns have also made extensive use of commercial advertising planning principles in their design and execution. Formative research, audience segmentation, and pretesting appear as key ingredients. Clearly delineated campaign goals are also highly important.

The effectiveness of PSAs is highly dependent on the extent of their dissemination by broadcast and print media, and such activity has shown a recent increase in some topic areas. The technical quality of PSAs is a clear factor in their success, as is their local community appeal. PSAs also are generally more effective when tied to more extensive campaigns, and/or when they ride on a wave of ongoing public opinion or concern.

PSAs are also likely to be more effective when they provide information about topics most people already generally agree on, and if their design takes into account not only existing awareness, attitudes, and behaviors of the target audience with respect to the topic, but their communication preferences and behavior as well.

Some of the more productive paths future research might follow include studying the modes of information processing for various types of PSAs by individuals. It seems apparent that PSAs attract different audiences than other forms of advertising. Messages promoting cognitive, attitudinal, and behavioral changes on issues or ideas rather than products may well require differing attention and processing strategies. Moreover, although the dominant medium for PSAs is clearly television, their use in other media deserves more study, including radio in particular (cf. Bauman et al., 1988).

Also needing further investigation is the role of PSAs in larger scale campaigns, and the ways in which PSAs interact with other mediated messages, as well as interpersonal communication. Do PSAs have a unique role in such a mix? How can the typical 30-second televised spot most effectively convey information that will reinforce or complement the array of other dissemination sources? This line of inquiry likely needs to include more detailed scrutiny of audience dispositions toward PSAs, perhaps focusing on the kinds of functions they serve for various individuals and the kinds of gratifications or utilities they provide.

In a broader sense, we need to be more concerned with the policy implications of such advertising. Paletz et al. (1977) raised the issue of a propagandistic role for PSAs in American society, particularly in terms of kinds of issues the Advertising Council, as well as television networks and individual stations, choose to promote. Emphasis on dissemination of one type of message, be it drug abuse, smoking, or AIDS, reduces the likelihood of other messages on other topics reaching the public. The responsibilities of the gatekeepers here obviously cannot be taken too lightly. The development of successful public service advertising remains part art, part science, and very much a consequence of political policy and social debate.

ACKNOWLEDGMENT

This chapter was in part supported by a grant from the National Partnership to Prevent Drug and Alcohol Abuse.

REFERENCES

ABC (1986a). *Alcohol and drug-related public service announcements.* New York: Social Research Unit, ABC.

ABC (1986b). *Major alcohol abuse-related public service announcements, 1970–1984.* New York: Social Research Unit, ABC.

Atkin, C. K. (1981). Mass media information campaign effectiveness. In R. Rice & W. Paisley (Eds.), *Public communication campaigns* (pp. 265–280). Beverly Hills, CA: Sage.

Atkin, C. K., Garramone, G., & Anderson, R. (1986, May). *Formative evaluation research in health campaign planning: The case of drunk driving prevention.* Paper presented at the annual convention of the International Communication Association, Chicago, IL.

Atkin, C. K., Hocking, J., & Block, M. (1984). Teenage drinking; Does advertising make a difference? *Journal of Communication, 34,* 157–167.

Bandura, A. (1977). *Social learning theory.* Englewood Cliffs, NJ: Prentice-Hall.

Bauman, K. E., Brown, J. D., Bryan, E. S., Fisher, L. A., Padgett, C. A., & Sweeney, J. M. (1988). Three mass media campaigns to prevent adolescent cigarette smoking. *Preventive Medicine, 17,* 510–530.

Black, G. S. (1987). *The attitudinal basis of drug abuse.* New York: Media-Advertising Partnership for a Drug-Free America.

Black, G. S. (1988). *Changing attitudes toward drug use.* New York: Media-Advertising Partnership for a Drug-Free America.

Blosser, B., & Roberts, D. F. (1985). Age differences in children's perceptions of message intent: Responses to TV news, commercials, education spots, and public service announcements. *Communication Research, 12,* 455–484.

Bogart, L. (1986). *Strategy in advertising.* Lincolnwood, IL: NTC Business Books.

Brown, J. D., Waszak, C. S., & Childers, K. W. (in press). Family planning, abortion and AIDS: Sexuality and communication campaigns. In C. T. Salmon (Ed.), *Information campaigns: Balancing social values and social marketing.* Newbury Park, CA: Sage.

Capalaces, R., & Starr, J. (1973). The negative message of anti-drug spots: Does it get across? *Public Telecommunications Review, 1,* 64–66.

Cartwright, D. (1949). Some principles of mass persuasion. *Human Relations, 2,* 253–267.

Chaffee, S. H., & Roser, C. (1986). Involvement and the consistency of knowledge, attitudes and behaviors. *Communication Research, 13,* 373–399.

Chaffee, S. H., Roser, D., & Flora, J. (in press). Estimating the magnitude of threats to validity of information campaign effects. In C. T. Salmon (Ed.), *Information campaigns: Balancing social values and social marketing.* Newbury Park, CA: Sage.

Christenson, P. (1982). Children's perceptions of TV commercials & products: The effects of PSAs. *Communication Research, 9,* 491–524.

Cohn, A. (1985). *The role of media campaigns in preventing child abuse.* Chicago, IL: National Committee for Preventing Child Abuse.

Douglas, D., Westley, B., & Chaffee, S. H. (1970). An information campaign that changed community attitudes. *Journalism Quarterly, 47,* 479–487.

Ettema, J., Brown, J., & Luepker, R. (1983). Knowledge gap effects in a health information campaign. *Public Opinion Quarterly, 47,* 516–527.

Evans, R. (1978). Planning public service advertising messages: An application of the Fishbein model and path analysis. *Journal of Advertising, 7,* 28–34.

Farquhar, J., Fortmann, S., Maccoby, N., Williams, P., Flora, J., Taylor, C. B., Brown, B., Solomon, D., & Hulley, S. (1985). The Stanford Five City Project: Design and methods. *American Journal of Epidemiology, 122,* 323–343.

Feild, T., Deitrick, S., Hersey, J., Probst, J., & Theologus, G. (1983). *Implementing public health education campaigns: Lessons from alcohol abuse prevention.* Summary report presented to the National Institute on Alcohol Abuse and Alcoholism, Washington, DC.

Feingold, P., & Knapp, M. (1977). Anti-drug abuse commercials. *Journal of Communication, 27,* 20–28.

Flay, B. R. (1983). *The role of mass media in community intervention for drug abuse prevention: Research Recommendation.* Prepared for NIDA/NIAAA Technical Review of Community Prevention Research, Washington, DC.

Flay, B. R. (1986, May). *Mass media and smoking cessation.* Paper presented at the annual convention of the International Communication Association, Chicago, IL.

Flay, B. R., & Sobel, J. L. (1983). The role of mass media in preventing adolescent substance abuse. In T. Glynn, C. Leukefeld, & J. Ludford (Eds.), *Preventing adolescent drug abuse* (pp. 5–35). Rockville, MD: National Institute on Drug Abuse.

Flora, J., Roser, C., Chaffee, S., & Farquhar, J. (1988, May). *Communication for heart disease prevention.* Paper presented to the annual conference of the International Communication Association. New Orleans, LA.

Flora, J. A., & Thoreson, C. E. (1988). Reducing the risk of AIDS in adolescents. *American Psychologist, 43,* 965–970.

Goodman, R.I. (1981). Selecting public service announcements for television. *Public Relations Review, 7,* 25–33.

Grunig, J. E., & Childers, L. (1988, July). *Reconstruction of a situational theory of communication: Internal and external concepts as identifiers of publics for AIDS.* Paper presented to the annual convention of the Association for Education in Journalism and Mass Communication. Portland, OR.

Grunig, J. E., & Ipes, D. A. (1983). The anatomy of a campaign against drunk driving. *Public Relations Review, 9,* 36–52.

Hanneman, G. H. (1973). Communicating drug-abuse information among college students. *Public Opinion Quarterly, 37,* 171–191.

Hanneman, G. H., McEwen, W., & Coyne, S. (1973). Public service advertising on television. *Journal of Broadcasting, 17,* 387–404.

Hochheimer, J. L. (1981). Reducing alcohol abuse: A critical review of education strategies. In M. Mark & D. Gerstein (Eds.), *Alcohol and public policy: Beyond the shadow of prohibition* (pp. 286–335). Washington, DC: National Academy Press.

Hornik, R. (in press). The knowledge-behavior gap in public information campaigns: A development communication view. In C. T. Salmon (Ed.), *Information campaigns: Balancing social values and social marketing.* Newbury Park, CA: Sage.

Hyman, H. H., & Sheatsley, P. (1947). Some reasons why information campaigns fail. *Public Opinion Quarterly, 11,* 412–423.

Klapper, J. T. (1960). *The effects of mass communication.* New York: The Free Press.

Kline, F. G., Miller, P., & Morrison, A. (1975). Communication issues in different public health areas. *Advances in Consumer Research, 4,* 290–294.

Kline, F. G., & Pavlik, J. (1981, May). *Adolescent health information acquisition from the broadcast media.* Paper presented to the annual convention of the International Communication Association and Convention, Minneapolis, MN.

Kotler, P. (1982). *Marketing for nonprofit organizations.* Englewood Cliffs, NJ: Prentice-Hall.

Lazarsfeld, P., Berelson, B., & Gaudet, H. (1948). *The people's choice.* New York: Columbia University Press.

Lynn, J. (1973). Perception of public service advertising: source, message and receiver effects. *Journalism Quarterly, 50,* 673–679.

Lynn, J. (1974). Effects of persuasive appeals in public service advertising. *Journalism Quarterly, 51,* 622–630.

Lynn, J., Wyatt, R., Gaines, J., Pearce R., & Bergh, B. (1978). How source affects response to public service advertising. *Journalism Quarterly, 55,* 716–720.

McGowan, A. (1980, June). Public service announcements: What, where, how. *Channels, 4,* 38–45.

McGuire, W.J. (1981). Theoretical foundations of campaigns. In R. E. Rice & W. J. Paisley (Eds.), *Public communication campaigns* (pp. 41–79). Beverly Hills, CA: Sage.

McLeod, J. M., Pan, Z., & Rucinski, D. M. (1988, July). *Processing news and advertising: Same strategies and same effects?* Paper presented to the annual convention of the Association for Education in Journalism and Mass Communication. Portland, OR.

McNamara, E., Kurth, T., & Hansen, D. (1981). Communication efforts to prevent wildfire. In R. Rice & W. Paisley (Eds.), *Public communication campaigns* (pp. 143–160). Beverly Hills, CA: Sage.

McQuail, D. (1987). *Mass communication theory* (2nd ed.). Newbury Park, CA: Sage.

Mendelsohn, H. (1973). Some reasons why information campaigns can succeed. *Public Opinion Quarterly, 37,* 50–61.

Merton, R. (1957). *Social theory and social structure* (Rev. ed.). Glencoe, IL: The Free Press.

National Association of Broadcasters. (1984). *1984 Public affairs survey regarding broadcasters' contributions to prevent drunk driving & alcohol misuse.* Washington, DC: Author.

National Association of Broadcasters. (1985). *The fight against alcohol misuse: Broadcasters' Contributions November 1984 through May 1985.* Washington, DC: Author.

National Highway Traffic Safety Administration. (1979). *Review of programs designed to encourage use of safety belts.* Washington, DC: U.S. Department of Transportation.

National Institute of Mental Health. (1982). *Television & behavior: Ten years of scientific progress and implications for the eighties.* Rockville, MD: Author.

Needham Porter Novelli. (1985). *Survey of public service directors from TV stations representing high and low play of high blood pressure messages.* Washington, DC: National High Blood Pressure Education Program, National Heart, Lung and Blood Institute.

O'Keefe, G.J. (1985). "Taking a bite out of crime": The impact of a public information campaign. *Communication Research, 12,* 147–178.

O'Keefe, G. J. (1986). The "McGruff" national media campaign: Its public impact and future implications. In D. Rosenbaum (Ed.), *Community crime prevention: Does it work?* (pp. 252–268) Beverly Hills, CA: Sage.

O'Keefe, G. J., Mendelsohn, H., & Liu, J. (1980, August). *The audiences for public service advertising: An exploratory view.* Paper presented to the annual convention of the Association for Education in Journalism, Boston, MA.

O'Keefe, G. J., & Reid, K. (in press). The McGruff crime prevention campaign. In R. E.

Rice & C. K. Atkin (Eds.), *Public communication campaigns* (2nd ed.). Newbury Park, CA: Sage.

O'Keefe, G. J., & Reid-Nash, K. (1987). *Promoting crime prevention competence among the elderly.* Washington DC: National Institute of Justice.

O'Keefe, M. T. (1971). The anti-smoking commercials: a study of television's impact on behavior. *Public Opinion Quarterly, 35,* 242–248.

Paisley, W. J. (1981). Public communication campaigns: The American experience. In R. E. Rice & W. J. Paisley (Eds.), *Public communication campaigns* (pp. 15–40). Beverly Hills, CA: Sage.

Paletz, D. L., Pearson, R., & Willis, D. (1977). *Politics in public service advertising on television.* New York: Praeger.

Pasick, R. J., & Wallack, L. (1988). *Mass media in health promotion: A compilation of expert opinion.* Unpublished manuscript, School of Public Health, University of California, Berkeley, CA.

Pavlik, J. V. (1987, August). *Campaign planning in public relations: Learning from the Minnesota Heart Health Program.* Paper presented to the annual convention of the Association for Education in Journalism and Mass Communication, San Antonia, TX.

Percy, L., & Rossiter, J. (1980). *Advertising strategy: A communication theory approach.* New York: Praeger.

Ray, M., & Ward, S. (1976). Experimentation for pretesting public health programs: The case of the anti-drug abuse campaigns. *Advances in Consumer Research, 3,* 278–286.

Roberts, D., Bachen, C., Christenson, P., & Gibson, W. (1979). *Children's responses to consumer information & nutrition, information television spots.* Paper presented at the meeting of the American Psychological Association, New York.

Roberts, D. F., & Maccoby, N. (1985). Effects of mass communication. In G. Lindzey & E. Aronson (Eds.), *The handbook of social psychology* (3rd ed., Vol. 2, pp. 529–598). New York: Random House.

Robertson, L. S. (1976). The great seat belt campaign flop. *Journal of Communication, 26,* 41–45.

Robertson, L. S., Kelley, A., O'Neill, B., Wixom, C., Eiswirth, R., & Haddon, W., Jr. (1974). A controlled study of the effect of television messages on safety belt use. *American Journal of Public Health, 64,* 1071–1080.

Rogers, E. M., & Storey, J. D. (1987). Communication campaigns. In C. R. Berger & S. H. Chaffee (Eds.), *Handbook of communication science* (pp. 817–846). Newbury Park, CA: Sage.

Rosengren, K. E., Wenner, L. A., & Palmgren, P. (1985). *Media gratification research: Current perspectives.* Beverly Hills, CA: Sage.

Roser, C., Flora, J., Chaffee, S. H., & Farquhar, J. W. (1988, July). *Who's listening? Predictors of learning from a heart disease prevention program.* Paper presented to the annual convention of the Association for Education in Journalism and Mass Communication, Portland, OR.

Salcedo, R., Read, H., Evans, J., & Kong, A. (1974). A successful information campaign on pesticides. *Journalism Quarterly, 51,* 91–95.

Salmon, C. T. (1986). Message discrimination and the information environment. *Communication Research, 13,* 363–372.

Schanie, C., & Sundel, M. (1978). A community mental health innovation in mass media preventive education: The alternatives project. *American Journal of Community Psychology, 6,* 573–581.

Schmeling, D. G., & Wotring, C. E. (1980). Making anti-drug abuse advertising work. *Journal of Advertising Research, 20,* 33–37.

Smith, K., Nelson S., & O'Hara, J. (1982). *Food for thought project.* Alexandria, VA: U.S. Department of Agriculture.

Solomon, D. S. (1981). Social marketing and health promotion. In R. Rice & W. Paisley (Eds.), *Public communication campaigns* (pp. 281–292). Beverly Hills, CA: Sage.

Star, S., & Hughes, H. (1950). A report on an educational campaign: the Cincinnati plan for the United Nations. *American Journal of Sociology, 55,* 389–400.

Swinehart, J. (1981). *A descriptive review of selected mass media campaigns on highway safety.* Springfield, VA: National Technical Information Service.

Udry, J. (1974). *The mass media and family planning.* New York: Ballinger.

Udry, J., Clark, L. Chase, C., & Levy, M. (1972). Can mass media advertising increase contraceptive use? *Family Planning Perspectives, 4,* 37–44.

Warner, K. (1977). The effects of the anti-smoking campaign on cigarette consumption. *American Journal of Public Health, 67,* 645–650.

PART II

REPORTS OF ORIGINAL RESEARCH

Roles and Program Evaluation Techniques Among Canadian Public Relations Practitioners

Jennie M. Piekos
Edna F. Einsiedel
University of Calgary

An increasing number of public relations researchers and practitioners have emphasized that public relations is a planned effort that must be managed efficiently (Cutlip, Center, & Broom, 1985; Grunig & Hunt, 1984; Nager & Allen, 1984). This strategic management of public relations requires a systematic planning process that integrates program evaluation and scientific research techniques into the public relations process.

Top management in many instances has begun to require objective information and statistics to show that public relations efforts contribute, not only to overall organizational effectiveness, but also to the bottom line (Chapman, 1982). As Nager and Allen (1984) contended, "CEOs demand that all managers be held accountable for what they produce. This is true of all departments. Public relations is no exception" (p. 3). The era of planning and implementing public relations programs based on hunches, guesswork, and "gut feelings" is virtually over, according to Lindenmann (1980). To facilitate systematic planning, it has been suggested that practitioners: (a) view public relations from an open systems perspective; (b) adopt a management-by-objectives philosophy in their work; and (c) follow a systematic planning model (Cutlip et al., 1985; Grunig & Hunt, 1984). The systems perspective encourages practitioners to systematically monitor their environment, to formulate solutions to problems identified in this manner, to design programs as part of these solutions, and to monitor these programs on their effectiveness (Grunig & Hunt, 1984).

Encouraging the move away from a profession largely based on intuition to one that relies more heavily on objective data are public relations societies in both the

United States and Canada. The Public Relations Society of American (PRSA), for example, strongly supports the movement toward program evaluation and in-creased use of scientific research. Based on results from a PRSA-sponsored study in 1980, the Society officially recognized the need for program objectivity in 1982. Since then, PRSA requires entrants to its Silver Anvil Awards competition to explain how programs are evaluated (Cutlip et al., 1985; Hill, 1982; Nager & Allen, 1984). In 1980, Hill (1982) noted that of that year's Silver Anvil Award entries, 70% offered no measure of results and another 70% made no reference to desired behavior of the audience.

The Canadian Public Relations Society (CPRS) has also been concerned with scientific research and program evaluation (Blagg, 1984, 1985; McIvor, 1986). The 1984 and 1985 annual CPRS conferences included discussions on measure-ment and evaluation in public relations.

Despite this encouragement from the professional societies, practitioners remain divided on the use of research and evaluation. On the one hand, a number of individuals see the need to incorporate scientific research and program evaluation into the public relations process. "With mass audiences breaking down into far narrower segments, each with its own interests and concerns, research is the only certain method for knowing that a communications program will reach its target" (Finn & Harrity, 1984, p. 286). On the other hand, various individuals object to the integration of scientific research and evaluation into the public relations process by claiming public relations is an art that cannot be measured. As Grunig (1983b) lamented:

> Lately, I have begun to feel more and more like the fundamentalist minister railing against sin, the difference being that I have railed for evaluation. Just as everyone is against sin, so most public relations people I talk to are for evaluation. People keep on sinning, however, and PR people continue not to do evaluation research. (p. 28)

Although a number of studies have been conducted in the United States on the extent of program-evaluation practices among public relations professionals (see, for example, Broom, 1983; Center & Broom, 1983; Dozier, 1984, 1985), hardly any literature exists on Canadian professionals. This chapter reports on a portion of a larger study on Canadian public relations professionals (Piekos, 1988) and focuses on the extent of systematic program evaluation within the Canadian public relations profession. Because the practice of program evaluation is often deter-mined by the practitioner's location within the organization's decision-making hierarchy and the nature and range of activities he or she engages in, we also examine the roles occupied by these practitioners according to the typology devel-oped by Broom (1982) and Broom and Dozier (1986).

Public Relations Roles

The study of public relations roles has been an important area of research because it provides greater explanatory insight into the work behavior of public relations practitioners. Beginning in the 1970s, Broom and his colleagues spearheaded a program of research to arrive at a typology of public relations roles (Acharya, 1981; Broom, 1982; Broom & Smith, 1978, 1979; Smith, 1978). In their effort to test how public relations roles affect client satisfaction with practitioners, Broom and Smith (1978, 1979) and Smith (1978) reviewed a wide range of "consulting" literature and from this information, they conceptualized five distinct consulting roles. These roles were then operationalized in a public relations context to represent various ways practitioners behave. The five role models were expert prescriber, communication technician, problem-solving process facilitator, communication facilitator, and acceptant legitimizer. Subsequent research demonstrated the efficacy of the first four roles, whereas the last was dropped from use.

The concept "role model" was defined by the researchers as "the patterned behavior of a public relations practitioner. The behavioral pattern represents the role occupant's strategy for dealing with recurring types of situations, based in part on the role occupant's recognition of others' expectations" (Broom & Smith, 1978, p. 4).

Broom and Smith (1978, 1979) pointed out that the office of a public relations practitioner incorporates a variety of activities or roles. However, he or she develops a dominant pattern of job-related behaviors through individual preference, training, and in response to others' expectations and situational constraints.

Broom's (1982) definition of each role is provided here. Where appropriate, reference is made to the consulting literature from which the role model was developed. The following descriptions of the four role models illustrate that they "systematically differ in the amount of input they contribute and the approach they use to help resolve problems" (Johnson & Acharya, 1982, p. 11). These models served as the basis for this study and were empirically measured.

Expert Prescriber. The practitioner occupying the role of expert prescriber operates as the authority on both public relations problems and their solutions. The client or management is generally content to leave public relations in the hands of the "expert" and to assume a relatively passive role. The practitioner researches and defines the problem, develops the program, and takes major responsibility for its implementation.

This public relations role model is partly based on a model of consultation known as "doctor–patient" (Schein, 1969). Organizational managers hire consultants to "look them over," in much the same way a patient might ask a doctor for a physical examination. "The consultants are supposed to find out what is wrong with which part of the organization and then, like a physician, recommend a program of therapy" (Schein, 1969, p. 6).

Communication Technician. Practitioners operating as communication technicians provide their organization or client with the specialized skills needed to carry out public relations programs. These practitioners are usually hired on the basis of communications and journalistic skills such as writing, editing, and working with the media. Communication technicians are not part of the management team. Instead, throughout the problem-solving process, practitioners handle the technical aspects, whereas management is concerned with problem definition and resolution.

Problem-Solving Process Facilitator.   Public relations practitioners who assume this role collaborate with others (e.g., line managers) throughout the organization to define and solve problems. As part of the management team, the problem-solving process facilitator helps guide other managers and the organization through a rational problem-solving process. The practitioner maintains a high level of management involvement in implementing all phases of the program.

Communication Facilitator.   This practitioner serves as a liaison, interpreter, and mediator between the organization and its publics. The emphasis is in maintaining a continuous flow of two-way communication. A person in this role is also concerned with removing barriers to keep channels of communication open.

A communication facilitator is primarily concerned with promoting two-way communication between the parties involved in a particular event or issue. Communication constraints are the major concerns of this practitioner (Broom & Smith, 1978, 1979).

Roles Research in Public Relations

There appear to be two streams of research underway in public relations regarding practitioner roles. One stream of research attempts to further the understanding of practitioner roles, whereas another examines the relationship between roles and other important variables in public relations (e.g., environmental uncertainty, gender, salary, and participation in management decision making).

Dozier (1981) elaborated on Broom's (1982) models by factor analyzing the latter's database and developing four empirical models of organizational roles: manager, technician, media relations specialist, and communications liaison.

According to Dozier's typology, managers engage in activities that involve expert prescription, communication facilitation, and problem-solving process facilitation. Technicians are involved in activities similar to those described by Broom and Smith (1978, 1979) for the communication technician role. Dozier noted that the manager and technician roles provide a parsimonious way of reducing major practitioner roles into two categories.

The two other roles Dozier identified are media relations specialist and communication liaison. Unlike technicians, media relations specialists do not become involved with internal communication and, like technicians, they do not make policy decisions. Communication liaisons act as senior ranking advisors to decision makers but they themselves do not make decisions. Other researchers exploring practitioner roles have found that the roles of manager and technician are consistent over time with evidence being less conclusive regarding a number of minor roles (Ferguson, 1987).

The second stream of research examines the effect of roles in public relations. Particularly relevant to this chapter are those that focus on program evaluation and research approach. Dozier has done extensive work in these areas as did Judd (1987a, 1987b) who focused on roles and formal (scientific) research.

Dozier (1981) tested the relationship between roles and research approach. The roles he employed in this study were manager, technician, media relations specialist, and communication liaison. Research approach was dichotomized to include scientific and individualistic (intuitive) techniques. Three content areas were examined: preparation evaluation, dissemination evaluation, and impact evaluation. Data were collected on roles and evaluation activities of 169 public relations practitioners in San Diego, California.

Study results showed that manager role scores were significantly and positively related to both research methods across three content areas of program evaluation. Similar relationships were found for communication liaison role scores. Communication technician role scores were not correlated with either scientific or seat-of-pants evaluation activities.

In another study, Dozier (1984) identified "styles" of evaluation. He isolated three major clusters of evaluation activities and labeled them as *scientific impact style, seat-of-pants style,* and *scientific dissemination style.* The scientific impact style stressed scientific measures of program impact before and after program implementation. The seat-of-the pants style emphasized personalized and subjective checks on all parts of the public relations process. The scientific dissemination style described numeric analysis of "clip files" or the maintenance of accurate records of messages produced, distributed, and used by the media. Practitioners can adopt more than one style of evaluation.

Consistent with his earlier (1981) findings, Dozier's results showed that: (a) manager role scores were significantly and positively correlated with "scientific impact" style of evaluation and "seat-of-pants evaluation" across three content areas, and (b) no style of public relations evaluation was related to communication technician role scores.

In a later study, Dozier (1986) focused on one area of program evaluation, problem definition, and measured the relationship between practitioner roles and environmental scanning. As predicted, he found that informal and formal scanning methods were positively correlated with the managerial role. Neither formal nor informal scanning were correlated with the technician role. Judd (1987a, 1987b) examined the relationship between practitioner roles and research approach. He selected at random 100 Texas members listed in the 1985–1986 Register of the *Public Relations Journal* to participate in a telephone survey. He found that practitioners who perceive themselves in the manager role were significantly more likely to conduct formal research than practitioners who perceive themselves as technicians.

Based on these previous studies, the major hypothesis explored in this chapter is that there will be a significant relationship between the three managerial roles and the use of scientific evaluation methods. No significant relationships are expected between managerial roles and intuitive evaluation approaches. No relationships are also predicted between the communication technician role and scientific or intuitive program evaluation methods.

It was recognized that top management support was critical for conducting systematic research in the practice of public relations. We therefore hypothesized that as top management support for systematic research in public relations increases, there will be a concomitant increase in the use of scientific evaluation methods.

METHODOLOGY

Sampling Frame. The most recent membership lists of the Canadian Public Relations Society (CPRS) and the International Association of Business Communications, Canada (IABC) were merged and used as the sampling frame for this study. Only members listed as being from 12 major urban areas in Canada were included. These areas were: Vancouver, Calgary, Edmonton, Regina, Saskatoon, Winnipeg, Toronto, Ottawa, Montreal, Moncton, Halifax, and St. John's. This includes a large majority of the membership of both organization. Only individuals whose titles indicated involvement in public relations work (e.g., director of communications, corporate relations, government relations, director of public affairs, etc.) were included in the study. Included in the sample were 700 respondents.

Survey Instrument. The survey instrument was designed to measure evaluation methods across four program content areas and practitioner roles. Also measured but outside the scope of this chapter were background attributes (professional, personal, and organizational), participation in decision making, and attitudes toward the job (e.g., satisfaction), and particular professional trends. The program-evaluation scale used in this study consisted of four content areas and two research approaches. Items measuring evaluation methods across four content areas were developed by Dozier (1981) and Broom (1982). A number of items were also designed specifically for this study based on a review of relevant literature (see Table 4.1).

Procedure. The questionnaire was first pretested on a small sample of 15 professionals. After minor revisions, the instrument was mailed to the 700 respondents across Canada, along with a cover letter and a postage-paid envelope in September 1987. The incentive offered to the respondents was a copy of the summary report of the research findings if they filled out the questionnaire and returned a request-for-results card included with the questionnaire.

A follow-up mailing was administered 1 month after the initial mailing. Ques-

TABLE 4.1
Items Measuring Scientific and Intuitive Evaluation Methods

Problem Definition

Scientific	Intuitive
Before developing communication strategies, I define a public relations problem/issue by using formal research methods, e.g., survey research, reviewing relevant published surveys.[a]	I diagnose public relations problems/issues by using a variety of scanning methods (e.g., talking with field personnel to find out about key publics, calling embers of target publics to keep in touch).[a]

Program Planning and Preparation

Scientific	Intuitive
1. During the planning stages of a program, I set goals and objectives that are well defined, realistic and measurable.[a]	1. I participate in informal discussions with top management to determine how programs should be developed.[a]
2. I prepare communications by testing preliminary message strategies and formats on groups drawn from publics involved.[b]	2. I prepare communications by drawing on my own professional experience and on files I have accumulated on the subject.[c]
3. After materials have been developed for a campaign, I assess the ease with which the material can be comprehended through the use of systematic research (e.g., readability tests).[a]	3. I check communications strategies during preparation by reviewing them with practitioner colleagues who apply their own professional standards.[c]

Implementation/Dissemination

Scientific	Intuitive
1. I keep record of the number of messages sent (e.g., news releases, letters, speeches, feature stories). That is, I note all the materials produced and distributed.[a]	1. I monitor dissemination of messages (press releases, etc.) through personal contacts with media professionals.[b]
2. I keep an accurate record of the number of messages *used* by the media.[a]	2. I monitor the dissemination of messages through periodic, formal meetings with senior media professionals.[c]
3. I measure potential exposure to program messages by reviewing circulation figures, audience size data, and attendance figures for events, meetings or exhibits.[a]	3. I judge the potential exposure to program messages by the number of brochures, press releases, etc., distributed to media representatives and/or other outlets.[a]
4. To help determine the number of people who attend to the prepared messages (audience attention), I undertake readership, listenership, viewership studies.[a]	4. I judge the levels of audience attention to prepared messages by monitoring public feedback (e.g., the number of phone calls made).[a]

(continued)

TABLE 4.1   *(Continued)*

Problem Definition

Scientific	*Intuitive*
1. I use formal research methods to measure whether program goals and objectives (set out in the planning stage) have been met.[a]	1. I check PR impact by keeping my eyes and ears open to the reactions of my personal and public contacts.[c]
2. I check program impact through interviews with a scientifically selected cross-section of significant publics.[b]	2. I check PR impact by attending meetings and hearings of groups representative of significant publics.[b]
3. When appropriate, I use indirect methods for observing desired behavioral changes (e.g., observation of turnstyles at events, head counts at meetings).[a]	3. I check PR impact by the reaction the program receives from senior management.[a]

[a] Piekos (1988).
[b] Broom and Dozier (1983).
[c] Dozier (1984).

tionnaires, cover letters, and postage-paid envelopes were sent to every other nonrespondent on the list. Budgetary constraints precluded a follow-up to all nonrespondents. Both mailings were disrupted by nation-wide postal strikes.

RESULTS

Return Rate and Sample Representativeness.   The first mailing resulted in 277 usable questionnaires, whereas the second wave yielded only 32 more. The final response rate was 47.4%. Because of the unexpected postal strikes right after the mail-outs, it is possible that the uncertain postal situation might have discouraged some individuals from returning the questionnaire. Because only an English version of the questionnaire was used, it is also possible this might have accounted for the low response rate of 30% from Montreal.

To validate the representativeness of the respondents, we examined the CPRS membership by gender. The membership distribution was 56.5% male and 43.5% female. Of the survey respondents who cited membership in CPRS (N = 187), 56.2% were males, whereas 43.8% were females. On this attribute at least, the respondents appear to be reasonably representative.

Item Reliability.   Reliability coefficients were determined for the practitioner role measures as well as for the program evaluation scales. The coefficients for practitioner roles (see Table 4.2) parallel closely those found by Broom and Dozier (1986) who used the longer version of the scale. Broom and Dozier (1986) found coefficients of .90 for expert prescriber; .73 for communication facilitator; .87 for problem-solving process facilitator; and .77 for communication technician.

TABLE 4.2
Cronbach's Alpha Reliability Coefficients for Scales
Measuring Practitioner Roles and Evaluation Methods

Practitioner Roles	Expert prescriber	.90
	Communication facilitator	.79
	Problem-solving process facilitator	.85
	Communication technician	.76
Evaluation Methods	Scientific preparation/planning	.68
	Scientific dissemination	.70
	Scientific impact	.61
	Overall scientific scale	.83
	Intuitive preparation/planning	.52
	Intuitive dissemination	.74
	Intuitive impact	.61
	Overall intuitive scale	.82

Work Profile of Respondents. Eight in 10 respondents were permanent employees of their organizations. About 25% had worked in public relations for 5 years or less, 30% had 6 to 10 years of public relations experience, whereas 44% had 11 years or more of professional experience. In terms of their rank in the public relations hierarchy, there was an even split between those who said they were the highest ranking PR practitioner and those who were not the highest ranking practitioner. The modal category in terms of organizational size was 1,000 or more employees.

Distribution of Dominant Roles

Table 4.3 shows the following:

- The single largest majority of respondents were categorized as communication technicians.

TABLE 4.3
Percentage Distribution of Respondents
With Dominant Roles

	Percent
Communication technician	41.7
Expert prescriber	16.2
Problem-solving process facilitator	15.2
Communication factilitator	12.3
Two-way tied scores	12.6
Three-way tied scores	1.9
N	309

- The most common managerial role is that of expert prescriber, followed by the problem-solving process facilitator, and communication facilitator.

About 4 in 10 respondents were labeled communication technician, whereas the various components of the managerial role were distributed as follows: 16% of respondents were designated as expert prescribers and an almost equal proportion was listed as problem-solving process facilitators. More than 10% of the sample was classified as communication facilitator. Scores for the remaining respondents (15%) were tied.

The Use of Program Evaluation Techniques

Tables 4.4 and 4.5 show the following:

- Overall, intuitive techniques are used significantly more often than scientific ones when evaluating public relations programs.
- During the problem-definition phase of program evaluation, intuitive methods are used significantly more often than scientific ones.
- Respondents apply intuitive evaluation techniques significantly more often than scientific ones when planning and preparing their programs.
- The situation is reversed during the implementation/dissemination phase of program evaluation. Scientific methods are used significantly more often than intuitive ones.
- To evaluate the impact of programs, respondents reported significantly greater usage of intuitive techniques than scientific methods.

Scientific Evaluation Methods.   As Table 4.4 demonstrates, a majority of respondents (44%) reported low usage of scientific research methods to help define public relations problems compared to almost one-fifth who described themselves as frequent users.

Three behavioral indicators measured scientific preparation and planning. Results show the use of scientific research methods is infrequent. A majority of respondents cited low usage of focus group testing (61%) and message comprehension testing (58%). However, the data show more than 50% of respondents take a management by objectives (MBO) approach to their work by frequently setting goals and objectives for their programs.

During the dissemination/implementation phase of a program, most respondents frequently monitor the distribution (56%) and placement (39%) of all communications materials produced. These tasks are considered scientific because all information is systematically recorded and maintained. The use of formal research methods appears to be limited. About 6 in 10 respondents reported low usage of scientific research methods to measure audience attention and 44% men-

TABLE 4.4
Percentage Distribution of Scientific Evaluation Methods
Across Four Program Content Areas

Program Content Area	% Rating 6/7	X̄	N
Problem definition:			
• Formal research methods.	17.5	3.8	309
Planning and preparation:			
• Set goals and objectives.	56.6	5.4	309
• Focus group testing.	10.4	3.2	309
• Test message comprehension via scientific methods.	12.4	3.3	307
X		3.9	
Implementation/dissemination:			
• Record all messages produced and sent.	56.2	5.1	306
• Record messages *used* by the media	38.7	4.3	305
• Measure potential exposure to messages by reviewing relevant data.	25.8	3.9	306
• Use scientific research to determine levels of audience attention.	11.1	3.0	305
X		4.1	
Impact assessment:			
• Use formal research methods to measure whether program goals and objectives attained.	13.1	3.3	306
• Interview scientifically selected, cross-section of significant publics to check PR impact	6.2	2.6	305
• Use indirect methods of observing	24.8	3.6	302
X		3.1	

Scale: Never (1) . . . . (7) Always

tioned infrequent reference to secondary sources to help measure potential exposure to messages.

Three items tapped the final program content area, impact evaluation. Results show that all three scientific techniques are seldom used by respondents. About 75% cited infrequent use of scientific research methods to check PR impact, 56% hardly ever apply formal research methods to measure whether program goals and objectives have been attained, and 50% reported low usage of indirect methods to observe desired behavioral changes. Table 4.5 shows a higher percentage of practitioners using intuitive methods almost all or all the time. The most common method was to use experience and the files to prepare communications during the planning and preparation phase. For implementation and dissemination, monitoring message dissemination via media contacts was done by three in ten respondents almost all or all the time. In terms of impact assessment, the majority said they checked program impact via the reactions of their contacts.

TABLE 4.5
Percentage Distribution of Intuitive Evaluation Methods
Across Four Program Content Areas

Program Content Area	% Rating 6/7	$\overline{X}$	N
Problem definition:			
• Informal methods to define problems	34.0	4.70	309
Planning and preparation:			
• Discuss program development with top management	58.1	5.40	308
• Prepare communications based on experience/files.	63.6	5.70	308
• Check communication strategies with colleagues.	29.7	4.15	306
$\overline{X}$		5.08	
Implementation/dissemination:			
• Monitor message dissemination via media contacts.	30.4	4.13	306
• Monitor message dissemination via meetings with media professionals.	12.7	2.83	306
• Judge message exposure by materials distributed.	18.4	3.65	305
• Judge audience attention via public feedback.	23.0	3.66	305
$\overline{X}$		3.58	
Impact assessment:			
• Check program impact via reactions of contacts.	62.2	5.64	307
• Check PR impact by attending meetings and hearings held by significant publics.	21.2	3.81	306
• Check PR impact via top management reaction.	36.1	4.45	305
$\overline{X}$		4.63	

A mean score was computed for each respondent on the frequency of use for all scientific and intuitive methods. Tests showed significantly higher use of intuitive rather than scientific methods with the exception of the implementation phase where scientific methods were used more frequently (Table 4.6). Looking back at Table 4.4, however, the method used most frequently was the recording of all messages produced and sent rather than the more formal research methods.

Dominant Roles and Evaluation Methods

The data from Table 4.7 show that:

• As predicted, positive and significant correlations were found between each of the three managerial role and scientific evaluation methods.

TABLE 4.6
Mean Evaluation Scores Across Four Program Content Areas

	Mean Evaluation Scores	
Program Content Area	Scientific	Intuitive
Problem definition	3.80	4.70*
Planning & preparation	3.92	5.08*
Implementation/dissemination	4.06	3.54*
Impact assessment	3.13	4.62*
Overall mean score	3.76	4.37*

*$p < .05$ using pair-wise t test.

- Contrary to expectations, positive and significant correlations were also found between each of the three managerial roles and intuitive evaluation methods. It was predicted that these relationships would be insignificant.

- Also contrary to expectations, positive and significant correlations were found between the communication technician role and both scientific and intuitive evaluation methods. It was expected the relationships would not be significant.

Top Management Support for Systematic Research

According to study results, 42% of respondents said senior management in their organization is not very supportive of systematic research, compared to 25% who perceived senior management as very supportive. In light of this finding it is not surprising that intuitive techniques are applied significantly more often than scientific ones during program evaluation.

On the other hand, this study had hypothesized that as top management support for systematic research increases, there will be an increase in the use of scientific evaluation methods. To test this hypothesis, an overall mean scientific evaluation score was calculated for each respondent based on his or her scores across all scientific evaluation measures. A coefficient of determination was then

TABLE 4.7
Correlation of Overall Evaluation Methods Scores With Dominant Role Scores
(Pearson's R)

Overall Evaluation Methods Scores	Dominant Roles			
	E.P.	C.F.	P.S.P.F.	C.T.
Scientific	.38*	.56*	.49*	.44*
Intuitive	.42*	.77*	.63*	.51*
N	50	38	47	129

Pearson's r significant at $p < .05$.

TABLE 4.8
Top Management Support and Use of Scientific Evaluation Methods

Source of Variation	Sum of Squares	df	Mean Square	F	p
Top mngt. support	66.14	1	66.14	63.77	.000
Residual	312.18	301	1.04		
Total	378.31	302			

$r = .418$
$R^2 = .175$
$SE = 1.018$

calculated to measure the proportion of explained variance in the dependent variable.

Regression results (Table 4.8) show that top management support is indeed correlated with use of scientific evaluation methods and that this support explains about 18% of the variance in use of scientific methods. Further analysis also showed that this relationship remained significant despite variations in type and size of organization and size of PR department.

DISCUSSION

The major finding of this study—that intuitive techniques are used more widely than scientific ones—was not unexpected. Although a majority, or 87%, said systematic research will have or is having an overall positive impact on the field (suggesting that practitioners are favorably disposed to the scientific approach), in practice, it appears Canadian practitioners are not yet prepared to actually apply it in their work. Researchers in the United States have found similar patterns (Dozier, 1985; Grunig, 1983a).

Scientific approaches are avoided partly because most practitioners lack the training to use this approach. Less than 3% of respondents indicated they had any background in scientific research methods. This study found that participation in continuing education programs is fairly high: About 66% of practitioners have taken courses offered by continuing education departments. Because practitioners are already inclined to further their education, they could get this training either through workshops or through university course.

Dominant Roles and Evaluation Methods. The relationships between dominant roles and evaluation methods were explored and a number of hypotheses tested. The first hypothesis, that positive and significant correlations would be found between each of the three managerial roles and scientific evaluation methods scores, was supported. Generally, correlations were strongest for the role of communication facilitator, indicating these practitioners apply scientific techniques more often than those in the other managerial roles. This finding could be a function of the responsibilities assumed by this type of manager. Perhaps communication facilitators require more objective information than the others in order to keep channels of communication open between various parties.

Expert prescribers, problem-solving process facilitators, and communication facilitators are the individuals who manage public relations in organizations and should be on the vanguard of the movement toward application of scientific research techniques. Without managerial initiatives, intuitive techniques will continue to pervade program evaluation in public relations. In addition, those working at the lower levels will not have progressive role models to emulate.

Practitioners who assume a technical role are expected to primarily write and edit communication materials and deal with the media. This study unexpectedly found they also perform the managerial task of program evaluation. In contrast, studies undertaken in the United States have found technicians are not involved in program evaluations (Dozier, 1981, 1984; Judd, 1987a, 1987b). A number of explanations are possible.

Practitioners function in a variety of organizational roles but generally, a dominant one emerges. In this study, almost 50% of all communication technicians indicated they are the highest ranking public relations practitioner in their organization. As the highest ranking practitioner, the individual may take on managerial responsibilities, such as evaluating programs, in addition to technical tasks. This may account for the significant relationship between the technician role and the use of scientific methods. On the other hand, the scientific methods used more frequently by the various roles—both technician and managerial—tend to be those involving systematic record-keeping and simple counts.

Significantly more technicians than those assuming managerial roles work in public relations departments ranked as small, employing one to five individuals. Perhaps in smaller public relations departments, technicians are expected to go beyond performing strictly technical tasks and take on managerial ones. Also, the type of organization may affect responsibilities assumed by the technicians. Significantly more technicians work for nonprofit organizations and private companies (not traded publicly) than do those in the other three roles. One can speculate that the factors just given, alone or in combination, may have contributed to the unexpected relationships between the communication technician role and program evaluation.

When evaluating programs, technicians follow in the footsteps of managers by applying intuitive methods more often than scientific ones. With little top management support for systematic research, limited training in scientific research methods and few public relations role models, the finding is not completely unexpected.

Top Management Support for Scientific Evaluation Methods. This study had found that although there was generally little overall support for scientific approaches, when such support was available, there was also a likelihood for conducting scientific research. Support for research is likely limited partly because public relations is perceived simply as an output function, producing, and distributing communications materials. Under these circumstances, research might be considered a waste of time and money or given a low priority. Without top management understanding and support, some argue systematic research in public relations will not be commonplace (Cutlip et al., 1985).

Comparisons Between Canadian and U.S. Findings

Some of the findings from this study can be compared with those obtained by researchers in the United States. Communication technicians in Canada are involved in all phases of program evaluation whereas in the United States, technicians generally do not conduct evaluations. On the other hand, in both countries, managerial practitioners apply intuitive and scientific evaluation techniques but rely more heavily on intuitive ones.

It is certainly possible that the greater extent of specialization among practitioners in the United States might account for the more marked distinctions in job activities. With a large number of technicians in the Canadian sample operating as the highest ranking practitioner in their organizations, it is possible their range of functions might be more diffuse.

Implications for the Profession

One of the major concerns facing public relations is the slow integration of scientific evaluation techniques into the public relations process. Two major barriers must be overcome before the scientific approach is entrenched: little top management support for systematic research and lack of practitioner knowledge and understanding of research methods.

Senior management support is a critical factor affecting the use of scientific research in public relations. Generally, Canadian practitioners' perceptions of top management support for research are not very encouraging. In some ways, this might be seen as a Catch-22 situation. On the other hand, one might argue that practitioners can and should take the initiative to get their company managers to buy into the importance of public relations to the overall effectiveness of the organization and to demonstrate this importance through the results of scientific approaches to program evaluation. Ideas on how to accomplish this are not lacking (Baer, 1983).

Canadian professionals' attitudes toward systematic research are favorable but attitudes alone are not enough to spur research activity. To encourage widespread use of scientific techniques, more practitioners must learn what they are and how they are applied.

Limitations and Questions for Further Research

The scale measuring practitioner roles was developed in the United States ad used in its entirety in this study. Statistical measures of internal consistency (Cronbach's alpha) match those obtained by U.S. researchers and are considered to offer relatively high measurement reliability. However, one of the problems encountered in this study was the relatively large number of respondents with tied scores (15%). These subjects were not assigned a dominant role and were thus excluded from analyses involving dominant roles. Broom's (1982) study used the longer version of the role scale consisting of 28 items and found that only 7% of his sample had tied scores.

It is also clear that some of the program evaluation measures need some refinement and validation. The reliability coefficients, particularly for measures of scientific impact and intuitive preparation/planning, show the need to examine more closely these measures and to further test them on other groups.

On the whole, the findings do not present a totally dismal picture of the state of public relations practice in Canada. However, the profession has a long way to go for it to earn the support of top-level management and to achieve greater control and effectiveness in the practice of public relations.

REFERENCES

Acharya, L. (1981). *Effect of perceived environmental uncertainty on public relations roles.* Paper presented to the Foundation of Public Relations Research and Education, Wisconsin University, Madison, WI.

Baer, D. M. (1983). Selling management on public relations research. *Public Relations Quarterly, 28,* 9–11.

Blagg, M. (1984). *Intimations of the future in public relations from the annual 1984 CPRS conference.* Ottawa: CPRS.

Blagg, M. (1985). Perspectives on public relations from the 1985 Annual Conference of the Canadian Public Relations Society. Ottawa: CPRS.

Broom, G. M. (1982). A comparison of sex roles in public relations. *Public Relations Review, 8*(3), 17–22.

Broom, G. M. (1983). An overview: Evaluation in public relations. *Public Relations Quarterly, 28,* 5–8.

Broom, G. M., & Smith, G. D. (1978). *Toward an understanding of public relations roles: An empirical test of five role models' impact on clients.* Paper presented to the Public Relations Division, Association for Education in Journalism Annual Convention, Seattle, WA.

Broom, G. M., & Smith, G. D. (1979). Testing the practitioner's impact on clients. *Public Relations Review, 5*(3), 47–59.

Broom, G. M., & Dozier, D. M. (1983). An overview: Evaluation in public relations. *Public Relations Quarterly, 28,* 5–8.

Broom, G. M., & Dozier, D. M. (1986). Advancement for public relations role models. *Public Relations Review, 12*(1), 37–56.

Center, A. H., & Broom, G. M. (1983). Evaluation research. *Public Relations Quarterly, 28*, 2–3.

Chapman, R. (1982). Measurement: It is alive and well in Chicago. *Public Relations Journal, 38*, 28–29.

Cutlip, S. M., Center, A. H., & Broom, G. M. (1985). *Effective public relations* (6th ed.) Englewood Cliffs, NJ: Prentice-Hall.

Dozier, D. M. (1981). *The diffusion of evaluation methods among public relations practitioners.* Paper presented to the Public Relations Division, Association for Education in Journalism Annual Convention, East Lansing, MI.

Dozier, D. M. (1984). Program evaluation and the roles of practitioners. *Public Relations Review, 10*(2), 13–21.

Dozier, D. M. (1985). Planning and evaluation in PR practice. *Public Relations Review, 11*(2), 17–24.

Dozier, D. M. (1986). *The environmental scanning function of public relations practitioners and participation in management decision making.* Paper presented to the Public Relations Division, Association for Education in Journalism and mass Communication Annual Convention, University of Oklahoma, Norman, OK.

Ferguson, M. A. (1987). *Utility of roles research to corporate communications: Power, leadership and decision making.* Paper presented to the International Communication Association, Public Relations Interest Group, Montreal.

Finn, D., & Harrity, M.-K. (1984). Research. In B. Cantor (ed.), *Inside public relations* (pp. 273–287). New York: Longman.

Grunig, J. E. (1983a). *Organizations, environments and models of public relations.* Paper presented at the Annual Meeting of the Association for Education in Journalism and Mass Communication, Corvallis, OR.

Grunig, J. E. (1983b). Basic research provides knowledge that makes evaluation possible. *Public Relations Quarterly, 28*, 28–32.

Grunig, J. E., & Hunt, T. (1984). *Managing public relations.* New York: Holt, Rhinehart & Winston.

Hill, D. (1982). In search of excellence. *Public Relations Journal, 38*, 36–37.

Johnson, D. J., & Acharya, L. (1982). *Organizational decision making and public relations roles.* Paper presented to the Public Relations Division, Association for Education in Journalism, Annual Convention, Athens, OH.

Judd, L. R. (1987a). *Relationships of perceived public relations role with use of formal research and organization type.* Paper presented to the Annual Convention of the Association for Education in Journalism and Mass Communication, San Antonio, TX.

Judd, L. R. (1987b). Role relationships using research and organization type. *Public Relations Review, 13*(2), 52–59.

Lindenmann, W. K. (1980). Hunches no longer suffice. *Public Relations Journal, 36*, 9–13.

McIvor, G. K. (1986). *Evaluation and measurement of public relations programs: CPRS seminar* (Toronto). Ottawa: CPRS.

Nager, N. R. & Allen, T. H. (1984). *Public relations management by objectives.* New York: Longman.

Piekos, J. M. (1988). *An empirical analysis of the impact of practitioner roles and gender on decision-making and program evaluation in public relations.* Unpublished master's thesis, University of Calgary, Calgary, Alberta, Canada.

Schein, E. (1969). *Process consultation.* Reading, MA: Addison-Wesley.

Smith, G. D. (1978). *Public relations roles: An empirical study of public relations consulting.* Unpublished master's thesis, University of Wisconsin-Madison, WI.

Chapter 5

Power in the Public Relations Department

Larissa A. Grunig
University of Maryland at College Park

PURPOSE OF THE STUDY

Professionalism remains an elusive goal for public relations practitioners. Even in an era of unprecedented growth for the field and of concomitant academic programs, most public relations practitioners remain at the technical level. That is, they engage in typically journalistic activities—informing their relevant publics about organizational decisions through press releases, speeches, or newsletters. However, they tend to remain "outside the door" when those top-level decisions are being made. They rarely ascend to the managerial level that would make them part of the decisional process.

Informing target audiences about decisions made by others results in one-way communication that may be inadequate for coping with the turbulent environment most organizations encounter in the 1980s. It also inhibits the professional development of individual practitioners and of the entire field of public relations.

Because the exclusion of most public relations practitioners from managerial decision making seems counterproductive for them, for their field, for their organizations, and perhaps even for the broader society in which those organizations operate, this study of power in public relations seems overdue.

To date, little has been written about the extent of power public relations practitioners experience. We lack a taxonomy of characteristics of power in public relations. We do not know from whence that power may come, nor can we say why some practitioners enjoy more influence than others in similar positions.

This chapter addresses the gaps that remain in our understanding of the role power plays in the practice of public relations. It takes a structural approach. That is, relationships are viewed in the context of Hage–Hull's (1981) typology of organizational structure: traditional (small-scale, low-knowledge complexity), mechanical (large-scale, low-knowledge complexity), organic (small-scale, high-knowledge complexity), and mixed mechanical/organic (large-scale, high-knowledge complexity).

Through personal interviews and survey data gathered in the Washington DC area this chapter fills many of the gaps in our understanding of power in public relations. Through that knowledge, a future generation of public relations practitioners may learn to spot organizations where their ability will be matched with a corresponding degree of power. At the same time, public relations departments may learn to spot employees with the potential for exercising power in a way that benefits both the organization and its relevant external environment.

CONCEPTUALIZATION

In this section a number of important concepts are defined and explored. These concepts suggest the theoretical links among power, organizational structure, and the practice of public relations. Together they lead to the hypotheses that shaped the research design and analysis of this study.

The complexity of the theoretical notions—especially their interrelationships and the nuances of their conceptual definitions—necessitates a thorough review of the literature. However, key elements of this literature are reiterated in capsule form along with the hypotheses at the end of this section.

Definition of Concepts

Public Relations. Public relations, typically part of the managerial subsystem of organizations, can be defined many ways. In a definition consistent with systems theory, however, J. Grunig and Hunt (1984) defined it best: the management of communication between an organization and its publics. The key term relevant to this study is *management*, because management implies a role for public relations practitioners that goes beyond the technical.

Broom and Dozier (1985) agreed that involvement in managerial decision making is fundamental to any definition of public relations. Isolation of the public relations department from top administration, in their view, limits its practice to the role of "explaining and justifying" others' decisions. As long as this technical role dominates, they argued, professional status for the field is unlikely.

Instead, Broom and Dozier (1985) held that involvement of practitioners in the organization's dominant coalition is "perhaps more important to the profession of public relations than any other measure of professional growth" (p. 8). J. Grunig and Hunt (1984) went even further in asserting that there is little justification for any practice of public relations unless practitioners are included in the dominant coalition. If the assertions of these scholars are well founded, then empirically determining the nature of the relationship between the distribution of power in organizations and the practice of public relations seems necessary.

Power. First, however, one must understand the concept of *power.* Organizational theorists have posited many definitions,[1] just as communication scholars have sought to define *public relations.* Common elements include the force necessary to change others' behavior (Emerson, 1962), an imbalance in the relationship between those with power and those without power (Simon, 1953) and the control of some over others (Morgenthau, 1960). Gaski (1984) considered the underlying theme to be "the ability to evoke a change in another's behavior" (p. 10).

Considered in this context, power is a personal attribute. It also can be seen as departmental or organizational. Its relevance in this study is to the relative position the public relations subsystem occupies within the organizational structure. It refers at least in part to the department's ability to mobilize what are typically scarce resources.[2] A related basis for power is being situated in an environmentally critical function (Hambrick, 1981). Crozier (1964) called power the unit's ability to deal with environmental uncertainty (see also Perrow, 1961, and Hickson, Hinings, Lee, Schneck, & Pennings, 1971).

Power may come to public relations practitioners from different sources. The value the dominant coalition attaches to the public relations function is one way. The expertise of practitioners, leading to increased professionalism, is another. Aldrich and Herker (1977), in their work on boundary spanning, alluded to this factor as follows:

> The power of boundary role incumbents will vary inversely with boundary role routinization, and directly with their own expertise in accomplishing role requirements and with the costliness and unpredictability of interorganizational transactions. (p. 277)

J. Grunig (1976), describing the relationship between placement in the hierarchy and power of the public relations department, reasoned:

> In a decentralized organization, the public relations unit's power probably would not depend upon its location in the hierarchy, since discretionary power is delegated

---

[1]To understand how the organizational literature has tended to define power, see Doob (1983), Hagberg (1984), and Cuming (1985).

[2]Extensive studies of organizational and departmental power, where power has been equated with obtaining critical resources, have been conducted by Levine and White (1961), Thompson (1967), Warren (1967), Aiken and Hage (1968), Zald (1970), Jacobs (1974), Benson (1975), Van de Ven (1976), Cook (1977), Pfeffer and Salancik (1978), Aldrich (1979), and Whetten and Leung (1979).

throughout the organization. In a centralized organization, however, the unit would have little power unless it is located at the top of the hierarchy, since rules prevent decision making (uncertainty resolution) at the other levels. But it is also possible for administrators to place public relations high in the organization in a deliberate effort to keep the unit under their control. (pp. 19–20)

Influence. Often, boundary personnel such as public relations practitioners lack the formal authority for action. As a result, they rely on subtle means of influence that include expertise, friendship, ingratiation, and even derision of the organization (Organ, 1971). This occupational hazard, according to Bales (1984), goes with the public relations territory.[3]

However, scholars rarely have distinguished between power and influence (Provan, 1980). One notable exception is the work of Katz and Kahn (1966), who said:

influence is a transaction in which one person (or group) acts in such a way as to change the behavior of an individual (or group) in some intended fashion. Power is the *capacity* to exert influence. Power does not have to be enacted for it to exist, whereas influence does; it is the demonstrated use of power. (p. 550)

Exchange theorists have implied that power does indeed have both potential and enacted components (Blau, 1964; Cook, 1977; Emerson, 1962, 1972).[4] Provan (1980) explained that the extent to which power can be enacted in a relationship depends on the relative dependencies of one actor on another.[5] (The

---

[3]Often, too, this results in the boundary-role incumbent leading in essence a double life when representing the organization to the environment and vice versa. Ensuing role conflict may lead to job dissatisfaction (Miles, 1977).

On the other hand, Sieber (1974), Keller and Holland (1975), and Keller, Szilagyi, and Holland (1976) explored the positive aspects of boundary spanning. Together their studies show that job satisfaction can result from the multiple relationships inherent in the activity of public relations practitioners. Aldrich (1979), too, contended that theorists may have over-emphasized the degree of role stress experienced by people in boundary-spanning roles.

[4]Other critical dimensions of power often discussed in the academic literature include internal versus external, vertical versus lateral and legitimate versus illegitimate. According to Farrell and Peterson (1982), these dimensions represent continua along which activities or choices may be ordered when people or groups try to influence the distribution of organizational resources.

Kanter (1979) distinguished between "productive" power and "oppressive" power, that which is used to punish, to prevent, to sell off, to reduce, to fire, and so on.

A recent article in the popular press added the further distinction between power used to control and manipulate others and personal power, which people use to control their own lives (Buffington, 1986). The author considered the first aspect to be primarily negative—manipulative and exploitive. The second, or personal, aspect can be a positive force when equated with will power and self-control.

[5]Cook (1977) contended that this exchange theoretic approach dominates the study of interorganizational relations. Skinner and Guiltinan (1986) explained that "through exchange relations, organizations which perform specialized functions can obtain resources critical to their operations" (p. 702).

actual exercise of power, according to Merton, 1940, is called *authority*.) Influ-ence, on the other hand, derives from the informal power accorded those whose personal attributes lead to an ability to persuade others (Hage & Aiken, 1970). Like power, however, influence often derives as well from the control of resources others value (Blau, 1964).

More recently, Cobb (1984) went a long way toward integrating these related yet distinct conceptions of power (whether potential or enacted) and influence. He argued that power is "the ability or potential to influence others or to control a situation" (p. 483).

Cobb further explained the role that power and influence play in decision making, in behavioral outcomes, and in situational outcomes. Power may figure in the dynamics of decision making, in behavioral outcomes, and in situational out-comes. Power may figure in the dynamics of decision making, he believed, when the target consciously considers the wishes of the agent; in such an instance, power is more appropriately conceived of as influence. Power is manifest, on the other hand, when the agent gets the target to do something he or she would not do otherwise. Power also is manifest in situations when the agent is unilaterally in control.

Coalitions. The related concept of *coalition* remains conceptually and opera-tionally distinct from *power* and *influence*. Because the focus of this study is on groups rather than on individuals, an understanding of coalitions seems vital.

Stevenson, Pearce, and Porter (1985), whose definitive work on coalitions appeared just 2 years ago, found fewer than a handful of previous studies on coalitions in organizations. The major explanation for this dearth of scholarly research is the difficulty both in defining the concept and in studying coalitions in the organizational setting.[6]

The notion of coalitions, however, has existed in the organizational literature for at least 25 years. Cyert and March were the first to focus on this aspect of organizational power (Cyert & March, 1963; March, 1962). By 1973 (Cyert & March, 1973) they had gone so far as to propose that an organization's behavior is determined by the values of its dominant coalition.

Why? With James Thompson (1967) in the vanguard and their own studies in sociology's political-value paradigm as confirmation, Cyert and March came to realize that no single (albeit powerful) person could head an organization operating

---

[6]Coalitions typically rely more on informal interaction than formal rules to define their membership. As a result, according to Stevenson et al. (1985, p. 263), their boundaries may be "fuzzy and ill-defined." Further, membership often shifts and is considered "illegitimate" by others in the organiza-tion, making coalitions difficult for researchers to identify—let alone study.

However, Hage (1980, pp. 131, 151) contended that changes in coalition membership do not necessarily result in changes in the coalition's power structure. The coalition will remain stable until it no longer is effective. As he put it, "Leaders come and go but dominant coalitions remain."

within the context of today's complex technology and environment. Later, Hage (1980) summed up this realization:

> The team approach, the variety of specialists, the complexity of the environment, the need for joint decision-making make the stamp of one man or woman less and less likely. This is the era of the dominant coalition. (p. 158)

Central to any study of coalitions is an operational and conceptual definition of the term. Such a definition had remained elusive until the recent work of Stevenson et al. (1985). They characterized the coalition in a way that makes the concept empirically verifiable:

> an interacting group of individuals, deliberately constructed, independent of the formal structure, lacking its own internal formal structure, consisting of mutually perceived membership, issue oriented, focused on a goal or goals external to the coalition, and requiring concerted member action. (p. 251)

Other scholars have examined the make-up of the coalition. Mintzberg (1983), for example, developed a typology of coalitions based on external versus internal influence. External coalitions may include stockholders, suppliers, clients, labor unions, the community, and government. Internal coalitions are comprised of full-time employees, those who make decisions and take action on a permanent and regular basis. Their make-up often includes the operators (workers who either produce the products or services or provide direct support to them), staff specialists, support staff, and top management.

Management, of course, normally is included (Cyert & March, 1963). Axelrod (1970) and Rosenthal (1970) added the understanding that people with similar ideologies are most likely to form coalitions.[7] Pfeffer (1981), who has studied the concept extensively, determined that coalitions consist of those who agree on a desired organizational outcome. Stevenson et al. (1985) reasoned that those with more discretion in carrying out their job responsibilities would have more opportunity to become part of a coalition.

With the understanding that different coalitions represent different goals, different ideologies, and different expertise, Thompson's (1967) concept of the "dominant" coalition becomes important.[8] He called it simply the "inner circle." He

---

[7]In 1978, however, Murnighan found only limited support for the contention that coalitions form among actors with compatible ideologies.

[8]Essentially, this notion is the same as Mintzberg's (1983, Part II) concept of the internal coalition. Mintzberg described five types or systems of internal influence: personalized (dominated by a particularly powerful CEO), bureaucratic (based on a formal system of institutionalized authority), ideologic (whose members are bound together by their shared beliefs), professional (where power accrues from knowledge or technical skills most needed by the organization), and politicized (characterized by political game-playing that weakens other, more legitimate power bases).

reasoned that one group of influentials or powerful people must prevail at any given time. Robbins (1983) explained that "any coalition that can control the resources on which the organization depends can become dominant" (p. 173). Mintzberg (1983, Part III) concluded that members of the power elite stand "ready to exploit discretion in terms of their own goals."

Structural Imperative. Other researches have looked at structural characteristics affecting coalitions. Bacharach and Lawler (1980), for example, determined that increasing centralization and formalization decrease the likelihood of coalition formation. Schneider (aka L. Grunig, 1985) looked specifically at the relationship among structure, communication, and power. She found that the managerial role for public relations dominates only in the mixed mechanical/organic type of organization.[9] Power correlated negatively with small-scale, traditional type organizations. Together these data suggest that the public relations professional sits closer to the top of the hierarchy in large-scale organizations than he or she does in the organization of simple machines, few employees, and relatively low productivity.

Thompson (1967), who believed that coalitions by definition remain "in process," also believed that coalitions are threatened by structural or environmental changes because change necessarily affects the organization's dependencies. Pfeffer (1981) agreed. He held that the coalition's need for organizational power explains its attempts at maintaining control over the environment: if it can manage its environment, it can avoid making structural changes within the organization; such change would interrupt the balance of power. Broom and Dozier (1985), however, pointed out that the relationship between public relations roles, organizational structure, and what they called the "management core" remains unclear.

This structural approach to the study of power in organizations is compatible with most research cited in this conceptualization section. Structural–functionalism focuses on how organizations design their internal departments contingent on the environment. It also acknowledges the complexity of the relationship between technology and dimensions of structure. Because of the lack of support for many hypotheses and the small size of many correlation coefficients found in previous studies, however, the theory that emerges in this study should be considered more normative than descriptive.

Technological Influence. Hage and Hull (1981) regarded scale and complexity as the key determinants of organizational structure. (These components formed their four-cell typology of organizations previously described.) Others, especially Woodward (1965), considered technology the most critical variable. Contrasting a

---

[9]This organizational type, first described by Hage and Hull (1981), is characterized by large scale of the environment and knowledge or task complexity. The other three Hage–Hull types are traditional or craft (small-scale, simplistic technology), mechanical (large-scale, simplistic technology), and organic (small-scale, sophisticated technology).

technological imperative with a technological influence helps make sense of this heterogeneous body of research in both the technological and structural schools.

Robbins (1983), for example, pointed out that because technology and struc-ture are both multidimensional concepts, "technology can have an important effect on structure without being imperative" (p. 134). Perhaps more important, Pfeffer (1978) explained the relationship among technology, environment, and structure when he talked about organizational management: "Choice of a domain, and a set of activities and tasks, tends to constrain the organization's technology, but the domain is still chosen" (p. 99). In other words, technology constrains managers because they have little choice over their organization's technological processes; they do have a choice of environment, however, and that environment influences their organizational activities.

Finally, Aiken and Hage (1971) suggested that as the speed of technological change increases, so will cooperative relationships between an organization and its environment via the communication link. This cooperative situation could encom-pass both organic and mixed mechanical/organic organizations, because both are characterized by high rates of knowledge change and growing complexity. Implica-tions for public relations personnel, as boundary spanners, are obvious.

Significance of Concepts

The foregoing review of relevant theoretical concepts from the literature of so-ciology, political science, public policy, psychology, public relations, and business management suggests that "power" is an important subject in the study of organi-zations, their boundary personnel and their environments. Allen (1979) said it most forcefully; he believed that the dominant coalition dictates organizational action to a far greater degree than does even the environment, a long-cherished predictor of organizational structure and decision making.

The key question that remains is why the inclusion of public relations practi-tioners within the dominant coalition is important. Before attempting to answer the question, this chapter addresses what is known about the relationship between public relations and organizational power.

Previous studies have documented the exclusion of public relations practi-tioners from the dominant coalition—whether it is called the inner circle, the power elite, or simply an internal influencer (Anshen, 1974; Brown, 1980; Close, 1980; Greyser, 1981; Lesly, 1981; Lindemann & Lapetina, 1981; Newman, 1980).

Some of these studies and still others have suggested reasons for public rela-tions' lack of representation in top management circles. Management itself is one important factor. Its perception of public relations as a "necessary evil" (Strenski, 1980) and its myopic, self-interested concentration on the free-enterprise system (Forrestal, cited in Baxter, 1980) both contribute to its lack of confidence in public relations. CEOs tend to consider public relations as a marginal function at best, according to Burger (1983).[10]

Characteristics of practitioners themselves, however, are a significant factor in their exclusion from the dominant coalition. Explanations include their lack of broad business expertise (Lesly, 1981; Lindemann & Lapetina, 1981); their passivity (Anshen, 1974); their naivete about organizational politics (Nowlan & Shayon, 1984); and their inadequate education, experience, or organizational status (Anshen, 1972). Other determinants of public relations role in the organization relative to power include gender and longevity in the job (Johnson & Acharya, 1981).

For whatever reason, public relations professionals rarely enjoy an influential position within their organization. As a result, one only can hypothesize about the effects of a powerful public relations department. The next section of this chapter deals with possible impacts of power on the individual practitioner, on the field of public relations, on the organizational system, and on society.

Effects on Public Relations Practitioners. Managers earn more than do technicians. Broom (1982), considered to be the "father" of public relations roles research, characterized the technical role as relatively underpaid and confined to the rank of lower staff. Communication managers, on the other hand, are more highly paid; they help make decisions, rather than simply implementing the decisions of others (Dozier, 1981). (On the negative side, of course, is the accompanying responsibility for the success or failure of decisions implemented.)

Perhaps more important than salary is the level of job satisfaction that often accompanies a rise from technical to managerial level. Dozier (1981) found that satisfaction increases with increasing professionalism. Finally, staffs in public relations departments should experience increased job satisfaction as their superiors become increasingly influential (Jablin, 1980).

Effects on the Field of Public Relations. Newman (1980) contended that public relations has evolved from its roots in the technical aspects of the field to a second phase of professional development. From that initial beachhead, he wrote, "we are ready to move inland, toward the command posts of corporate management" (p. 11). One former president of the Public Relations Society of America argued that the field would never attain professional status, however, until its practitioners regard themselves as part of a managerial team rather than as craftspeople (Hawver, cited in Baxter, 1980).

---

[10]Pennings and Goodman (1977) found, however, that the values of any group depend on who is a member of the group. It stands to reason, then, that if public relations managers become part of the dominant group, other members of that coalition would come to understand and to support their function.

Effects on the Organization.   The professional practice of public relations, more as a managerial than technical process, undoubtedly would have positive effects on the organizational system. As the chairman of the board at Spring Mills, Inc., put it to a group of public relations practitioners, "Let's face it, in a climate of special interests and over-regulation, inflated dollars here and deflated dollars there, . . . the chief executive can use your help—if management is convinced you *can* help" (Close, 1980, p. 11).

Given the broadening challenges facing corporate management—witness the environment Close described—including public relations in the dominant coalition seems vital. Professional public relations practitioners can share in the decision-making process and in the responsibility for the public's orientation toward the organization.

Enhancing the power base of public relations in the organization gives the department a greater capacity to influence events (Quinn, 1980). This becomes increasingly important in situations of great uncertainty or dissensus about choices (Pfeffer, 1981).

Professionals who want to influence strategic decisions have more effect when they are part of a group than when they act as organizational entrepreneurs. Thus, the public relations practitioner with the potential to contribute to organizational goals would be more effective as a member of the dominant coalition than as an independent actor in the organizational system. The group, rather than any one leader, typically makes decisions. Hage and Dewar (1973) found that the values of the power elite largely set organizational policy. Public relations, in its boundary-spanning role between organization and environment, warrants input into that policy process of strategic choices.

Effects on Society.   Relevant publics in the broader organizational suprasystem could be affected by a burgeoning managerial role for public relations practitioners. Anshen, writing about 16 years ago (1974), emphasized the corporation's social responsibility and the part that public relations plays in managing that obligation. More recently, Grunig and Grunig (1989) suggested that only as part of the dominant coalition could public relations professionals be influential enough to shape the organization's ideology. Presumably, these boundary spanners would appreciate the point of view both of their employers and of their relevant external publics.

Empowerment Strategies

Because the effects of power for public relations described here are primarily positive for all sectors involved, the next logical step in this conceptualization is a discussion of empowerment strategies. How can public relations practitioners enhance their power base? And given the power struggles within organizations and between powerful coalitions, why should any influentials share their power with others?

Kanter's (1979) work, although not related strictly to public relations, provides the most insightful answers. She took into account both powerfulness and power-lessness. The latter, she said, breeds bossiness—one main reason for empowering any bosses in organizations, including the head of the public relations department. She also linked powerlessness with job dissatisfaction, explaining that accountabil-ity without power (responsibility for results without the resources to get them) creates frustration or failure or both.

More important, however, are the advantages to sharing power Kanter cited. Her revelation is that organizational power can grow—rather than shrink—by being shared. In Kanter's words, delegation does not mean abdication. Why? People with information and support make more informed decisions, act more quickly, and often accomplish more than those who are powerless.

Thus, the leader who empowers others actually increases his or her own power via increased productivity.[11] The true sign of power, in Kanter's view, is accom-plishment. And, she believed that even the powerless would increase what little power they do have by sharing it with others. She recommended that organizations work toward team-oriented, participatory, power-sharing management.

Current Research on Power and Public Relations

With the notable exception of the work of Anshen (1974), most research on power as it relates directly to public relations has been conducted in this decade. Predict-ably, many of the studies have taken the form of graduate theses or dissertations. Because of their recency, their focus specifically on public relations and their empirical findings, these studies deserve special attention here.

Pollack (1986), for example, looked at the support of top management for public relations in scientific organizations. She found that the dominant coalition tends to support the public relations department at least moderately; the power elite considers the department's functions important. The department itself is located at the middle or top managerial level; about half of its major recommendations are implemented by the organization.

Pollack did not determine the influence the public relations director enjoys in the typical scientific organization, nor did she explain his or her involvement in major organizational decisions. She did discover, however, that when public rela-tions practitioners are represented in the dominant coalition, they are likely to

---

[11]The effectiveness that power brings evolves from two capacities, according to Kanter (1979): access to the resources, information, and support necessary to carry out tasks and the ability to get cooperation.

practice two-way symmetrical communication. They conduct more managerial and somewhat more liaison activities.

Further, Pollack found that practitioners included in the inner circle tend to have more training in public relations (greater percentage of graduate and bachelor's degrees in the field) as opposed to just a few courses or seminars or no formal education in public relations. This finding is consistent with that of Lawler and Hage (1973), who more than a decade earlier had established that professional training, along with professional activity, decreases at least felt powerlessness. (In their study of social workers, they also found a significant relationship between professionalism and work autonomy.)

Nelson (1986) attempted an in-depth study of the dominant coalition in two organizations. She found that top management's concept of public relations dictates what type of program (such as media relations, employee relations, community relations) dominates within the organization. Because that program emphasis or the model of public relations practiced may be inappropriate for the organization, given its environment, she recommended including public relations practitioners in the dominant coalition.

Grunig and Grunig (1989) integrated these and other recent findings into a program of research that approaches a general systems theory of public relations. They found that, in general, managerial support for and understanding of public relations correlated with the most sophisticated, two-way models of public relations (both balanced and imbalanced).[12] Based primarily on Pollack's (1986) study, Grunig and Grunig (1989) posited two explanations for the inclusion of public relations practitioners in the dominant coalition: either public relations departments represented in the power elite are empowered to practice a two-way model of communication or only those practitioners with the expertise to practice such a model would be included in that inner circle. Because of the significant correlations between inclusion in the dominant coalition and both education and experience in public relations, they favored the latter explanation.

In the most recent study, Ossareh (1987) hypothesized that the values of the dominant coalition would be a more significant predictor of use of technology for public relations tasks than would be the orientation or professionalism of public relations practitioners themselves. Through a nationwide survey of almost 500 practitioners, her assumption was confirmed. Again, as with the Pollack (1986) and Grunig and Grunig (1989) studies, representation of the public relations department in the managerial elite seems appropriate. Otherwise, a technological advance with potential for enhancing the practice of public relations may be ignored; inappropriate yet expensive technologies may be adopted.

---

[12]For a comprehensive discussion of the four major models of public relations (press agentry or publicity, public information, two-way asymmetrical and two-way symmetrical) see J. Grunig and Hunt (1984, chapter 2).

Hypotheses and Research Questions

The preceding conceptual framework created by reviewing classical and more recent, exploratory research leads to the hypotheses that follow. Where the literature is inadequate for such predictions, research questions are posed. Questions deal with the relationship between power and involvement with the dominant coalition and between power and professionalism in public relations.

H1: Public relations departments in traditional organizations have the least authority of those found in any of the organizational types.

H2: Traditional organizations require the most policy clearance of the public relations department of any of the organizational types.

J. Grunig (1976) contended that the public relations unit in a centralized operation would have little power unless it sits at the top of the hierarchy. Because most traditional organizations are at least moderately centralized, their rules should preclude much autonomous decision-making at the level of what the literature has established as the typical public relations department.

The dearth of professionals expected in public relations units of traditional organizations also should lead to little autonomy there. Finally, Schneider's (aka L. Grunig, 1985) study showed that traditional organizations are characterized by the least power and authority of any Hage–Hull type. Both clearance process and public relations activities were most centralized in these small-scale, noncomplex types.

H3: Superiors in traditional organizations value the public relations function less than do superiors in any of the other organizational types.

Allen (1979) contended that managers value the organizational roles that are part of their management teams. When public relations is excluded from the decision-making process (largely through the dominant coalition), as it tends to be in the typical traditional organization, one would expect managers to value its role less than in the other organizational types.

H4: Public relations departments in mechanical organizations have more authority than do traditional and organic organizations but less than does the mixed organization.

H5: Mechanical organizations require less clearance for public relations than do traditional organizations but more than do organic and mixed organizations.

Ryan and Martinson (1983) argued that with growing environmental scale, boundary spanners are accorded greater autonomy to go beyond the organization and collect the information necessary for disposing of outputs in that market context. Schneider (aka L. Grunig, 1985) found that mechanical organizations do indeed have more power and less centralization of the clearance process than their small-scale counterparts, the traditional organizations. However, their typical assembly-line process led to less autonomy than in the mixed mechanical/organic type or the organic type.

H6: Superiors in mechanical organizations value the public relations function more than do superiors in traditional organizations but less than in the other two types.

Maples (1981) found that managers value organizational roles that demand autonomous decision making. Thus, the greater the autonomy, the greater the value that managers should hold for public relations practitioners. This also echoes the contention of Allen (1979) that when organizational members become an integral part of the management team, they are valued.

H7: Public relations departments in organic organizations have more authority than in traditional organizations but less than in mechanical and mixed organizations.

H8: Organic organizations require less clearance for public relations than do traditional and mechanical types but more than does the mixed type.

According to Ryan and Martinson (1983), with professionalism comes autonomy necessary to do the job without undue interference from higher-ups in the organizational structure. However, an earlier study (Schneider, aka L. Grunig, 1985) found that organic organizations accord less power and authority to their public relations departments than do mixed types (which also employ a high proportion of professionally oriented public relations practitioners). The small size of the typical public relations department in an organic organization helps to explain why it should have less power than in the mixed mechanical/organic type.

H9: Superiors in organic organizations value the public relations function more than do superiors in traditional and mechanical types but less than in mixed types.

J. Grunig (1984) and Nanni (1980) both contended that politically liberal managers, who accept the notion of social responsibility for their organizations, would advocate symmetrical communication. This balanced communication might lead to adaptation to the needs of their publics, rather than manipulation or domination of those external groups. Because organic organizations tend to emphasize two-way, symmetrical public relations, their managers probably value that function highly.

H10: Public relations departments in mixed organizations have the most authority of any type.

H11: Mixed organizations require the least clearance for public relations of any type.

The large size of the typical public relations department in a mixed mechanical/organic organization, coupled with the professionalism of its employees, should lead to a high degree of autonomy (Schneider, aka Grunig, 1985). Public relations practitioners in these large-scale, high-complexity operations spend much of their time actually counseling management (Schneider, aka Grunig, 1985). Their clearance process was found to be less centralized than in any other Hage–Hull type. They enjoyed the most power and authority.

H12: Superiors in mixed organizations value the public relations function more than in any other type.

Managers who advocate symmetrical communication, between organization and relevant external publics, also should value the people responsible for such two-way, balanced public relations (J. Grunig, 1984; Nanni, 1980). Such interaction is necessary for organizational adaptation to a dynamic, large-scale environment (typical of the mixed organizational type). And, public relations professionals in the mixed mechanical/organic organization, more than in any other Hage–Hull type, should be part of the management team (Allen, 1979; Ryan & Martinson, 1983).

H13: Assembly-line technology in mixed organizations is associated with less autonomy for public relations—as evidenced by an extensive clearance process—than in mixed organizations with any other kind of technology.

Correlations between technology variables (both degree of routinization and Thompson's, 1967, concepts of long-linked, mediating and intensive) and organization type in an earlier (Schneider, aka Grunig, 1985) study failed to show significant associations in three of the four Hage–Hull types: traditional, mechanical, and organic.

That same study, however, established that organizations with long-linked or assembly-line technology tend to have larger public relations departments than in organizations with either mediating or intensive technology. Research also showed that in the case of the mixed organizational type, long-linked technology diminishes the likelihood of decentralized clearance process for public relations. Thompson (1967) reasoned that long-linked technology requires more efficiency and coordination among activities than does any other kind of technology (because of the fixed sequence of repetitive steps that characterize the assembly line).

RQ1: What is the relationship between professionalism and the four Hage–Hull organizational types?

Presumably, expert, professional practitioners who can act as the corporate conscience are accorded the autonomy necessary to deal effectively with the company's relevant external constituents. The need to cope with such external pressure might depend in part on the environmental niche represented by each Hage–Hull type.

RQ2: How does the involvement of public relations practitioners in the dominant coalition—and vice versa—vary by organizational type?

At times CEOs and other managers engage in activities commonly associated with public relations. This might happen particularly when administrators understand, support, and value the function of public relations and also when they have some education or training in the field. A related issue is the involvement of public relations practitioners in the activities of the dominant coalition.

METHODOLOGY

The research design was comparative, as recommended by Stinchcombe (1965) to deal with complex research problems. The historical–critical method contributed the bulk of the data; the quantitative portion helped guard against bias and subjective, perceptual data as reported by interviewees.

The study included both in-depth personal interviews with public relations managers and a self-administered, eight-page questionnaire. Forty-eight organizations in the Washington, DC area (12 representing each of the Hage–Hull types) were included in the purposive sample. Trained interviewers talked with two high-ranking individuals in the public relations departments of the 48 organizations.[13] Interviews with the 87 practitioners[14] lasted between 1 and 2 hours.

Internal media and mass media were analyzed for an initial assessment of organizational type. Finally, as Pavlik and Salmon (1983) recommended, current

---

[13]Interviewing two professionals rather than a single administrator should help to avoid idiosyncratic responses. Trying to talk with more than two practitioners might eliminate smaller organizations, those with correspondingly limited public relations departments. To do so also seems unnecessary in light of Grunig's (1983) findings that individuals closest to the top of the hierarchy have the greatest understanding of the organizational situation.

[14]In some cases, two public relations practitioners were unavailable in a single organization. This was especially true in the mid-sized companies—those large enough to employ one public relations expert but too small for an entire department. For this reason, the total number of interview respondents was 87, rather than the 96 possible if two practitioners had been available from all 48 organizations studied.

organizational publications such as company newsletters, annual reports, memoranda, organization charts, news releases, and public service announcements were examined.

Like Stinchcombe, Sanders (1982) suggested that such a combination of qualitative and quantitative research provides "stronger analyses than would have been possible by collecting either type alone" (p. 359), especially in the study of organizations. She advocated collecting phenomenological information and quantitative data concurrently from the same organizational setting.

Questionnaires, publications, and interviews all measured the internal and external public relations activities of the four types of organizations. They also tested for structural characteristics of scale and complexity, the intervening variable of technology and the relevant aspects associated with power as identified in the review of the literature. Computer analysis of the responses suggested the theoretical and operational linkages between power and public relations, dependent on organizational structure.

FINDINGS

Authority and the Clearance Process for Public Relations

During the in-depth interviews, respondents did not distinguish between the concepts of authority and clearance required for public relations in their department. Consequently, these notions were grouped to form an "autonomy" variable (see Tables 5.1 and 5.2). However, they are discussed separately in the ensuing section of the findings. Together they represent the ability of the public relations practitioner to function without undue interference or supervision from above. Responses were coded from *high* degree of autonomy to *some* autonomy or *little or no* autonomy.

TABLE 5.1
Indicators of Power in Public Relations Correlated with Organization Type

Organization Type	Autonomy	Level of Education	Training in PR	Professional Involvement
Traditional	−.12	−.44****	−.19*	−.12
Mechanical	.06	−.04	.08	.18**
Organic	−.07	.11*	−.13	−.13
Mixed	.13	.26***	−.02	.08

*p < .10.
**p < .05.
***p < .01.
****p < .001.

TABLE 5.2
Mean Scores of Autonomy and Professional Variables in Public Relations
Broken Down by Organization Type

Autonomy/Professional Variables	Entire Population (N = 81)	Organization Type			
		Traditional (N = 16)	Mechanical (N = 21)	Organic (N = 23)	Mixed (N = 21)
Autonomy	2.01	1.81	2.10	1.19	2.19
F = 1.10					
(3 DF)					
p < .36					
Training in PR	1.95	1.56	2.05	2.13	1.95
F = 1.22					
(3 DF),					
p < .31					
Prof. Involvement	4.98	4.00	5.23	4.87	5.07
F = 1.57					
(3 DF)					
p < .21					

Authority. A response typical of some authority came from the communications division of an association representing the liquor industry. The division's director explained that within his budget of line items, he has the authority to shift funds within major categories but not between them. Presidential approval is required for hiring even temporary help, but much of his media relations work (such as setting up interviews with VIPs) can be carried out on his authority alone.

Another instance of limited authority came from the Public Affairs Office of a governmental aerospace agency. Although the Agency's deputy of PA did not explain why, her remark enlightens the situation somewhat: "I usually feel that my decisions are autonomous, but anyone up the ladder can change them, saying, 'No way, honey.'"

Another possible explanation for limited authority (in addition to the sexism just suggested) may be the newness of the employee. According to the catalogue coordinator of a marketing department, another woman, "Most decisions related to my job have to be okayed. I've only worked here for six months, though, and I feel they already have more confidence in me by now."

Other determinants of autonomy mentioned frequently during the interviews include distance from headquarters, routineness of the activity in question, and the amount of money involved. One final contingency affecting the amount of authority granted the public relations department was cited by the senior director of employee communications and special events for a rail company. He associated autonomy with the values of the dominant coalition, and membership in that group changes from time to time. He explained that "Although we're a new company, I've served under four presidents. Each has been different in approach. Some have regarded our department highly, and others are stubborn as hell."

Extensive authority was reported by the area executive director of a national not-for-profit organization, who described its manifestations as "authorization to hire and fire and to set salaries." The director of information and volunteer services in a county government described complete authority over his department, too. He said, however, that "as a matter of courtesy and to avoid mistakes, I provide copies of news releases to county officials who are being quoted by the Office of Information." The community relations coordinator for the county's school system expressed a similar degree of autonomy, which she termed *enormous*, tempered only by her "sensitivity to issues without being a mouthpiece for the administration."

Some interviewees were their organization's CEO rather than a public relations practitioner per se. Such a respondent was the chief of a fire district. As chief, he had a great deal of autonomy (although he emphasized the constraints that a limited budget imposes). And, he indicated that he normally consults with the fire department's Board of Trustees before launching any major media campaign.

A small public relations and advertising firm is an example of the lack of authority accorded public relations people in some organizations. The seemingly autonomous decisions made by its public relations executives are really more constrained, according to the firm's public relations coordinator. She said, "We're all given an opportunity to say what we think, but in the end decisions are made for us."

Most interviewees (57%) indicated that they experience a limited degree of authority. Responses at either end of the continuum between autonomy and constraint were approximately balanced: 19 interviewees considered themselves highly autonomous and 14 highly constrained.[15]

Clearance Process. The process by which news releases, feature articles, and other information from the organization are okayed for dissemination is a second measure of autonomy in the public relations department. The necessity of receiving such approval from higher-ups is not emphasized in the literature of power; however, as a typical phenomenon in public relations, it bears examination here as one indicator of power.

A complex, highly formalized process for clearing news indicates a lack of autonomy. By asking respondents about the clearance process in their organizations, interviewers could help gauge the relative autonomy they enjoyed.

Respondents cited the following contingencies requiring clearance: if a direct quotation is used in the release, if the release is on a crisis subject or what the dominant coalition considers "major action," specialized content such as financial information or ad copy, novel—rather than routine—situations, political ramifications, and status of the person involved in the news.

In some organizations, time available seems to dictate the amount of clearance that actually takes place. As the director of the communication division of a trade

---

[15]Three interviewees did not hazard an opinion in this area of investigation.

association said, "Our president likes to review press releases before they go out, whenever it's possible for him to do so."

Other organizations require clearance for virtually all public relations materials. A large auto maker is such a company. The director of the Washington Department of Public Affairs said, however, that he would submit releases to headquarters in Detroit even if clearance were not necessary because he believes in keeping top management informed.

Several layers of clearance are required at other companies. At the information services component of a large electronics firm, for example, necessary clearance comes from the marketing communications group, the legal department, the internal products manager and others—depending on the issue involved.

Most governmental agencies require extensive clearance. At one, for instance, materials produced by the Information Office first are discussed within the office and then are sent up to the associate or head of the agency himself for clearance (especially if TV will be used). At another government agency, news releases require the following clearances: from the scientists, from the program personnel, from the director of the agency, from the department that oversees it, and—at times—even from the Office of Management and Budget.

Table 5.2 shows no significant differences in concepts related to autonomy among the four organization types. In Table 5.1, however, one distinction is obvious. The mixed mechanical/organic organization has a significantly higher degree of autonomy than do the other three types. Even there, however, the correlation coefficient is small ($.13, p <.10$).

Hypotheses 1, 4, 7, and 10; Hypotheses 2, 5, 8, and 11

These eight predictions deal with the relationship between the power of the public relations department—as measured by its authority and required clearance policy—and organizational type.

Hypotheses 1 and 2 relate specifically to traditional organizations. The first predicted that public relations in these craft types have the least authority and the second, that they require the most policy clearance. Neither was supported. However, they could not be disconfirmed either.

Only one statistically significant difference among the four types of organizations was apparent in Table 5.1, and that showed that mixed organizations tend to have more autonomy than do the other three types. With a more clear-cut distinction between authority and clearance policy, the relative position of public relations in traditional organizations might become obvious. Finally, this type of organization was represented by its CEO or another member of the dominant coalition in many cases. As a result, responses were not truly comparable with those of the public relations personnel, operating at lower levels, who were interviewed in other types of organizations.

Hypotheses 4 and 5 deal with mechanical organizations. Once again, the distinction between authority and the clearance process was blurred. As in all hypotheses of this kind, the concepts were consolidated into a single variable termed *autonomy*. The typical public relations department in the mechanical organization has no more autonomy than it does in the traditional. It has no less than does the organic, either, so only the final part of these hypotheses was confirmed: the mechanical organization does have less autonomy than the mixed mechanical/organic organization.

Hypotheses 7 and 8 predict the relationship between power and the organic organization. More specifically, Hypothesis 7 predicted that departments in organic organizations would have more authority than in traditional organizations but less than in the other two types. Hypothesis 8 predicted that organic organizations would require less clearance for public relations than would traditional and mechanical types but more than would the mixed type. These hypotheses were not confirmed, because no significant differences emerged regarding extensiveness of clearance process or level of autonomy hypothesized: that the public relations in organic organizations has more authority than in traditional organizations but less than in mechanical and mixed organizations and that organic organizations require less clearance than do traditional and mechanical organizations but more than does the mixed organization.

Hypotheses 10 and 11 are the last two in the group of predictions about power and clearance process, related specifically to mixed mechanical/organic organizations. They predict that public relations departments in mixed organizations have the most authority of any type and that they require the least clearance. Both hypotheses were supported. In fact, the only significant relationship between autonomy and the Hage–Hull types occurred with the mixed organization. It does, indeed, enjoy more autonomy than the other three types.

Professionalism

Professionalism was gauged by asking about the education, specialized training, and professional involvement of members of the public relations staff. Professional involvement encompasses membership in professional associations, attending meetings of those groups, and holding office in them. All of these measures were included in the questionnaire, to help answer the research questions and to explore the hypotheses as well.

Level of Education. The survey asked about respondents' highest level of education. Nearly 60% of the sample were college graduates. Almost equal proportions (3% and 4%) fell at the ends of the scale—high school or less and PhD.

Table 5.1 shows correlations between level of education and organizational type. Traditional organizations are strongly and negatively associated with a high level of education ($-.44$, $p < .001$). Statistically significant correlations of modest size are positive with both mixed mechanical/organic and organic organizations ($.26$, $p < .01$ and $.17$, $p < 10$, respectively).

Training in Public Relations. A second aspect of professionalism, specialized training in the field, was gauged by asking respondents, "Have you had any formal training in public relations?" Overall, little specialized training was evident. Only 10% of respondents had a graduate degree in the field and another 14% had a bachelor's degree in public relations. Remaining responses were evenly divided between some courses and no formal training (38% each).

Few statistically significant differences emerged across organizational types. Correlations in Table 5.1, although weak, show that mixed mechanical/organic organizations tend to hire or to attract people with specialized training in public relations and that traditional organizations do not.

Professional Involvement. The final measure of professionalism dealt with involvement in professional associations. Suggested organizations included the Public Relations Society of America (15%) and the International Association of Business Communicators (7%).

Responses to the open-ended "other" category included references to several more specialized groups: women's or regional organizations or associations appealing to special occupational interests. These specialized associations accounted for about 19% of all respondents. Almost half indicated that they belong to no professional associations.

Slightly more than half the respondents, however, showed some degree of professionalism. Their responses to questions about belonging to professional associations, attending their meetings, and holding office in any of those organizations were recoded to form a scale of professionalism.

The relationship between professionalism and the four Hage–Hull types of organizations is shown in Tables 5.1 and 5.2. Findings show that the organizational typology contributes little to the understanding of professionalism. Professionalism is negatively associated with the traditional type ($-.23$, $p < .05$) and positively with the mechanical type ($.18$, $p < .05$). Across the four types, however, differences are minimal.

Research Question 1

The first research question asked about the relationship between the professionalism of public relations practitioners and organizational type. Professionalism was determined by level of education, specialized training in public relations, and involvement in a professional association.

Traditional organizations employ the fewest public relations practitioners with a high level of education and with a professional orientation. They also employ the fewest staff members in public relations who have specialized education in the field, although few organizations can boast of a highly specialized staff in public relations.

Mechanical organizations tend to employ more professionally oriented person-

nel in public relations than do traditional organizations. Differences between mechanical and the other two organizational types, however, are insignificant.

Public relations practitioners in organic organizations have more education than
in the traditional and mechanical types, but not appreciably more than in the mixed
type. They have less training in the field of public relations than their counterparts
in mixed organizations do. Their involvement in professional associations is on a
par with public relations personnel in the other three organizational types.

Practitioners in mixed mechanical/organic organizations have a higher level of
education than their colleagues in traditional and organic organizations. Their
involvement in professional associations is not significantly different from the
involvement of practitioners in any of the other Hage–Hull types. However, they
have more specialized training in public relations than practitioners in any other
organizational type.

Managerial Values for Public Relations

Several items in the questionnaire and in the interviews gauged the degree to
which managers value public relations. A direct question to that effect was posed.
The literature indicates additional, related factors as well. They include understanding and support of administrators for the function of public relations, whether
they had had some education or training in the field, their involvement with public
relations and the involvement of public relations practitioners in the activities of the
dominant coalition. All of these factors relate to the shared ideology, common goals
and other aspects of the homogeneity typically found within the power elite.
Results appear in Tables 5.3 and 5.4.

Support for Public Relations. Managerial support for public relations was
measured by the question, "To what extent do the top administrators to whom the
public relations department reports support the public relations function in your
organization?" Possible responses ranged on a 5-point scale from *strongly support*
to *strongly oppose.* Answers to this question showed more uniformity than to any
other on the survey instrument. Only 1% of respondents indicated a neutral position (*neither support nor oppose*). No respondents answered *moderately* or *strongly
oppose.* Responses of *strongly support* and *moderately support* were 68% and 30%,
respectively.

As a result of this cross-organizational support for the role of public relations,
few significant differences appear in the analysis of variance and correlational
analyses shown in Tables 5.3 and 5.4. Managerial support is present unilaterally,
as indicated in the breakdown of Table 5.3 ($M = 4.67, 4.52, 4.78, 4.71$).

However, there are some statistically significant correlations between degree of
support and the four organizational types, which seem to reflect the difference
between moderate and strong support. Table 5.4 shows that strong support is
positively associated with both types of organizations that have high complexity:

TABLE 5.3
Mean Scores of Managerial Variables Broken Down by Organizational Type

Managerial Variables	Entire Population (N = 80)	Organization Type			
		Traditional (N = 15)	Mechanical (N = 21)	Organic (N = 23)	Mixed (N = 21)
Support for PR	4.68	4.67	4.52	4.78	4.71
$F = 1.05$					
(3 DF),					
$p < .3744$					
Understanding of PR	3.44	3.67	3.24	3.52	3.38
$F = 1.69$					
(3 DF),					
$p < .1770$					
Values toward PR	2.28	2.37	2.24	2.04	2.52
$F = 1.85$					
(3 DF),					
$p < .1459$					
Education in PR	2.00	1.94	1.86	2.13	2.05
$F = 2.63$					
(3 DF),					
$p < .0059$					
Involvement in PR	2.16	2.20	2.21	2.05	2.21
$F = .26$					
(3 DF),					
$p < .8558$					
Involvement of PR in mgt.	2.09	1.81	2.35	2.05	2.10
$F = 1.18$					
(3 DF),					
$p < .3237$					

TABLE 5.4
Correlates of Managerial Variables with Organization Type

Organization Type	Support for PR	Understanding of PR	Values toward PR	Education in PR	Involvement in PR	Involvement of PR in management
Traditional	.03	.17	.08	$-.12^*$	.02	$-.12^*$
Mechanical	$-.20^*$	$-.17^{**}$	$-.02$	$-.22^{**}$	.02	$.15^*$
Organic	$.13^*$	.09	$-.22^{**}$	$.25^{***}$	$-.13^*$	$-.03$
Mixed	.04	$-.07$	$.18^{**}$	.07	$.10^*$	$-.01$

$^*p < .10.$
$^{**}p < .05.$
$^{***}p < .01.$

organic and mixed mechanical/organic. Strong managerial support for public rela-tions is negatively associated with the two types of organizations with low task complexity: traditional and mechanical.

Understanding of Public Relations. A second, related survey question asked, "To what extent do these same top administrators understand the role of the public relations department?" The four possible responses were *clearly understand it, understand it somewhat, understand it very little,* and *do not understand it at all.* Once again, most organizational representatives indicated managerial understand-ing of the public relations function. Almost 50% claimed a clear understanding and another 43%, some understanding. Six percent indicated that their top admin-istrators understand the role of public relations very little, but none believed their managers fail to understand it at all.

Table 5.3 shows that differences among types of organizations are somewhat greater with the managerial-understanding variable ($p < .37$), although neither difference is significant. Mean score for the mechanical type of organization is lowest (3.24). Traditional organizations, surprisingly, indicate the most managerial understanding ($M = 3.67$). The only statistically significant differences ($p < .05$) related to this variable as indicated by the correlational data in Table 5.4 come with the two low-task complexity organizations. Respondents from traditional organiza-tions indicated a high degree of managerial understanding of the role of public relations and those from mechanical organizations a low degree.

Values Toward Public Relations. The value top administrators hold for the role of public relations was determined during the in-depth, personal interviews and from organizational publications. Organization charts, in particular, helped to corroborate or to challenge respondents' perceptions of the value and support top management holds for their public relations function.

Respondents' lengthy replies to this open-ended query were coded into three possibilities: *high, limited,* or *low* value.[16] Samples included here indicate how each category was determined.[17]

A response that would be coded to indicate *low* value for the role of public

---

[16]A related type of response indicated *growing* value for public relations. Typical of this category, although not included in the analysis, was the comment from the coordinator of community services at a medical association. She said: "I feel PR is becoming more valued. We have more commendations and awards in this area."

[17]In a few cases, the value was difficult to determine because members of the organization's dominant coalition could not be considered as a group with a single degree of value. A media specialist at the national headquarters of a large not-for-profit organization, for example, explained:

Our CEO is absolutely supportive He understands the need and importance of PR. He makes himself available for PR purposes. He give his own ideas on PR when asked to. He participates whenever requested. In fact, he initiates requests for PR activities. In contrast, the vice presidents know nothing about PR, the media, the energy required nor deadlines. They are a considerable handicap to Public Affairs.

relations came from the assistant vice president for corporate communication at a large rail company:

In my opinion, PR isn't sufficiently appreciated and top management doesn't participate enough in PR. They need a lot of education. Top management, mostly old railroad men, are very conservative; and mostly they feel that [this company] doesn't need the media.

The director of information for a county school system described a *limited* degree of value for public relations:

The school board is supportive of the Department of Information. They have never recommended a cut in the information budget. The superintendent also values public relations. But neither the superintendent nor the board understands PR. They tend to think of the Information Department as just a conduit for information to the public. "Get the word out." They emphasize the publicist aspect of the task and don't appreciate the counseling and public relations aspects.

A response that would be coded to indicate *high* value for the role of public relations came from a regional director of communications for a church:

Top management in the Church feels that public communication is very important to the proselytizing process. They feel that the media are important in the humanizing process.

Examples of evidence of high value for public relations included regular in-grade pay raises for government employees; an open door into the office of top management (including phoning administrators at their homes); regularly scheduled meetings to share information and to formulate policy; promoting public relations people to top jobs; giving them free rein to run their own department, including budget; enlarging the public relations staff; enhancing the budget for public relations; and including the head of the public relations department in a recognized policy-making group, such as a board of directors or executive council.

Differences among the four organizational types in terms of value toward public relations are not significant, as shown in Table 5.3. Mean scores range from 2.52 in mixed organizations to 2.04 in organic organizations, compared with an overall mean of 2.28. This indicates that in the opinion of respondents, top management in mixed organizations values the public relations function somewhat more than in the other three types. Correlations in Table 5.4 indicate a similarly high managerial value for public relations in the mixed mechanical/organic type ($.18, p < .05$) and the lowest value among organic organizations ($-.22, p < .05$).

Education in Public Relations. The education in public relations of top administrators is related to the support, understanding, and value they attach to this organizational function. As with values, this variable was measured during the personal interviews. Of the 81 who responded, 74 indicated that to their knowledge, members of the dominant coalition had little or no education in public relations.[18] Only four replied affirmatively to this question, and three did not know.

One interesting response attempted to explain the ramifications of lack of education in public relations. According to the public affairs director of a governmental agency:

> Top management, in respect to public relations, is like an elephant crossing a suspension bridge—it has to be led *very* carefully. PR is an uncertain business, which bothers the brass. In spite of the difficulties, our top offices have begun to understand the role and importance of PR, but they still need a lot of training.

Because the administration of this agency is not interested in disseminating information from what is essentially an information-gathering operation, the administration constrains the release of research news. This was apparent from the relative dearth of press releases contributed to the study. As the respondent said, "Not enough is being done to get out the accumulated information."

Typical explanations offered for the lack of education top management has in public relations include the busy schedule of members of the dominant coalition and innate or natural understanding as a substitute for formal training.

Tables 5.3 and 5.4 show that when broken down by organizational type, there are significant differences in this variable. Although most respondents indicated that their dominant coalition had no formal training in public relations, significantly more managers in organic organizations than in any other type had some education in the field. Mechanical organizations reported the least education in public relations among top administrators.

Hypotheses 3, 6, 9, and 12

This group of hypotheses relates to the value top management holds for the public relations function, dependent on organizational type. Hypothesis 12, the prediction that management in mixed mechanical/organic organizations would value public relations the most, was supported. This was the case when the question was posed directly. Another, more indirect indicator, however, told a somewhat different story. Education of the dominant coalition in public relations was significantly greater in organic organizations than in any other type.

The hypothesis that management in traditional organizations would value public relations the least was not supported, at least considering "value" in its strictest

---

[18]Willingness or the intention of becoming educated about public relations still was classified as *no education* in the field.

sense. Instead, management in organic organizations values public relations the least—despite the fact that top administration there is the most highly educated in the field and evidences the most support for the function. No other significant differences emerged to support or to disconfirm the other hypotheses in this group.

Involvement of Top Management in Public Relations

Another variable associated with the power organizational leaders lend to public relations is the extent to which management is willing to involve itself in the day-to-day activities of the public relations department. Responses gleaned during the interviews were coded into categories of *much, some, little or none,* and *don't know.*

More than half of the respondents (53%) indicated that top management was somewhat involved in public relations. About one-quarter considered their dominant coalition to be very involved. Only about 1 in 10 saw little or no involvement.

Activities typical of managerial involvement in public relations include speech making, participating in press conferences, and giving interviews. All of these are instances of cooperation with the press, including mass media and trade publications. Additional examples of managerial involvement include participating in trade shows and other special events. Almost all organizations that indicated managerial involvement pointed to frequent meetings between top administration and the public relations department.

Negative expressions of a high degree of managerial involvement included terms such as *meddling, interfering, always looking over my shoulder,* and *having the final say on everything.* More often, however, involvement was considered a plus for the department. Typical was the following response, indicating a high degree of managerial involvement, from the director of public relations for a chemical association:

> Public relations demands about 10% of the time of the chairman, the president and vice presidents. They are all responsive to requests for participation in PR.

A response indicating only some involvement came from an electric company's manager of headquarters communications:

> Probably 5% to 10% of the so-called 'Senior Management Group's' time here is spent on PR activities, but they have only average knowledge of it. They are accessible and cooperative, but we have to request their involvement in press conferences and interviews.

A response typical of the few who indicated little or no involvement of top administrators in public relations came from a public relations expert at an defense contractor:

We're typically handed a problem to solve. Management wants the corporation to be perceived accurately, which we consider our job. But we do try to keep management aware of what they're doing and how that affects PR.

Because more than half of all interviewees considered their top administrators to be somewhat involved in activities of the public relations department, that involvement varies little by type of organization. Table 5.3 shows no statistically significant differences. Correlations in Table 5.4 show some statistically significant, although weak ($p < .10$), associations between involvement and the two organizational types with complex technology. Administrators in the mixed type tend to be more involved in public relations than are executives in the other types. The dominant coalition in organic organizations, by contrast, is least involved.

Involvement of Public Relations in Activities of the Dominant Coalition

An interesting, related variable to managerial involvement in public relations is the involvement expected of public relations people in activities of the dominant coalition.[19] Again, this variable was explored during the in-depth interviews. Responses were coded into categories of *much*, *some* and *little or no* involvement. Findings were more varied than in the case of managerial involvement in public relations: 40%, 33%, and 25%, respectively.

A high degree of involvement was indicated primarily in the areas of policy and issues management. This role, however, tends to be advisory or counseling rather than actual policy making. As the director of communications for a church said:

Only the president himself can speak for the official church position on an issue, but public communications people sit in the highest council of the Church and participate in policy and operating decisions.

Many respondents indicated that they participate in weekly sessions dealing with operating decisions and problems of management. These respondents tend to be the number-one person in the public relations department. They characterized their involvement as "intimate," "regular," "integral," "daily," and "close."

Interviewees implying a moderate level of involvement with the dominant coalition include an auto maker's director of public affairs. He said that he and other executives in this office have "a voice" in corporate policy and operating decisions that affect at least public relations, marketing, and advertising. Others charac-

---

[19]In some cases, of course, the interviewee was a member of the dominant coalition. This occurred in the smallest organizations, such as a bagel bakery, where no formalized public relations position exists. It also was typical of respondents with the title of "vice president" in companies that included the world's largest seller of spices, an advertising/public relations firm and a large metropolitan hospital.

terized their limited involvement as "by invitation," "sometimes," "occasional," "situational," and "ad hoc."

A response typical of virtually no involvement with the power elite came from a governmental agency's director of public information. Although he described "easy access" to the chief on matters of policy and administration, he never participates in the weekly top staff conferences with the chief. Instead, the deputy chief for administration briefs him on discussions that concern his work.

Although Table 5.3 shows that mean scores of involvement in management vary across organizational types, these differences are statistically insignificant. Differences exposed in Table 5.4 are similarly minor. Apparently, type of organization is not a strong predictor of the involvement of public relations personnel in the dominant coalition.

Research Question 2

The second research question explores the involvement of public relations in the dominant coalition, and vice versa. Findings show that such involvement varies somewhat by organizational type. Public relations practitioners in traditional organizations are somewhat less likely to be included in their dominant coalitions. However, the number of interviewees who consider themselves part of the dominant coalition was remarkably high across organizations. Such self-reports are suspect, of course, but more than 4 out of 10 indicated considerable involvement with top management.

Top management in organic organizations is somewhat less likely to involve itself in public relations efforts than is the power elite in the other three Hage–Hull types. (That involvement is typically considered positive, showing support and appreciation for and understanding of the function.) As with public relations' involvement in the dominant coalition, however, such involvement was relatively high in all types of organizations.

Technology

During the initial contextualizing necessary for determining organizational type, organizations were placed into one of three Thompson (1967) categories of technology. *Long-linked* or assembly-line technology is characteristic of a serially interdependent process, as in the manufacture of trucks. *Mediating* technology links customers or clients who would be independent otherwise. A savings and loan association is an example of mediating technology. *Intensive* technology, as exemplified in a hospital, relies on extensive feedback from customers, clients, or consumers.

Of course, some organizations (especially those in the mixed mechanical/organic type) depend on a combination of technologies. However, the final hypothesis in

TABLE 5.5
Comparison of Organizational Types by Technology

Organization Type	N	Technology					
		Long-Linked		Mediating		Intensive	
		%	N	%	N	%	N
Traditional	16	18.3	3	43.8	7	37.5	6
Mechanical	21	14.3	3	57.1	12	28.6	6
Organic	23	17.4	4	47.8	11	34.8	8
Mixed	21	42.9	9	38.1	8	19.0	4
N	81	23.5	19	46.9	38	26.9	24

Chi square = 6.83, 6 DF, $p < .3367$.

this study is based on the *predominant* technology. Determination was based largely on organizational publications provided, especially annual reports.

Mediating technology was most common (47%), followed by intensive (30%), and long-linked (23%). Table 5.5, a crosstabulation of organizational type by technology, shows that all Hage–Hull types employ long-linked, mediating, and intensive technologies. Because one third of the cells have fewer than five cases in each, the value of chi square may not be meaningful. As a result, determining whether one technology dominates in one organizational type to a significant degree is difficult.

A couple of obvious differences, however, deserve mention. Mediating technology dominates in the traditional (43.8%), the mechanical (57.1%), and the organic (47.8%) organization. Long-linked technology prevails in the mixed organizational type (42.9%).

Table 5.6 uses Kendall's tau correlations to show the covariation by type of technology (within each organizational type) with the autonomy measure. The two large-scale organizational types, mixed and mechanical, show no significant correlations between technology and autonomy. However, traditional organizations with long-linked technology give significantly less autonomy to their public relations department than do those with mediating technology. This is also the case in organic organizations. There, with increased environmental complexity, the small manufacturing operation gives significantly more autonomy to the public relations department than when technology is mediating.

Hypothesis 13

The final hypothesis predicted a relationship between the power of the public relations department and mixed organizations with assembly-line technology. Presumably, this long-linked process would necessitate more clearance or less autono-

TABLE 5.6
Correlates of Technology Variables with Autonomy of PR
Within Each Organizational Type

	Technology		
Organization Type	Long-Linked	Mediating	Intensive
Traditional (N = 15)			
Autonomy	−.40**	.50***	−.18
Mechanical (N = 21)			
Autonomy	−.07	−.02	.08
Organic (N = 23)			
Autonomy	−.44***	.28**	.05
Mixed (N = 21)			
Autonomy	−.18	.12	.07

**$p < .05$.
***$p < .01$.

my for the public relations department there than in mixed organizations with other kinds of technology. (Differences among technologies in the remaining three types of organizations were not projected because the literature did not indicate the likelihood of such variation.)

The hypothesis was not supported. No significant variation between the three kinds of technology and autonomy (the variable that includes clearance policy along with authority) occurred. However, both organic and traditional organizations did vary significantly in terms of technology and autonomy; this consideration begs further study.

CONCLUSIONS

Summary

This study found the perception of almost unilateral support for the public relations function across organizations. Interviewees reported virtually no opposition from top management to their role in the organization. Management also seems to have a clear understanding of public relations. Executives often involve themselves integrally in activities of the public relations department, and this is perceived as a positive indication of understanding and support.

Apparently, however, support and understanding do not go hand in hand with value. Respondents indicated medium to high levels of value for their role on the part of the organization's power elite. Perhaps this explains the limited degree of authority that respondents reported. Their power within the organization was rarely unbridled.

Explanations frequently cited for lack of autonomy include sexism, newness to the organization, being in a regional office rather than at the headquarters and restrictive government policy. Most constraining, however, is the lack of education in public relations on the part of the dominant coalition. Many reportedly equate public relations with publicity or—a related problem—believe the organization does not "need" the media.

Even in the relatively rare instances of powerful public relations practitioners, some qualifications exist. Respondents indicated that their autonomy may be contingent on dealing with routine situations; small amounts of money; the traditional areas associated with public relations, such as media relations; and a busy CEO. Others who reported a high degree of power qualified their status by alluding to practices such as "keeping the higher-ups informed as a courtesy" and the constraints imposed by budget or an even-more-powerful board.

The study revealed surprisingly extensive involvement of public relations practitioners with the dominant coalition. Even in the critical area of issues management, though, their role is more advisory than actual policy making

This exploratory study is as important for what it did not find as for what it was able to establish about power in public relations. For example, responses indicated little specialization in public relations, a low degree of professionalism, little education in the field on the part of top management, and only limited power in public relations departments across organizations. That power was further limited to the technical or typically journalistic activities of public relations, rather than to the managerial role of counseling, planning, evaluation, and decision making. Finally, responses in many key areas varied insignificantly if at all among the four organizational types. Thus the Hage–Hull typology was not such a strong predictor of characteristics related to power and public relations as expected.

Profiles of Power in the Four Organizational Types

Respondents in *traditional* organizations implied a high degree of managerial understanding of their field. Understanding does not lead to support for the public relations function, however, at least in the case of the traditional organization. Practitioners in this type indicated little managerial advocacy. (Of course, public relations is considered a staff—rather than managerial—function in traditional organizations.) Low professionalism also characterizes this organizational type; and this finding is consistent with the organization whose knowledge complexity is low and thus needs less innovation than do other types to survive or to increase their market share.

Managerial support for public relations is weaker in the *mechanical* organization than in both organic and mixed organizations. One explanation might lie in the limited understanding and value that most managers in mechanical organizations have for public relations. Also, their executives have the least education in the field of public relations. However, a more reasonable explanation probably is that these operations tend to be market oriented. They need public relations to dispose of their products or services in their vast market. At the same time, because their market is relatively stable, they need to gather little information from their environment.

Beyond that, however, the potential of public relations rarely is realized in the typical mechanical organization. Even the fact that practitioners there are more professional than in the other three types of organizations does not preclude their doing little more than disseminating information. When the power elite does not value nor understand their capabilities, practitioners may violate their professional norms or standards—thus compromising their professional judgment and even ignoring the public interest.

Managers in *organic* organizations support the public relations effort to a significantly greater degree than in both types of organizations with low task complexity (traditional and mechanical). Although most survey respondents said their top executives have little or no education in public relations, organic organizations reported significantly more members of the dominant coalition with such specialized knowledge. Employees in the public relations department there have a relatively high level of education in general.

Members of the power elite in *mixed mechanical/organic* organizations involve themselves in public relations activity somewhat more than in the other three types. Perhaps because top management is so intimately involved, it strongly supports and values the public relations department. A second outgrowth may be the autonomy granted public relations practitioners in the typical mixed organization: significantly more independence than in any other type. A second factor accounting for the high degree of autonomy (in addition to managerial support and appreciation) may be the kind of person typically working in these public relations departments. Administrators might feel secure in giving them free rein because of their high educational level and—probably more important—their specialized training in public relations.

Limitations of the Study

Using the Hage–Hull typology turned out to be only moderately useful as a theoretical approach to studying power and public relations. The typology does explain about 10% of the variance. However, correlations are small and so, much remains to be explained. However, mediating influences affect both organizational structure and power in public relations. Two major forces are managerial values for the public relations function and professionalism of staff members in public relations. The two are related: if top executives of the corporation do not value the role that public relations can play there, even the professional employee may compromise his or her judgment to keep the job.

Undoubtedly, the small size of the sample also accounts for some of the insignificant effects by organizational type. Because of the combined methodology, a larger sample size[20] was prohibitive in terms of cost and of time in particular. However, the few cases distributed across several variables may not have produced the significant results that a larger sample would.

A third, related limitation is the fact that some respondents are not public relation practitioners per se. Instead, they are presidents, vice presidents, or general managers—whoever is responsible for whatever public relations is done in an organization with no formalized public relations position. This confounds the results somewhat, since the study tried to gauge the involvement of practitioners in the dominant coalition, and vice versa. In some cases, the interviewee is a member of that power elite. This happens especially often in small-scale organizations.

Also, this field study relies heavily on verbal reports from the participants. Tan (1985) described one relevant problem inherent in this methodology: interviewees undoubtedly consider certain responses more prestigious than others, such as the extent of their association with top management or their degree of professional involvement.

Finally, the precise measurement of "autonomy" proved problematic. Although interviewers tried to distinguish between the admittedly related concepts of "authority" and "clearance process," interviewees could or would not. As a result, responses were grouped into a single variable called *autonomy*. At least in the case of the traditional organization, where the respondent most often is a CEO or other member of the dominant coalition but not in public relations per se, this distinction might have provided important insights. As it is, responses are not truly comparable with those of public relations personnel working at a lower level of the organizational hierarchy.

Implications

In spite of its limitations, this study has important implications both for public relations practitioners and for students planning to enter the field.

Practitioners. The management vacuum in public relations is what a lead article in *pr reporter* (Must busy, 1984) called the "opportunity of a century." Filling the vacuum would allow public relations professionals to add to their skills and to realize their aspirations for leadership roles in organizations. The same article in *pr reporter* pointed out that practitioners are more concerned over their role in the future of the field than any other topic. They note with anxiety that nonpublic relations people are getting top spots in public relations.

A managerial (rather than technical) approach to the practice of public relations would add to practitioners' acceptance and respect within their organizations and

---

[20]According to Tan (1985), "It is easy to get 'significant' effects with large samples" (p. 188). Ideally, this study would have involved several hundred public relations practitioners.

with the public at large. The lack of credibility is often a problem with boundary spanners. By increasing the probability that public relations practitioners attain managerial status, the field moves from a practice toward a profession. At that point, the organization gets its money's worth from employees who allocate their public relations budgets—typically in the hundreds of thousands of dollars—based on scientific monitoring of relevant concerns in the environment. This sensitivity and resultant ability to innovate benefit the larger society.

Practitioners, too, would benefit through the predictable increase in job satisfaction that accompanies growing power. When those in the dominant coalition become willing to share their power, the productivity of the organization as a whole should increase as well.

All of this implies delegating more authority to the department. Public relations practitioners can be more than journalists-in-residence, more than communications technicians. They can be managers or part of the power elite themselves. As it is, however, they need more autonomy—especially in organic and traditional organizations where public relations departments have the most stringent clearance processes and the least power. Finally, public relations practitioners themselves will not meet the challenge until they have more education specifically in their field, especially at the graduate level.

Students. Decision making separates managers from nonmanagers. The ability to make valid decisions in public relations partly depends on the knowledge of communication theory and research methods that comes with a university education in the field—primarily as a master's or doctoral student. Advanced training also leads to professionalism: taking advantage of the theoretical body of knowledge to build a practice based not on isolated experiences but on generalizable findings that apply to organizations beyond the individual cases studied or experienced.

Specialized training in public relations also leads to professionalism in the sense that it indoctrinates students in the culture of the field. This, in turn, lays the groundwork for involvement in professional associations such as the PRSA and the IABC.

Perhaps most important, students reading this study can project their career path. They can learn to avoid mechanical organizations, where top management is least educated in public relations and where they could expect the least involvement with the dominant coalition. For that same reason, they also should avoid traditional organizations—especially when the technology there is long-linked.

On the other hand, if autonomy is the deciding factor for students anticipating a career in public relations, then the mixed mechanical/organic organization should be the first choice. Top management there is the most involved with public relations. Unfortunately, these large-scale, high complexity types hire the fewest beginners.

Organic organizations offer a logical alternative. Especially in the case of these small-scale, high complexity organizations with assembly-line technology, the in-ner circle values public relations highly. Although least involved with public rela-tions of the four Hage—Hull types, they exhibit the most education of top manage-ment in public relations. However, both this type and the mixed organization indicate the strongest support for public relations.

Because longevity in the organization emerged as a possible predictor of power, those same students might consider staying in the organization that initially hires them. Findings also indicate that throughout their tenure, PR practitioners should be educating top brass in the need for sophisticated, two-way public relations—helping the dominant coalition understand that the field can and should be more than simple, one-way dissemination of information.

REFERENCES

Aiken, M., & Hage, J. (1968). Organizational interdependence and intra-organizational structure. *American Sociological Review, 33,* 912–930.

Aiken, M., & Hage, J. (1971). The organic organization and innovation. *Sociology, 5,* 63–82.

Aldrich, H. E. (1979). *Organizations and environments.* Englewood Cliffs, NJ: Prentice-Hall.

Aldrich, H. E., & Herker, D. (1977). Boundary spanning roles and organization structure. *Academy of Management Review, 2,* 217–230.

Allen, T.J. (1979). *Managing the flow of technology; Technology transfer and the dis-semination of technological information within the research and development organization.* Cambridge, MA: MIT Press.

Anshen, M. (Ed.). (1974). *Managing the socially responsible corporation.* New York: Macmillan.

Axelrod, R. (1970). *Conflict of interest.* Chicago: Markham.

Bacharach, S. B., & Lawler, E. J. (1980). *Power and politics in organizations.* San Francis-co: Jossey-Bass.

Bales, R. W. (1984, May). *Organizational interface: An open systems, contingency ap-proach to boundary-spanning activities.* Paper presented at the meeting of the Interna-tional Communication Association, San Francisco, CA.

Baxter, W. (1980). *Our progress and our potential* (Working paper). Norman, OK: School of Journalism, University of Oklahoma.

Benson, J. K. (1975). The interorganizational network as a political economy. *Admin-istrative Science Quarterly, 20,* 229–249.

Blau, P. M. (1964). *Exchange and power in social life.* New York: Wiley.

Broom, G. M. (1982). A comparison of sex roles in public relations. *Public Relations Review, 8*(3), 17–22.

Broom, G. M., & Dozier, D. M. (1985, August). *Determinants and consequences of public relations roles.* Paper presented at the meeting of the Association for Education in Journalism and Mass Communication, Memphis, TN.

Brown, D.A. (1980). Public affairs/public relations. *Public Relations Journal, 36,* 11–14.

Buffington, P. W. (1986, August). The powers that be. *SKY*, pp. 97–100.

Burger, C. (1983). How management views public relations. *Public Relations Quarterly*, 27(4), 27–30.

Close, H. W. (1980). Public relations as a management function. *Public Relations Journal*, 36, 11–14.

Cobb, A. T. (1984). An episodic model of power: Toward an integration of theory and research. *Academy of Management Review*, 9, 482–493.

Cook, K. S. (1977). Exchange and power in networks of interorganizational relations. *The Sociological Quarterly*, 18, 62–82.

Crozier, M. (1964). *The bureaucratic phenomenon.* Chicago: University of Chicago Press.

Cuming, P. (1985). *Turf and other corporate power plays.* Englewood Cliffs, NJ: Prentice-Hall.

Cyert, R. M., & March, J. G. (1963). *A behavioral theory of the firm.* Englewood Cliffs, NJ: Prentice-Hall.

Cyert, R. M., & March, J. G. (1973). *A behavioral theory of the firm* (2nd ed.). Englewood Cliffs, NJ: Prentice-Hall.

Doob, L. W. (1983). *Personality, power and authority: A view from the behavioral sciences.* Westport, CT: Greenwood Press.

Dozier, D. M. (1981, August). *The diffusion of evaluation methods among public relations practitioners.* Paper presented at the meeting of the Association for Education in Journalism, East Lansing, MI.

Emerson, R. M. (1962). Power-dependence relations. *American Sociological Review*, 27, 31–43.

Emerson, R. M. (1972). Exchange theory, part 2: Exchange relations, exchange networks, and groups as exchange systems. In J. Berger, M. Selditch, & B. Anderson (Eds.), *Sociological theories in progress* (Vol. 2)(pp. 58–87). Boston: Houghton Mifflin.

Farrell, D., & Peterson, J. C. (1982). Patterns of political behavior in organizations. *Academy of Management Review*, 7, 402–412.

Gaski, J. F. (1984). The theory of power and conflicts in channels of distribution. *Journal of Marketing*, 48, 9–29.

Greyser, S. A. (1981). Changing roles for public relations. *Public Relations Journal*, 18, 18–25.

Grunig, J. E. (1976). Organizations and public relations: Testing a communication theory. *Journalism Monographs*, 46.

Grunig, J. E. (1983). Basic research provides knowledge that makes evaluation possible. *Public Relations Quarterly*, 28(3), 30.

Grunig, J. E. (1984). Organizations, environments, and models of public relations. *Public Relations Research and Education*, 1(1), 6–29.

Grunig, J. E., & Grunig, L. S. (1989). Toward a theory of the public relations behavior of organizations: Review of a program of research. In J. E. Grunig & L. A. Grunig (Eds.), *Public relations research annual* (Vol. 1, pp. 27–63). Hillsdale, NJ: Lawrence Erlbaum Associates.

Grunig, J. E., & Hunt, T. (1984). *Managing public relations.* New York: Holt, Rinehart & Winston.

Hagberg, J. (1984). *Real power: The stages of personal power in organizations.* Minneapolis, MN: Winston Press.

Hage, J. (1980). *Theories of organizations: Form, process, and transformation.* New York: Wiley.

Hage, J., & Aiken, M. (1970). *Social change in complex organizations.* New York: Random House.

Hage, J., & Dewar, R. A. (1973, September). Elite values versus organizational structure in predicting innovation. *Administrative Science Quarterly, 18,* 279–290.

Hage, J., & Hull, F. (1981). *A typology of environmental niches based on knowledge technology and scale: The implications for innovation and productivity* (Working Paper 1). University of Maryland: Center for the Study of Innovation, Entrepreneurship and Organization Strategy.

Hambrick, D. C. (1981). Environment, strategy, and power within top management teams. *Administrative Science Quarterly, 26,* 253–276.

Hickson, D. J., Hinings, C. R., Lee, C. A., Schneck, R. E., & Pennings, J. M. (1971). A strategic contingencies theory of intraorganizational power. *Administrative Science Quarterly, 16,* 216–229.

Jablin, F. M. (1980). Superior's upward influence, satisfaction, and openness in superior-subordinate communication: A reexamination of the "Pelz" effect. *Human Communication Research, 6*(1), 210–220.

Jacobs, D. (1974). Dependency and vulnerability: An exchange approach to control of organizations. *Administrative Science Quarterly, 19,* 45–59.

Johnson, D. J., & Acharya, L. (1981, August). *Organizational decision making and public relations roles.* Paper presented at the meeting of the Association for Education in Journalism, Athens, OH.

Kanter, R. M. (1979, July–August). Power failure in management circuits. *Harvard Business Review.*

Katz, D., & Kahn, R. L. (1966). *The social psychology of organizations.* New York: Wiley.

Keller, R., & Holland, W. (1975). Boundary-spanning roles in a research and development organization: An empirical investigation. *Academy of Management Journal, 18,* 388–393.

Keller, R., Szilagyi, A., & Holland, W. (1976). Boundary-spanning activity and employee relations. *Human Relations, 29,* 699–710.

Lawler, B. J., & Hage, J. (1973). Professional-bureaucratic conflict and intraorganizational powerlessness among social workers. *Journal of Sociology and Social Welfare, 1* (3), 92–102.

Lesly, P. (1981). The stature and role of public relations. *Public Relations Journal, 37,* 14–17.

Levine, S., & White, P. E. (1961). Exchange as a conceptual framework for the study of interorganizational relationships. *Administrative Science Quarterly, 5,* 583–601.

Lindemann, W., & Lapetina, A. (1981). Management's view of the future of public relations. *Public Relations Review, 81*(3), 3–13.

Maples, S. F. (1981). *Relationship of organizational structure to public relations decision-making.* Unpublished master's thesis, California State University, Fullerton, CA.

March, J.G. (1962). The business firm as a political coalition. *Journal of Politics, 24,* 662–678.

Merton, R. K. (1940, May). Bureaucratic structure and personality. *Social Forces, 18,* 560–568.

Miles, R. H. (1977, August). *Boundary relevance.* Paper presented at the meeting of the Academy of Management, Kissimmee, FL.

Mintzberg, H. (1983). *Power in and around organizations.* Englewood Cliffs, NJ: Prentice-Hall.

Morgenthau, H. (1960). *Politics among nations.* New York: Knopf.

Murnighan, J. K. (1978). Models of coalition behavior: Game theoretic, social psychological and political perspectives. *Psychological Bulletin, 85,* 1130–1153.

Must busy professionals be concerned about education for the field while battling issues like achieving top management decision making? (1984). *pr reporter, 27*(48), 1–2.

Nanni, E. C. (1980). *Case studies of organizational management and public relations practices.* Unpublished master's thesis, University of Maryland, College Park, MD.

Nelson, D. (1986). *The effect of management values on the role and practice of public relations within organizations.* Unpublished master's thesis, University of Maryland, College Park, MD.

Newman, L. (1980). Public relations phase II: Adviser becomes decision maker. *Public Relations Journal, 36,* 11–13.

Nowlan, S. E., & Shayon, D. R. (1984). Reviewing your relationship with executive management. *Public Relations Quarterly, 39*(1), 5–11.

Organ, D. W. (1971). Linking pins between organizations and environments. *Business Horizons, 14*(12), 73–80.

Ossareh, J. C. (1987). *Technology as a public relations tool: Theoretical perspectives, practical applications, and actual use.* Unpublished master's thesis, University of Maryland, College Park, MD.

Pavlik, J. V., & Salmon, C. T. (1983, August). *Theoretic approaches in public relations research.* Paper presented at a meeting of the Association for Education in Journalism and Mass Communication, Corvallis, OR.

Pennings, J. M., & Goodman, P. S. (1977). Toward a workable framework. In P. S. Goodman & J. M. Pennings (Eds.), *New perspectives on organizational effectiveness* (pp. 146–184). San Francisco: Jossey-Bass.

Perrow, C. (1961). Organizational prestige: Some functions and dysfunctions. *American Journal of Sociology, 66,* 335–341.

Pfeffer, J. (1978). *Organizational design.* Arlington Heights, IL: AHM Publishing.

Pfeffer, J. (1981). *Power in organizations.* Boston: Pitman.

Pfeffer, J., & Salancik, G. R. (1978). *The external control of organizations: A resource dependence perspective.* New York: Harper & Row.

Pollack, R. (1986). *Testing the Grunig organizational theory in scientific organizations: Public relations and the values of the dominant coalition.* Unpublished master's thesis, University of Maryland, College Park, MD.

Provan, K. G. (1980). Recognizing, measuring, and interpreting the potential/enacted power distinction in organizational research. *Academy of Management Review, 5,* 549–559.

Quinn, J. B. (1980). *Strategy for change: Logical incrementalism.* Homewood, IL: Richard Irwin.

Robbins, S. P. (1983). *Organization theory: The structure and design of organizations.* Englewood Cliffs, NJ: Prentice-Hall.

Rosenthal, H. (1970). The study of coalition behavior. In S. Groennings, E. W. Kelley, & M. Leiserson (Eds.), *The study of collective behavior* (pp. 43–59). New York: Holt, Rinehart & Winston.

Ryan, M., & Martinson, D. L. (1983). The PR officer as corporate conscience. *Public Relations Quarterly, 38*(2), 20–23.

Sanders, P. (1982). Phenomenology: A new way of viewing organizational research. *Academy of Management Review, 7,* 353–360.

Schneider, L. A. (1985). The role of public relations in four organizational types. *Journalism Quarterly, 62*(3), 567–576, 594.

Sieber, S. (1974). Toward a theory of role accumulation. *American Sociological Review, 39,* 567–578.

Simon, H. (1953). Notes on the observation and measurement of political power. *Journal of Politics, 15,* 500–516.

Skinner, S. J., & Guiltinan, J. P. (1986, March). Extra-Network linkages, dependence, and power. *Social Forces, 64*(3), 702–713.

Stevenson, W. B., Pearce, J. L., & Porter, L. W. (1985). The concept of "coalition" in organization theory and research. *Academy of Management Review, 10*(2), 256–268.

Stinchcombe, A. L. (1965). Social structure and organizations. In J. G. March (Ed.), *Handbook of organizations* (pp. 142–193). Chicago: Rand McNally.

Strenski, J. B. (1980). The top 12 public relations challenges for 1980. *Public Relations Journal, 36,* 11–14.

Tan, A. S. (1985). *Mass communication theories and research* (2nd ed.). New York: Wiley.

Thompson, J. D. (1967). *Organizations in action.* New York: McGraw-Hill.

Van de Ven, A. H. (1976). On the nature, formation, and maintenance of relations among organizations. *Academy of Management Review, 1,* 405–416.

Warren, R. L. (1967). The interorganizational field as a focus for analysis. *Administrative Science Quarterly, 12,* 396–419.

Whetten, D. A., & Leung, T. K. (1979). The instrumental value of interorganizational relations: Antecedents and consequences of linkage formation. *Academy of Management Journal, 22,* 325–344.

Woodward, J. (1965). *Industrial organizations: Theory and practice.* Oxford: Oxford University Press.

Zald, M. N. (1970). Political economy: A framework for comparative analysis. In M. N. Zald (Ed.), *Power in organizations* (pp. 221–261). Vanderbilt, TN: Vanderbilt University Press.

Chapter 6

Community Size, Perceptions of Majority Opinion, and Opinion Expression

Charles T. Salmon
University of Wisconsin—Madison

Hayg Oshagan
University of Michigan

The concept of public opinion has been central to the practice and study of public relations since the early writings of Edward L. Bernays (1923) on the "crystalliz-ing" of public opinion. The Silver Anvil, the most prestigious honor bestowed by PRSA for excellence in public relations, is awarded annually for an organization's ability to "forge public opinion." Yet despite the centrality of the concept to the field, little theory building of public opinion has occurred in recent years, and the area has been described as theoretically barren (Blumer, 1948; Goldner, 1971). In large measure, this is due to the overwhelming and uncritical acceptance of the dominant model of public opinion research, namely that public opinion is merely the arithmetic sum of individual's opinion on an issue of public importance (Blumer, 1948; Pavlik & Salmon, 1984).

This chapter describes the merger of two research traditions, Noelle-Neumann's "spiral of silence" theory (Noelle-Neumann, 1973, 1974, 1977, 1979, 1981, 1984) and Tichenor, Donohue, and Olien's structural model of mass communica-tion (Donohue, Tichenor, & Olien, 1973; Olien, Donohue, & Tichenor, 1968; Tichenor, Donohue, & Olien, 1973, 1980), to provide a theoretical framework for understanding public opinion processes. Specifically, this chapter examines struc-tural influences on individuals' willingness to express opinions on two social issues, the propriety of the sale of pornographic materials, and passage of a pro-posed mandatory seat-belt law in the state. In both cases, the issues have been the subject of intense public relations efforts by interest groups, businesses, and gov-ernment seeking to manage the economic, political, and social environments in which they operate.

THE "SPIRAL OF SILENCE" MODEL

One of the few attempts to introduce theory into the otherwise atheoretical area of public opinion research has been made by Elizabeth Noelle-Neumann, a noted German pollster and political scientist. Noelle-Neumann's model is predicated on the work of the German sociologist Tonnies, who considered public opinion to be a mechanism of social control: "[Public opinion] demands consent or at least compels silence, or abstention from contradiction" (Noelle-Neumann, 1974, p. 44). The model can be divided into three distinct segments, referring to elements of the mass media environment, individuals' scanning of information environment, and implications for social change.

To start with, Noelle-Neumann argued, the mass media are ubiquitous and consonant; that is, mass media messages are virtually inescapable in contemporary society, and the ideological origin of these messages is largely homogeneous. Media professionals, Noelle-Neumann claimed, tend to be disproportionately liberal in their political orientations. This ideological preference is manifested in news content, thus allowing journalists to be in the vanguard of social change through constructing a social reality that is more liberal in appearance than in substance. The combination of these two forces creates opinion environments that envelop individuals in society. Because most persons have an innate fear of isolation or ostracization, she contended, they constantly scan the information environment to determine which opinions are popular and which are not. The most important cue in the information environment is that structured by the ubiquitous mass media, meaning that the media exert a powerful potential influence over the cognitions of individuals. If an individual perceives that his or her opinion is shared by the majority, he or she will feel sufficiently confident to express that opinion in public without fear of social sanction. Conversely, if an individual senses that his or her opinion is unpopular, he or she will remain silent. Implications of this process are that, over time, popular opinions will increasingly dominate social discourse; policy decision makers, in turn, will base their decisions on those opinions that are expressed, not withheld. The importance of this model for public relations practitioners is obvious; to the extent that campaign planners can control an information environment and make it appear that their viewpoint or opinion dominates, they can create a self-perpetuating system in which their opinion actually will become dominant over time. This is the rationale for the organizing and staging of newsworthy "events" that draw media attention, thereby granting legitimacy to holders of a particular issue position and implicitly demonstrating that individuals who similarly hold that issue opinion are not isolated in society. Thus, the model has direct applications to the work of public relations professionals and issues managers who attempt to shape the opinion environment on such topics as the legitimacy of smoking in public, abortion, environmental pollution, or the national debt. It is a major strategic advantage in policy disputes for an organization to be able to create a climate conducive to the expression of opinion on one side of an issue—

concomitantly with a climate that inhibits the expression of opinion on an opposing side.

The static version of this model (i.e., that individuals perceived and are influenced by opinion climates at any one point in time) has been subjected to a number of empirical tests, mostly in West Germany and the United States, with mixed support (e.g., Bergen, 1986; Glynn & McLeod, 1984; Rucinski, Lee, & Salmon, 1987; Salmon & Neuwirth, in press; Salmon & Rucinski, 1988). Based on these studies, there is reason to believe that perceptions of majority opinion have a limited—but statistically significant—influence on willingness to express opinions publicly for some issues. On the other hand, little empirical data address the dynamic version of the model (i.e., the extent to which holders of a minority issue position are silenced over time). In addition, the model has been subjected to several critiques that have raised a number of questions regarding conceptual and operational considerations (e.g., Glynn & McLeod, 1985; Salmon & Kline, 1985). Summarizing research on the topic, Salmon and Neuwirth (in press) concluded that opinion expression appears to be a function of the issue itself, the form of expression required, issue knowledge and involvement, perceptions of majority opinion, and demographics.

The last set of influences, demographic characteristics, has been found to be a significant predictor of expression by Noelle-Neumann (1974), who concluded that individuals of higher levels of education and those from urban rather than rural communities were among those most likely to speak out. This latter serendipitous finding, which has not been explored by any research in either West Germany or the United States, suggests that certain structural variables may be important to an understanding of the conditions under which individuals will be more or less likely to express opinions on controversial issues.

THE STRUCTURAL MODEL OF MASS COMMUNICATION

Tichenor, Donohue, and Olien, social scientists at the University of Minnesota, have developed a research program that is relevant to the study of structural variables and opinion expression. Their model is predicated on the notion that the mass media represent one subsystem among many within the larger systemic framework, rather than an independent "Fourth Estate" operating in the absence of constraints or pressures from without. The media serve a dual control function in this context, providing both feedback control and distribution control. In the former case, the media basically provide the mechanism through which various subsystems communicate with other subsystems within the overall system. In the latter case, the media serve as a disseminator of information on the public agenda, a public record of community concerns and opinions. Through the interaction of these two functions, Tichenor, Donohue, and Olien argued, the media help define social norms through coverage of the positions of various subsystems.

The degree to which one or both functions is emphasized is a function of community size (Donohue et al., 1973). In a less complex system, the media tend to act more in a distributive role, whereas in more complex systems, the media provide more of a feedback function. In large measure, this is because more complex systems are, by nature, more heterogeneous, consisting of more and more diverse community power structures (Olien et al., 1968). Because the media selectively reflect concerns of dominant power groups, media coverage of community disputes necessarily will be greater in larger communities (i.e., those in which more competing groups co-exist; Tichenor et al., 1980).

In other words, community size in large measure determines the degree of reporting of conflict on a controversial issue and, as a result, the extent to which various community groups will be made aware of the opinions of others in the community. Because smaller communities tend to be more homogeneous than larger ones, social norms are more clearly established and more readily apparent to residents. Further, the reporting of conflict tends to be limited in smaller communities as a result of gatekeeping decisions by editors who often play a "community boosterism" role (Edelstein & Schulz, 1963; Olien et al., 1968). This editorial process may imply the presence of a consensus or dominant norm that, in turn, community residents may sense. Vidich and Bensman (1968), in their classic participant observation study of small-town life, essentially provided the linkage between the inculcation of social norms described by Noelle-Neumann in the small community setting:

> There is silent recognition among members of the community that facts and ideas which are distributing to the accepted system of illusions are not be be verbalized. . . . Instead, the social mores of the small town at every opportunity demand that only those facts and ideas which support the dreamwork of everyday life are to be verbalized and selected out for emphasis and repetition. (p. 303)

In contrast, editorial decision making in larger communities may suggest the lack of consensus or dominant norms, thereby allowing residents greater latitude in expressing opinions.

HYPOTHESES

Noelle-Neumann traditionally has described opinion climates as largely monolithic, the product of consonant mass media, and has not investigated different "levels" or "sources" of opinion climates. Yet the notion of a pluralistic society implies that different opinion climates will be associated with different social contexts and groupings. Therefore, we hypothesize that

> H1: Individuals will perceive differences in prevailing opinion climates in different communities to which they are oriented.

The second hypothesis involves a classic test of Noelle-Neumann's central tenet, namely that:

H2: There will be a relationship between opinion congruity and expression of opinion, such that congruity with the majority will be positively related to greater willingness to express an opinion, whereas congruity with the minority will be positively related to decreased willingness to express an opinion.

The third hypothesis integrates elements of the structural model with that of the spiral of silence. Tichenor, Olien, and Donohue found in their research that larger, more complex systems contain greater diversity of viewpoints as a function of more and more diverse social groups. Further, media reports of conflict in larger communities reflect this lack of consensus in reportage. We thus hypothesize that:

H3: Individuals from larger communities will be less certain of the majority opinion in their communities than will individuals from smaller communities.

Next, as a result of Noelle-Neumann's (1974) serendipitous finding that residents of urban areas are inherently more likely to express opinions than are residents of smaller communities, we hypothesize a main effect of community size on opinion expression:

H4a: Individuals from larger communities will be more likely to express their opinions than will residents of smaller communities.

However, the combination of Hypotheses 2 and 3 leads to the possibility that in a small community, a system characterized by greater face-to-face interaction and more clearly specified norms, congruity with majority will be a more important determinant of personal expression than it will be in the larger, more heterogeneous communities in which the existence of diverse social groups legitimizes the holding of "minority" opinions. We hypothesize then, that:

H4b: The magnitude of the relationship between opinion congruity and opinion expression will be greater in the small community than in the large.

METHODOLOGY

Four hundred and seventy-eight university students were surveyed regarding their willingness to express opinions on two social issues, regulation of the availability of pornographic materials and a proposed mandatory seat-belt law. Both of these meet Noelle-Neumann's criteria that issues employed in tests of this model should have a moral component and be controversial. Pornography is an "older" issue in the sense that it has received media attention for a number of years, whereas the mandatory seat-belt issue is more recent. Further, the issue of pornography is more likely to elicit considerations of sensitivity or discomforture when an individual considers the ramifications of discussing the issue publicly. Both of these issue dimensions are expected to result in different patterns of opinion expression.

Student subjects were enrolled in a large introductory public relations class at the University of Wisconsin—Madison, and originally were from communities scattered throughout the midwest and, to a lesser extent, other regions of the country. Because the goal of this study is to compare effects of structural influences on decisions regarding opinion expression—rather than to establish specific opinions or level of support for a specific issue—there is no reason to expect that generalizability is limited by the use of students in this study. The only caveat that should be kept in mind with the data is that previous studies (Noelle-Neumann, 1974; Salmon & Neuwirth, in press) have established that level of education is related to greater overall willingness to express opinions and by using college students in this study we have essentially overestimated that behavior relative to its prevalence in the general population. But the relative contributions of various predictor variables should be generalizable in an ordinal sense without contamination.

Measurement

Personal Opinion and Opinion Congruity. Subjects were asked their opinion on two issues and then asked to estimate the opinion of: (a) most students in the university; (b) most residents of the community in which the university is located; and (c) most residents of their hometown. For each opinion item, a semantic differential format was used in which extreme opinion statements anchored each end of the 5-point scale. From these items, congruity scores were calculated, with a "1" being assigned to those individuals who perceived themselves as being in the minority, a "2" being assigned to those individuals who perceived themselves as neither in the minority nor majority, and a "3" being assigned to those who perceived themselves as in the majority. Further, subjects were asked how certain they were about their assessments of each of the three opinion climates.

Opinion Expression. Because previous research has demonstrated that differences in forms of opinion expression are inherently considered more or less attractive by individuals (Salmon & Neuwirth, in press; Salmon & Rucinski, 1988), three forms of expression were used in this study. Subjects were asked how willing they would be to: (a) participate in a demonstration with people who share their opinion on the issue; (b) wear a pin or button expressing their opinion on the issue; and (c) be interviewed by a TV reporter with camera and microphone for airing on the TV newscast. For all three modes of expression, subjects rated their willingness to participate in these activities in their hometown. These three forms of expression can be distinguished conceptually in terms of: (a) the degree to which each form of expression is public; and (b) the degree to which feedback will be immediate and perhaps unpleasant. The degree to which opinion expression is public is crucial in terms of Noelle-Neumann's theory; on the other hand, lack of willingness to engage in public expression in and of itself does not imply fear of isolation or censure.

Expressing an opinion to a TV reporter will ultimately result in a highly public form of opinion expression, yet one for which feedback will be delayed, if it occurs at all (i.e., it will occur only if others view the interview, recognize the interviewee and contact that individual). In contrast, wearing a pin or button is limited in terms of the degree to which it is public, yet will often result in immediate feedback. Participating in a demonstration is associated with a higher probability of confrontation or open conflict, yet may be considered less public than participating in a TV interview.

Structural Variables. Structural variables were measured in the following manner. Community size was measured with a 5-point scale, with points corresponding to: (1) less than 1,000 persons; (2) 1,000 to 10,000 persons; (3) 10,000 to 40,000 persons; (4) 40,000 to 100,000 persons; and (5) over 100,000 persons. Additional variables measured included: number of years lived in hometown [(1) less than 5; (2) 6 to 10; (3) 11 to 15; (4) 16 to 20; (5) more than 21] and year in college.

RESULTS

Perceptions of Opinion Climates

The first hypothesis, and a point of theoretical departure, was concerned with whether individuals could distinguish between different climates of opinions. To test this, a series of t tests was conducted comparing perceptions of majority opinion among students on campus, the community in which the university is located, and the subject's hometown communities (see Table 6.1 for univariate statistics). Presented first are data on the issue of pornography. Excluding those cases for which the university community was a subject's hometown (64 cases), significant differences were found between perceptions of the majority opinion among university students and university-community residents ($t = -17.58, p < .01$), between university students and hometown residents ($t = -16.75, p < .01$), and between university-community residents and hometown residents ($t = 2.45, p < .05$). For the issue of mandatory seat belts, there were significant differences between perceptions of majority opinion among university students and university-community residents ($t = 16.58, p < .01$) and between university students and hometown residents ($t = 15.21, p < .01$). There were no significant differences in opinion perceptions between university-community residents and hometown residents.

TABLE 6.1
Univariate Statistics

Variable	Large Hometown mean/st. dev. (n = 323)	Small Hometown mean/st. dev. (n = 91)
Hometown Opinion[a]		
Hometown majority opinion on pornography	3.29/1.02	3.67/0.91
Hometown majority opinion on seat belt use	2.35/1.09	2.65/1.20
Expression of Opinion[b]		
Join a demonstration on pornography in . . .	1.72/1.02	1.90/1.06
Wear a pin or button on pornography in . . .	1.97/1.18	2.06/1.33
Be interviewed on TV on pornography in . . .	2.89/1.43	3.19/1.40
Join a demonstration on seat belt use in . . .	2.29/1.25	2.53/1.24
Wear a pin or button on seat belt use in . . .	2.90/1.41	2.90/1.44
Be interviewed on TV on seat belt use in . . .	3.84/1.20	3.80/1.20
Years lived in hometown	3.43/1.03	3.30/1.10

[a]Hometown opinion variables scored: 1 = No regulation, personal choice, 5 = Strong regulation.
[b]Expression of opinion variables scored: 1 = Not willing at all, 5 = Very willing.

In general, the data provide support for the notion that individuals are capable of at least estimating differences in opinion climates. In this particular case, sub- jects consistently evaluated the opinion climate among students as the most toler- ant, followed by the opinion climate of the university community; the subjects' hometown community consistently was viewed as the least tolerant environment of the three. Possibly, this is due to the particular nature of the university community in general, which tends to be somewhat liberal and permissive relative to others in the state and region.

Opinion Congruity and Expression

In general, subjects were more likely to engage in some forms of opinion ex- pression than others—regardless of the prevailing climate of opinion. For both issues, subjects were most willing to agree to be interviewed by a television reporter ($x = 2.95$ for pornography; $x = 3.83$ for seat belt), somewhat less likely to wear a pin or button ($x = 1.98$ for pornography; $x = 2.89$ for seat belt), and least likely to participate in a demonstration ($x = 1.98$ for pornography; ($x = 1.78$ for pornography; $x = 2.34$ for seat belt). Differences in the three modes of opinion expression—for both issues—in all cases were statistically significant at the .001 level.

In terms of a specific expectation, the second hypothesis posited a positive relationship between opinion congruity and willingness to express an opinion. Support for this, the central element of Noelle-Neumann's model, is limited. Correlations between perceived congruity and expression are statistically significant and in the predicted direction for two forms of expression on the issue of pornography: participating in a demonstration ($r = .13$, $p < .05$) and for wearing a pin or button ($r = .17$, $p < .01$). For the seat-belt issue, the correlations were in the predicted direction, but not statistically significant. Thus, in only two of the six cases (two issues, three modes of expression for each) was the hypothesis supported.

Community Size, Opinion, and Opinion Expression

The third hypothesis was that individuals from large communities would feel less certain in their perceptions of majority opinion than would individuals from smaller communities. This hypothesis was supported for the issue of pornography ($r = .11$, $p < .01$), but not for the seat-belt issue ($r = -.04$, n.s.).

Relative Contributions of Community Size and Congruity on Opinion Expression

Tests of Hypothesis 4a (i.e., positing a main effect of community size on opinion expression) and Hypothesis 4b (i.e., an interaction between community size and congruity in predicting opinion expression) were done through the use of path analyses. In the path-analytic model, three exogenous variables—community size, number of years of residence in the community, and year in school—were employed. The endogenous variable was opinion congruity, and the dependent variable was opinion expression, again measured separately in terms of three modes of expression. Two approaches to the path analysis were employed. The first, employed to test Hypothesis 4a, was to use all subjects, and the second, to test the interaction hypothesized in 4b, was to conduct separate paths for residents of small communities (less than 10,000 residents) and large communities (more than 10,000 residents).[1]

---

[1] The test for interactions between community size and congruity was done by segmenting the sample into two groups, residents of small and large communities. This approach was chosen to present the interaction term because in our causal model one component of the term (community size) precedes the other (congruity). Typically, the interaction can be placed in a path as a "real" variable only if its component parts are not. In our path analysis, however, congruity was included because of its integral contribution to the model. Hayduk and Wonnacott (1980) recommend for such cases that analysts segment the overall sample by levels of the interacting variable if the two resulting groups can be reasonably seen as representing two different systems at work.

The three exogenous variables were expected to affect self expression directly, and also to affect congruity directly, and expression thus indirectly. Year in school was included because it represents exposure to the relatively cosmopolitan atmo-sphere of the University of Wisconsin—Madison campus. Greater exposure to this environment might directly increase willingness of self-expression generally, and do so indirectly by affecting the aspects of congruity dependent on the climate of opinion.

Years lived in the hometown was expected to have differential effects in large as opposed to small hometowns. The longer one had lived in a small community, the more one would have been exposed to the small-town-homogeneous climate of opinion, and the less willing one would be to express oneself, in general. A related effect of small community atmosphere would be a greater desire to conform to the majority position, thus creating a direct path to congruity. We had no apriori theoretical expectations of this variable in the overall sample analyses, but included it for symmetry in our models.

Hometown size, the main variable of interest, was included for essentially the same reason as year in school was. Small hometowns, with their homogeneous climates of opinion, would be expected to inhibit self expression, and also affect congruity directly by making siding with the majority more likely. The reverse was expected from larger communities.

All three analyses were conducted for each issue and for each form of opinion expression, but for ease of presentation, and because the models are recursive, all three forms of opinion expression are included in each model. The basic path diagram looks like the following:

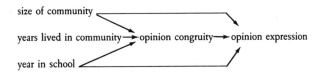

Hypothesis 4a. Considering first the overall samples, for pornography, only congruity, not size of the hometown community, predicts willingness to express opinions ($\beta=.14$, $p<.05$ for participating in a demonstration; $\beta=.17$, $p<.01$ for wearing a pin or button). Moreover, the directional relationship is as expected by the spiral of silence model in that one will be more likely to express oneself if one is in the majority. Again, hometown size has no direct effect on self expression, nor does it predict congruity. This, of course, does not rule out the possibility of an interaction between hometown size and congruity (the test of which is described here).

With the seat-belt issue, most path coefficients are summarily close to zero. The direct path between year in school and willingness to participate in a demonstra-tion (among residents of large communities) is the only significant path.

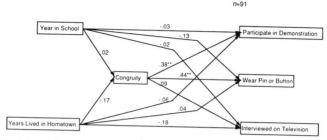

FIG. 6.1. Path analysis for the small hometown sample on the issue of pornography regulation (*$p < .05$, **$p < .01$).

Hypothesis 4b. As a comparison of Fig. 6.1 and 6.2 shows, for the issue of pornography the relationship between opinion congruity and willingness to participate in a demonstration is highly significant in the small community sample ($\beta = .37$, $p < .01$) and not significant in the large community sample ($\beta = .06$, n.s.). Similarly, the relationship between congruity and wearing a pin or button is significant in the small community sample ($\beta = .44$, $p < .01$) and not significant in the large-community sample ($\beta = .09$, n.s.). In both cases, the betas for the small-community samples are significantly greater than for the large-community samples ($t = 20.9$, $p < .01$ for willingness to engage in a demonstration; $t = 19.4$, $p < .01$ for willingness to wear a pin or button). Willingness to express opinions through a TV interview was not significantly predicted by opinion congruity in either the large or small community samples.

Although no other coefficients reach statistical significance, years lived in the hometown influences congruity ($\beta = -.17$) and willingness to be interviewed on TV ($\beta = -.18$) in the expected manner, in that the longer one has lived in a small hometown, the more one will want to side with the majority, and the less likely one will be to express oneself. Again, although these results are not significant, they are in the expected direction. The important conclusion, however, looking at congruity, is that there is a powerful interaction effect at work: In the small communi-

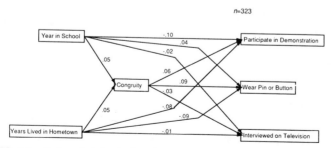

FIG. 6.2. Path analysis for the large hometown sample on the issue of pornography regulation.

n=91

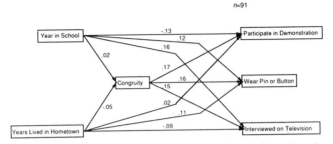

FIG. 6.3.   Path analysis for the small hometown sample on the issue of mandatory
seat belt use

n=323

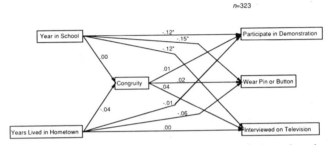

FIG. 6.4.   Path analysis for the large hometown sample on the issue of mandatory
seat-belt use (*p<.05).

ty, the more one is on the majority's side, the more likely one will be to express
oneself. These conclusions, moreover, do not hold for larger communities, in
which a heterogeneous climate of opinion legitimizes the expression of a wider
variety of opinion positions.

Looking at the seat-belt modes (Fig. 6.3, 6.4), we see no significant interactions
between perceived opinion congruity and community size. Instead, there is an
interaction between "year in school" and community size, with those individuals
absent from their (large) hometown community the longest less willing to express
opinions there. Conversely, although the path coefficients are not statistically
significant for the small-town sample, the opposite pattern is present; that is, those
respondents who have been absent from their (small) hometown community the
longest are more willing to express opinions there.

DISCUSSION

This study describes the application of two theoretical models of communication
and public opinion to the development of a theory of public opinion as a form of
social control, a social sanction that can be levied against individuals who do not

conform to majority opinion. First, the data indicate that individuals do indeed perceive differences in opinion climates. These perceived differences, in turn, have implications for individuals' willingness to express opinions publicly, especially those that may be unpopular in a particular reference group.

Evidence is quite clear that opinion expression is not a monolithic concept; general willingness to express opinions via a TV interview is greater than for wearing a pin or button which, in turn, is greater than for participating in a demonstration. Noelle-Neumann's model tends to explain significant amounts of variance for two forms of expression—wearing a pin or button and participating in a demonstration—but not participating in a TV interview. Thus, Noelle-Neumann's contention that "fear of isolation" is the mechanism that determines opinion expression is not fully supported with these results. The most potentially public form of expression—a TV interview—is the form of expression that is least responsive to the influence of an antagonistic climate of opinion. On the other hand, participation in a demonstration, in which one can maintain some semblance of anonymity depending on the circumstances, is the most responsive. This suggests that "fear of confrontation" may be a more compelling motivator than "fear of isolation," particularly on issues that arouse passions (i.e., the banning of pornography rather than the passage of a mandatory seat-belt law).

A second set of hypotheses was concerned with influences of structural variables on opinion expression. There was no significant main effect of community size on opinion expression. However, individuals from smaller communities were found to be less likely to express unpopular opinions in their communities than were residents of larger, more pluralistic communities.

Larger communities, by their nature, are characterized by greater diversity of points of view. The media, in performing a feedback-control function, portray this diversity or lack of consensus through the reporting of conflict. This, in turn, provides support for individuals who hold opinions that may be incongruent with the majority, but still held by others in the community. By downplaying community conflict in smaller communities, on the other hand, the media may create the illusion of a consensus where none actually exists, or they may be faithfully reflecting the greater homogeneity of the community. In either case, the appearance of consensus inhibits expression of minority opinions to a much greater degree than in larger communities.

These findings suggests the importance for public relations practitioners of being sensitive to environmental pressures on conformity, or at least to the reluctance of residents of small communities to speak against the perceived dominant opinion, for certain issues. Where an organization's position is congruent with the perceived majority opinion, communication efforts should actively reinforce this perception. On the other hand, in cases in which an organization's position is incongruent with the perceived dominant opinion, it is incumbent upon the organization to disrupt the consonance of media coverage of the dominant side and to demonstrate through pseudo-events or other tactics that individuals holding the minority opinion have social support and will not be ostracized. This is the theoretical rationale for demonstrations, rallies, and so on. This line of reasoning also suggests that a great deal of groundwork must be laid in terms of generating support for a candidate or issue position before staging public displays of support, particularly the types of displays of opinion that are inherently least attractive to individuals (i.e., demonstrations). To the extent that individuals feel that they have social support, they will be more likely to demonstrate their opinion publicly, thereby further strengthening the perception that their opinion is in the majority or at least gaining public support. Without prior coalition or consensus building (i.e., efforts to create a "community" or shared interest of supporters of a particular issue position,) an organization risks staging a public demonstration that will fail and accelerate a losing cause.

On the other hand, the formidable nature of opinion climates clearly is issue specific. That is, the impact of perceived opinion congruity appears to be much greater on newer, less involving issues (e.g., seat belt) than on more enduring and more involving or personal issues (e.g., pornography). In the absence of strong personal convictions or community norm regarding an issue, campaign planners and community relations specialists will likely be more able to overcome adverse opinion climates and to attract favorable media attention because the threat of open, rancorous conflict is not as great as more volatile issues (see Grunig & Hunt, 1984). Thus, new issue positions can be introduced and adopted in the small community, whereas conversion of attitudes on older, more involving issues will be greatly limited by prevailing opinion climates.

ACKNOWLEDGMENT

We are grateful to Kurt Neuwirth, doctoral candidate at the University of Wisconsin—Madison, for his assistance with this chapter.

REFERENCES

Bergen, L. (1986, May). *Testing the spiral of silence theory with opinions on abortion.* Paper presented at the annual meeting of the International Communication Association, Chicago, IL.

Bernays, E. L. (1923). *Crystallizing public opinion.* New York: Knopf.

Blumer, H. (1948). Public opinion and public opinion polling. *American Sociological Review, 13,* 542–554.

Donohue, G. A., Tichenor, P. J., & Olien, C. N. (1973). Mass media functions, knowledge and social control. *Journalism Quarterly, 50,* 652–659.

Edelstein, A., & Schulz, J. B. (1963). The weekly newspaper's leadership role as seen by community leaders. *Journalism Quarterly, 40,* 565–574.

Glynn, C., & McLeod, J. (1984). Public opinion du jour: An examination of the spiral of silence. *Public Opinion Quarterly, 48,* 731–740.

Glynn, C., & McLeod, J. (1985). Implications of the spiral of silence theory for communication and pubic opinion research. In K. Sanders, L. L. Kaid, & D. Nimmo (Eds.), *Political Communication Yearbook 1984* (pp. 43–65). Carbondale IL: Southern Illinois University Press.

Goldner, F. (1971, May). *Public opinion and survey research: A poor mix.* Paper presented at the annual meeting of the American Association for Public Opinion Research.

Grunig, J. E., & Hunt, T. (1984). *Managing public relations.* New York: Holt, Rinehart & Winston.

Hayduk, L. A., & Wonnacott, T. H. (1980). "Effect equations" or "effect coefficients": A note on the visual and verbal presentation of multiple regression interactions. *Canadian Journal of Sociology, 5*(4), 399–404.

Noelle-Neumann, E. (1973). Return to the concept of powerful mass media. *Studies of Broadcasting, 9,* 68–105.

Noelle-Neumann, E. (1974). The spiral of silence. *Journal of Communication, 24,* 43–51.

Noelle-Neumann, E. (1977). Turbulences in the climate of opinion. *Public Opinion Quarterly, 41,* 113–58.

Noelle-Neumann, E. (1979). Public opinion and the classical tradition. *Public Opinion Quarterly, 43,* 143–156.

Noelle-Neumann, E. (1981). Mass media and social change in developed societies. In E. Katz & T. Szecsko (Eds.), *Mass media and social change* (pp. 137–165). Beverly Hills, CA: Sage.

Noelle-Neumann, E. (1984). *The spiral of silence.* Chicago, IL: University of Chicago Press.

Olien, C. N., Donohue, G. A., & Tichenor, P. J. (1968). The community editor's power and the reporting of conflict. *Journalism Quarterly, 45,* 243–252.

Pavlik, J. V., & Salmon, C. T. (1984). Theoretic approaches in public relations research. *Public Relations Research & Education, 1*(2), 39–49.

Rucinski, D., Lee, H. R., & Salmon, C. T. (1987, Chicago). *Audience perceptions of media consonance.* Paper presented at the annual meeting of the Midwest Association for Public Opinion Research, Chicago, IL.

Salmon, C. T., & Kline, F. G. (1985). The spiral of silence ten years later: An examination and evaluation. In K. Sanders, L. L. Kaid, & D. Nimmo (Eds.), *Political communication yearbook 1984* (pp. 3–30). Carbondale IL: Southern Illinois University Press.

Salmon, C. T., & Neuwirth, K. (in press). Perceptions of opinion "climates" and willingness to discuss the issue of abortion. *Journalism Quarterly.*

Salmon, C. T. & Rucinski, D. (1988, May). *Fear of isolation from whom? Environmental cues and willingness to express opinions on controversial issues.* Paper presented at the annual meeting of the International Communication Association, New Orleans, LA.

Tichenor, P. J., Donohue, G. A., & Olien, C. N. (1973). Mass communication research: Evolution of a structural model. *Journalism Quarterly, 50,* 419–425.

Tichenor, P. J., Donohue, G. A., & Olien, C. N. (1980). *Community conflict and the press.* Beverly Hills: Sage.

Vidich, A. J., & Bensman, J. (1968). *Small town in mass society.* Princeton, NJ: Princeton University Press.

Chapter 7

Internal Communication and Job Satisfaction Revisited: The Impact of Organizational Trust and Influence on Commercial Bank Supervisors

J. David Pincus
California State University, Fullerton

Janice E. Knipp
Mitsubishi Bank

Robert E. Rayfield
California State University, Fullerton

The critical importance of communication to an organization's effectiveness has long been established by scholars, ranging from Barnard (1938), to Redding (1979), to Ruch and Goodman (1983). Unfortunately, most organizational communication research over the past four decades has been primarily descriptive in nature (Grunig, 1973; Richetto, 1977). Further, many of the most prominent studies have used such widely diverse instruments and methodologies as to be noncomparable (Pincus & Rayfield, 1989).

Some major studies in the past decade, however, have developed useful theoretically based research or validated standard research tools. Dennis (1974) contributed such a tool for the conceptualization and measurement of *communication climate*, a construct increasingly attracting the attention of organizational communication researchers. Dennis defined communication climate as:

> a subjectively experienced quality of the internal environment of the organization; the concept embraces a general cluster of inferred predispositions, identifiable through reports of members' perceptions of messages and message-related events, occurring in the organization. (p. 29)

The study reported here used Dennis' (1974) communication climate structure as the basis for investigating the relationship between communication climate and job satisfaction among supervisors of commercial banks in southern California.

173

This chapter discusses the implications of the results of this research effort from both conceptual and applied perspectives. First, prior literature on organizational and communication climates, and their relationship to job satisfaction, is reviewed. Second, the hypotheses that guided the study are forwarded. Third, the methodology is explained. Fourth, key results are presented. And finally, conceptual and practical implications of the findings are discussed, and several recommendations for future research are suggested.

ANALYSIS OF RELEVANT LITERATURE

Organizational Climate

Before focusing on the concept of communication climate, the broader construct from which it emanated—organizational climate—should be examined and understood.

Organizational climate has been defined and operationalized in a variety of ways. Generally speaking, however, organizational climate has been perceived as "a summative variable representing the individual's filtering of various stimuli impinging on him from the organization" (Knipp, 1985, p. 11), which is "assumed to influence motivation and behavior" (Litwin & Stringer, 1968, p. 143).

Inherent within the multiplicity of organizational climate characterizations are various combinations of direct communication or communication-related dimensions. For example, Litwin and Stringer (1968) identified the following dimensions of organizational climate: organizational structure, individual responsibility, warmth/support, rewards/punishment, conflict resolution, performance standards, and organizational identity. In contrast, Taylor and Bowers (1972) pinpointed a different series of dimensions, which included human resources primacy, communication flow, motivational climate, and upward influence. And Campbell, Dunnette, Lawler, and Weick (1970) included individual autonomy and support from superiors in their inventory of organizational climate dimensions.

However climate has been defined as a concept or operationalized as a variable, researchers have consistently attempted to understand and predict its effects on organizational members (Falcione & Werner, 1978). For example, in studies where climate was positioned as a dependent variable, perceptions of climate have been found to vary between types of employees (Litwin & Stringer, 1968), organizational levels (Porter & Lawler, 1965), and managers and assistant managers (Schneider & Bartlett, 1970). Where climate has been examined as an intervening variable, it has been linked to dependent variables, such as job satisfaction and job performance (Hellriegel & Slocum, 1974; Pritchard & Karasick, 1973). And as a predictor variable, organizational climate has been positively correlated with job satisfaction (Cawsey, 1973; Kaczka & Kirk, 1968) and job performance (Kaczka & Kirk, 1968).

Based on the thrust of organizational climate research, Campbell, Dunnette,

Lawler, and Weick (1970) argued the existence of "an inherent logic in the reasoning that the organization, as perceived by the individual, can exert influence over behavior" (pp. 385–386). A significant contributor to organizational climate is the multidimensional variable referred to as communication climate, which has not been adequately isolated and examined (Lawler, Hall, & Oldham, 1974), despite the fact that most organizational research instruments incorporate communication climate dimensions (Falcione & Werner, 1978).

Communication Climate

Communication climate has long been believed by researchers to contribute to organizational climate, and thus to measurable elements of management effectiveness (Likert, 1967). The concept has been variously defined as the pattern of how people communicate (Johnson, 1977), the degree to which individuals perceive organizational communication to be supportive (Schneider, Donaghy, & Newman, 1976), and as a subjective experience identified through members' perceptions of organizational messages (Dennis, 1974). Regardless of the particular definition, it is generally agreed that each employee has a perception of the quality of the environment within his or her organization—a perception constructed by personal evaluations of elements of communication within the organization. And, most researchers would agree, an important purpose of communication climate research is to be able to predict and influence organizational effectiveness. "Communication climate," according to Ireland, Van Auken, and Lewis (1978), "must be viewed as having an intimate relationship with patterns of organizational success" (p. 9).

Research on the factors composing communication climate over the past two decades has been infrequent, but enlightening. One of the earlier efforts was Gibb's (1961) identification of two communication climate types: the supportive/open climate, which facilitates effective message transmission and the defensive/closed climate, which impedes successful message transmission. A number of subsequent studies were conducted based on Gibb's work. Likert (1967) posited that the hierarchy above each work group forms a climate within which a lower level must function. He found that in the defensive/closed climate, where decisions are centralized at the top, motivation is low and communication is infrequent and distorted. DeCharms (1968) found that individuals want to change their organizational environments to be more supportive/open. Seventeen years after Gibb's research, Ireland et al. (1978) used Gibb's typology as a framework for illustrating the effects of various management behaviors on shaping different aspects of communication climate.

Several other, more focused attempts to define communication climate have been reported. Redding (1972) identified five dimensions of communication climate: supportiveness, participative decision making, trust, openness/candor, and emphasis on high performance goals. Building on Redding's work, Dennis (1974) pinpointed a somewhat varied set of five perceptual factors for supervisory personnel: superior–subordinate communication, quality and accuracy of downward communication, supervisor empathy with subordinates, quality and accuracy of upward communication, and information reliability. A number of other closely related communication climate typologies have surfaced over the years, such as Roberts and O'Reilly's (1974) 16-dimension climate measure, which incorporates both communication and noncommunication factors.

Thus, the concept of communication climate has been crafted and refined over time. Professionals and researchers alike seem to believe that employees who perceive the communication climate in their organizations in positive ways will likely develop positive perceptions toward their work and organizations. And evidence is emerging that management's actions can substantially influence employees' perceptions of communication climate (Kulhavy & Schwartz, 1981). Nevertheless, research to date presents an inadequate understanding of which communication actions by managers will most probably bring about desired results, such as greater employee job satisfaction.

Communication Climate and Job Satisfaction

Much communication climate-based research has focused on the relationship between various communication factors and job satisfaction, generally believed to be a desirable organizational objective. Job satisfaction, which has been the object of considerable organizational research, is the favorableness or unfavorableness with which employees view their work (Applebaum & Anatol, 1979). As a research construct, however, job satisfaction has been operationalized in a multiplicity of ways.

Wanous and Lawler (1972) examined nine different operational definitions of job satisfaction, distinguishing between overall job satisfaction measures and satisfaction with particular facets of the job. More recently, Richmond and McCroskey (1979) outlined three conceptualizations of job satisfaction research: (a) a global or one-factor approach, which is a general response to one's work environment (e.g., Ewen, Smith, Hulin, & Locke, 1966); (b) a two-factor theory comprised of motivators (e.g., recognition) that influence satisfaction, and hygiene factors (e.g., pay) that cause dissatisfaction (Herzberg, Mausner, & Snyderman, 1959); and (c) a multiple-factor approach in which each dimension represents a satisfaction–dissatisfaction continuum (e.g., Falcione, Daly, & McCroskey, 1977; Pincus, 1986; Wheeless, Wheeless, & Howard, 1982). Smith, Kendall, and Hulin (1969) first operationalized the multiple-factor approach. They isolated five dimensions of job satisfaction: supervision, the work itself, pay, promotion, and co-workers. Their Job Description Index (JDI) has been widely employed and adapted to job satisfaction research.

In their meta-research perspective of the body of communication-job satisfaction research, Pincus and Rayfield (1989) concluded that, despite varying definitions, instruments, and methodologies used in relevant research, "a positive, but complex relationship exists between employees' perceptions of various types of organizational communication and their perceived job satisfaction" (p. 27). An array of communication variables has been shown to be positively linked to job satisfaction, such as superior–subordinate communication (Jablin, 1977; Pincus, 1986; Plunkett, 1982), employee-centered leadership style (Richmond, Wagner, & McCroskey, 1983), information flow (Coan, 1984; Sussman, 1974; Weatherford, 1982), feedback (Ivancevich & McMahon, 1982; Pincus, 1986), and role perceptions (Schuler, 1979).

In studies where communication climate per se was related to job satisfaction, results have been mixed. Although Roberts and O'Reilly (1974) and Muchinsky (1977) found significantly positive results, Dennis' (1974) often cited study of insurance and automotive manufacturing supervisors reported only modestly positive and significant correlation results between each of five communication climate factors and job satisfaction. Only superior–subordinate communication correlated significantly with satisfaction with the "boss" and downward communication correlated significantly with overall satisfaction with the organization. Nevertheless, Dennis believed his limited significant findings suggested an important relationship between managerial communication and organizational effectiveness. Further, he was encouraged by the potential viability of his communication climate factor structure for future research:

> It is important to re-emphasize that the communication climate factor-structures of the two contrasting organizations were found to be nearly identical. This finding. . . certainly suggests that the communication climate measure may indeed have generalizability beyond the present research. (p. 54)

In a later study using Dennis' (1974) communication climate factors, Krivonos (1978) found among supervisors at two large manufacturing companies only slight support for the notion that intrinsically motivated individuals would perceive the communication climate as more open than those who are extrinsically motivated. The conclusion, then, is unavoidable: The viability of Dennis' communication climate construct and its relationship to organizational effectiveness measures, such as job satisfaction, remains unclear.

Hypotheses

This study, then, sought to clarify the communication climate–job satisfaction relationship using Dennis' (1974) communication climate construct as the predictor variable. Confirmation of the existence of this relationship via experimental and field research, allowing isolation of key variables, can bolster theory-building efforts. In addition, such information can provide vital data to managers and supervisors on how to increase employees' job satisfaction.

Two hypotheses were generated to guide this study, one designed to confirm the existence of a positive relationship between organizational communication and job satisfaction and the other to investigate the varying degrees of influence of different communication factors.

H1: Employees' perceptions of communication climate will be positively and significantly ($<.05$) correlated with their job satisfaction.

This hypothesis was predicated on the largely consistent pattern of communication–job satisfaction research (see Pincus & Rayfield, 1989). However, this prediction takes on added importance in light of Dennis' (1974) and Krivonos' (1978) relatively weak results using Dennis' five-factor communication climate measure.

H2: Among the communication climate factors, employees' perceptions of superior–subordinate communication will account for the greatest amount of variance in their job satisfaction.

A growing body of research has strongly argued that an employee's communication relationship with his or her immediate supervisor may play *the* major role in predicting that employee's job satisfaction (see Falcione et al., 1977; Jablin, 1977; Pincus, 1986). Therefore, of Dennis' five communication factors (superior–subordinate communication, downward accuracy, supervisor empathy, upward influence, information reliability), superior–subordinate communication was expected to be the strongest influence on job satisfaction.

METHODOLOGY

This survey and analysis sought to validate Dennis' (1974) communication climate instrument and test the relationship between perceptions of communication climate and job satisfaction of supervisory employees in a field not previously examined, the banking industry. The Dennis model is particularly useful. It outlines communication climate as encompassing significant organizational people (superiors, subordinates, peers), significant organizational groups (management and work groups), as well as the organization as a whole.

The banking industry is particularly interesting to investigate at this time. Recent deregulation has created an increased competitive marketplace for banks. As a result, many banks have undergone a flurry of bank closings, increased centralized control and a dwindling of middle management (Nadler, 1985). These industry disturbances have inevitably affected the communication environment within bank cultures. It should be useful to professionals and researchers in the communication and banking fields to better understand how these changes are impacting on communication climate, and subsequently job satisfaction. This study should be especially valuable to an industry that, despite its growing awareness of communication's importance, still has segments that do not see it as a management function (Vinson, 1978).

Sample

From a list of the 68 commercial banks existing in Orange County, California, in the spring of 1985, 13 were selected via a systematic random-sampling procedure. All 13 banks agreed to participate in the study. Among those banks, 137 supervisory personnel were identified and 98 of those subjects returned usable questionnaires, representing a 71% response rate.

Predictor Variable: Communication Climate

The predictor, or independent, variable in this study was perceptions of communication climate, as outlined in Dennis' (1974) model. It was slightly modified to control for response set by randomly reversing questions. In addition, several questions concerned with top management communication, based on those used by Pincus (1984), were added. The questionnaire was structured to measure perceptions of superior–subordinate communication (21 questions), reliability of organization information (12 questions, 3 of which related to top management), supervisors' empathy for subordinates (5 questions), upward communication and influence (5 questions), and reliability of information from subordinates and peers (2 questions). Possible responses were along a 5-point Likert scale ranging from "strongly agree" to "strongly disagree," with "neutral" as the midpoint.

Criterion Variable: Job Satisfaction

The criterion, or dependent, variable was job satisfaction, based on Taylor and Bowers' (1972) instrument and used by Dennis (1974). One question each examined: compatibility with fellow employees; adequacy of immediate supervisor; satisfaction with job as a whole; effectiveness of the organization; and satisfaction with economic rewards. Two questions addressed satisfaction with present and future progress within the organization. Possible responses were along a 5-point Likert scale ranging from "very satisfied" to "very dissatisfied."

The questionnaire was pretested among 30 supervisors at two banks in Orange County not included in the sample. The minor changes recommended by the participants were incorporated.

Data Collection

Each subject was given a blank questionnaire accompanied by a cover letter explaining the identification of the researcher, guaranteeing confidentiality, outlining the purpose of the survey, and providing necessary instructions. Question-naires were completed by individuals during work hours. In three cases, managers requested that participants complete them during preset on-site group sessions. All completed questionnaires were deposited in sealed drop boxes placed in each bank.

RESULTS

The analysis of data sought to explain the relationship between supervisors' per-ceptions of their communication climate and job satisfaction and to explore the viability of Dennis' (1974) five-factor communication climate construct frame-work. Factor analysis, correlation analysis, and multiple regression analysis were employed to test the hypotheses.

Reliability of Instruments

Crobach's alpha was used to measure the internal consistency of the communica-tion climate and job-satisfaction scales. Both scales were found to be highly reli-able, based on Carmines and Zeller's (1979) guideline that reliabilities for widely used scales should be near .80. The communication climate scale had a Cron-bach's alpha of .93 and the job satisfaction scale was .79.

Factor Analysis: Comparison With Dennis

Factor analysis (principal factoring with iteration and varimax rotation) was used to compare the communication climate factors generated in this study with those derived by Dennis (1974). Results revealed partial replication of Dennis' factor loadings—three of the five factor domains mirrored Dennis' findings, whereas two new factors were formed. These new factors might be accounted for by differences across industries or by changes in employees' values and communication needs since Dennis' (1974) study.

The three factors remaining similar to Dennis' findings were superior–subordi-nate communication, supervisor empathy with subordinates, and information relia-bility. However, the items comprising Dennis' upward influence factor combined with some items of his downward accuracy factor to form a new factor, which we labeled *organizational trust and influence*. These items reflected employees' con-cerns with their perceptions of their organization as a whole and top management, and their ability to influence organizational decisions affecting the workplace.

A second new factor identified in this study, called *information satisfaction*, drew strength from the remaining items in Dennis' downward accuracy factor. These items revealed employees' satisfaction with information about the organiza-tion and their immediate work environment. Table 7.1 depicts the communication

TABLE 7.1
Communication Climate Factors

Dennis (1974)	Pincus, Knipp, and Rayfield (this chapter)
Superior–subordinate communication	Superior–subordinate communication
Downward accuracy	Organizational trust and influence
Supervisor empathy with subordinates	Supervisor empathy with subordinates
Upward influence	Information satisfaction
Information reliability	Information reliability

climate factors from both this and Dennis' (1974) studies. Table 7.4 (see later) details the factor-item loadings in this study.

The two new factors identified in this study appear to reflect contemporary trends revealed by recent research efforts. The essence of the items forming these factors emphasizes the increasing importance of organizational members' desire for an opportunity to participate in and influence organization decisions (see meta-analytic review in Miller & Monge, 1986), and members' desire for more open, trusting communication with top management (Pincus & Rayfield, 1986).

This new set of communication climate factors—superior–subordinate communication, organizational trust and influence, information satisfaction, supervisor empathy with subordinates, and information reliability—was used as the basis for subsequent statistical analyses.

Correlation Analysis: Communication Climate and Job Satisfaction

Pearson product-moment correlation analysis was performed to test the efficacy of Hypothesis 1, which predicted that perceptions of communication climate will be positively and significantly correlated with job satisfaction. Hypothesis 1 was, for the most part, supported. Four of the five communication climate factors were positively correlated with job satisfaction at $p < .05$; only supervisor empathy with subordinates was not statistically significant.

The strongest correlation between job satisfaction and the communication factors examined in this study was with organizational trust and influence ($.55$, $p = .001$). Similarly strong associations were also found with superior–subordinate communication ($.46$, $p = .001$) and information satisfaction ($.35$, $p = .001$). Table 7.2 contains complete results.

Interestingly, these strongly supportive results are substantially different from Dennis' (1974) findings. He reported extremely weak, nonsignificant relationships between the five communication climate factors and job satisfaction (see Table

TABLE 7.2
Pearson Correlation Analysis: Communication Climates and Job Satisfaction,
1974 vs. 1985

Dennis (1974)			Pincus, Knipp, & Rayfield (this chapter)
Superior–subordinate communication	.02	.46 ($p = .001$)	Superior–subordiante communication
Downward accuracy	−.02	.55 ($p = .001$)	Organizational trust & influence
Supervisor empathy w/subordinates	.02	.12	Supervisor empathy w/subordinates
Upward influence	.05	.35 ($p = .001$)	Information satisfaction
Information reliability	.03	.27 ($p = .004$)	Information reliability

7.2). He suggested that his disappointing findings might have been due to a deficiency in the criterion measure itself or the inherent weakness in one-time data-collection studies. In order to further compare this study's results with Dennis', another correlation analysis using Dennis' 1974 factor loadings and job satisfaction scores of respondents in this sample was done. Results revealed that three of Dennis' factors correlated positively and significantly with job satisfaction: downward accuracy (.51, $p = .001$), superior–subordinate communication (.46, $p = .001$), and upward influence (.47, $p = .001$). This finding may be attributable to the nature of the sample, the different industries under study, or may reflect more fundamental underlying changes in employees' preferences/expectations.

Not surprisingly, the superior–subordinate communication factor was positively and significantly related to job satisfaction, as prior studies have consistently shown (e.g., Jablin, 1979; Pincus & Rayfield, 1989). Somewhat less expected, however, was the strong relationship between job satisfaction and the downward accuracy and upward influence factors. Items from these factors combined to shape the new factor, organizational trust and influence, which was found to be the predominant influence in both correlation and multiple regression analyses (see next section). This seems to suggest that employees' perceptions of their ability to participate in meaningful two-way communication with top-level management may rival immediate supervisor communication as a meaningful predictor of job satisfaction.

In summary, Hypothesis 1—that perceptions of communication climate will be positively and significantly correlated with job satisfaction—was strongly supported via correlation analysis. More specifically, results indicated that employees' views of communication with their immediate supervisors and top managers, as well as their ability to participate in the organizational decision-making process, is strongly associated with their work satisfaction.

Regression: The Influence of Superior–Subordinate Communication

Hypothesis 2 stated that perceptions of superior–subordinate communication will account for the greatest variance in job satisfaction. Because of the likelihood that the communication climate factors are highly correlated with each other, stepwise multiple regression analysis was used to test this hypothesis. The stepwise form of multiple regression determines if the last-entered variable should be retained in the equation or eliminated because it is highly correlated with a subsequently entered variable (Green, 1978).

Overall, about 40% of the variance in overall job satisfaction was explained by the five factors comprising communication climate (r-square $= .405$, adjusted r-square $= .371, p = .001$). Hypothesis 2 was only partially supported. Contrary to predictions, the strongest contributor to job satisfaction was organizational trust and influence, which accounted for almost three-fourths of the variance (r-square $= .287, p = .001$). The second most influential factor was superior–subordinate communication, which combined additively with organizational trust and influence to explain most of the variance in overall job satisfaction (r-square $= .377, p = .001$). Table 7.3 contains complete results.

Although Hypothesis 2 was not confirmed completely, the multiple regression

TABLE 7.3
Stepwise Multiple Regression*: Communication Climate Factors
and Job Satisfaction

Comm. Climate	Mult R	R-Square	Overall F	P-Value
Organizatonal trust and influence (and)	.53	.29	36.65	.001
Superior–subordinate communication (and)	.61	.37	27.30	.001
Information satisfaction (and)	.62	.39	18.85	.001
Information reliability (and)	.62	.40	14.44	.001
Supervisor empathy with subordinates	.63	.41	11.85	.001

*Due to high correlations among the variables, stepwise multiple regression was used because it considers each variable one at a time and determines its value to the equation additively.

results reinforced the correlation analysis, which highlighted the powerful relationship of organizational trust and influence, and superior–subordinate communication, with job satisfaction. These results suggest that the influence of employees' perceptions of communication with immediate supervisors on job satisfaction remains strong, as predicted in Hypothesis 2. A slightly modified picture
emerged in this study, however. A new factor, organizational trust and influence—
which encompasses employees' perceptions of top-level management's communication practices and employees' role in important organization decisions—appears to also positively and definitively impact worker satisfaction, according to
results from this study.

DISCUSSION

This study of 98 supervisory personnel representing 13 commercial banking organizations examined the relationship among various organizational communication
factors and job satisfaction. The results provided insights into the importance of
employees' perceptions of the communication climate in their organizations on
their job satisfaction. The following discussion highlights some of the implications
of these findings and relates them to prior research efforts.

Communication–Job Satisfaction Link.   Results confirmed, in a general sense,
the long-held notion that positively perceived organizational communication is
positively and significantly related to job satisfaction (Downs, 1979; Pincus &
Rayfield, 1989). In this case, a five-factor communication climate construct, mod-
eled after Dennis' (1974) factor structures, revealed strong support via correlation
and multiple regression analyses for the existence of a definitive association between communication climate and job satisfaction. Previous research has encompassed many different types of organizations; however, whether these results are
unique to this particular banking organization or banks in general will require
additional research among bank employees.

On a micro-level, the data analysis revealed a substantially positive link between
organizational trust and influence, a newly formed factor, and superior–subordinate
communication, which was, based on prior research, hypothesized to be the most
influential factor (Jablin, 1979; Muchinsky, 1977; Pincus, 1986). Moderately
positive and significant relationships were also found between the information
satisfaction and information reliability factors and job satisfaction.

Influence of Top Management Communication.   An especially interesting,
consistent finding in this study was that the major contributor to supervisors' job
satisfaction was their communication with top management and their ability to
influence workplace decisions—not their communication with immediate supervisors. Although superior–subordinate communication was found to be a strong

influence on employees' job satisfaction, it was not *the* most powerful influence, as was originally predicted.

In contrast, the communication factor that accounted for most of the explained variance in job satisfaction, organizational trust and influence, did not surface as an independent factor in Dennis' study (1974). This unexpected result may signal subtle shifts in employees' workplace values and motivations since Dennis' study in 1974, as well as changes in what they expect from communication with manage-ment at different organizational levels. Indeed, recent studies have reported an increasingly significant influence of employees' perceptions of top management on job satisfaction and job performance (Petelle & Garthright-Petelle, 1985; Pincus & Rayfield, 1986; Ruch & Goodman, 1983).

The emergence of the power of employees' views of upper-level management in explaining organizational effectiveness measures does not, as Pincus (1986) ar-gued, "necessarily diminish the importance of the employee-immediate supervisor communication" (p. 414), but may suggest that employees today are more aware of and want to increase their active participation within the organizational system.

Beyond the Superior–Subordinate Relationship. Results from this study, which are based on supervisory personnel only, suggest that as individuals rise in the organizational hierarchy and get closer to the top, their desire for communica-tion with top management may increase. Concomitantly, the importance that supervisors' attach to communication with their immediate supervisors may drop off accordingly. For instance, in Pincus' (1986) study of hospital nurses, most of whom were not supervisors, despite the strong influence of perceptions of top management communication, immediate supervisor communication was neverthe-less the most significant contributor to job satisfaction and job performance. In this study, superior–subordinate communication was, as anticipated, a substantial ex-planatory force, yet organizational trust and influence accounted for most of the explained variance in job satisfaction.

This finding might be accounted for by natural and normal differences between managers and nonmanagers. As organizational members assume more supervisory responsibilities, their self-perceptions, ambitions, and general view of the organiza-tion may change. Their need for direct supervision may lessen. Their desire to participate in decisions (Miller & Monge, 1986) that influence the organization and thereby impress their superiors may increase. Their management role may require that they receive more and have greater access to information about the organization as a whole—information that frequently emanates from top-level management.

The implication for organizational decision makers is that they must develop and implement more effective two-way communication mechanisms that allow supervisors to offer input and feedback regularly to top-level management. To deter supervisors' initiative in becoming more involved and feeling greater ownership in the organizational system could severely reduce job satisfaction and performance.

Bank Communication Strategies. Findings in this study may reflect some of the changes occurring within the banking industry in particular, and service industries in general, that could affect management's creation of the most appropriate organizational communication strategies. For example, deregulation of the banking industry has substantially altered the organizational structure and concerns of banks. Increasing emphasis on cost efficiency in a highly competitive marketplace has contributed to more frequent branch closings, an increase in centralization and a flatter organizational structure as middle managers become obsolete (Nadler, 1985). As a result, supervisors, located at far-flung branch offices and perhaps feeling increasingly isolated from their bank's headquarters, seem to want top management to play a more active and substantive role in shaping the organization's communication climate. In this service-intensive industry, if bank personnel, both supervisors and employees, are not well informed and do not feel positive about their work, such negative attitudes can damage their regular contact with customers.

FUTURE RESEARCH RECOMMENDATIONS

As a one-shot study of supervisors at banks located in one metropolitan area in the United States, results from this study cannot be generalized widely. Nevertheless, this research effort uncovered a number of areas that demand further exploration:

1. The factor structures comprising the communication climate construct differed somewhat from Dennis' (1974) original factor loadings. Are these factor variations due to differences across industries or more permanent differences in supervisors' communication needs? How stable are these factors over time? Only application of these instruments to other diverse populations can provide such answers.

2. This study, as have several others recently, has shed light on the emerging importance of employees' communication with top management and employees' desire to take a more active role in workplace decisions. However, the number of studies that have investigated this area are relatively few. Clearly, more studies should be focused on the contribution of top management communication, and organizational trust and influence, in addition to the more traditional communication factors (e.g., superior–subordinate communication), to job satisfaction and job performance.

3. This study and Dennis' (1974) study incorporated supervisory personnel only. Based on some comparisons between these results and other studies of either nonsupervisors or a mix of supervisors and nonsupervisors, different communication factors may be most influential on job satisfaction. To more closely examine

TABLE 7.4
Communication Climate Factor Loadings

No.	Title	Loading
	Factor I: Superior–Subordinate Communication	
1	Supervisor makes you feel free to talk with him.	.83
2	Super really understands your job problems.	.77
3	Super wants you to let him know when things go wrong.	.77
4	Super makes it easy for you to do your best work.	.79
5	Super expresses confidence in your ability to do job.	.75
6	Super encourages you to bring new info. even when bad.	.71
7	Super makes you feel things you tell him are important.	.75
8	Super tolerates argument, fair hearing to all views.	.75
9	Super has your interests in mind when he talks to boss.	.79
10	Super is a competent, expert manager.	.72
11	Super listens when you tell things that bother you.	.77
12	It is safe to say what you really think to your Super.	.70
13	Super is really frank and candid with you.	.50
14	You can "sound off" about frustrations to your Super.	.57
15	You can tell Super how you think he manages work group.	.64
16	You are free to tell your Super you disagree with him.	.74
17	You can tell "bad news" to Super without fear of retaliation.	.65
18	You think your Super *believes* he really understands you.	.56
20	Your Super really understands you.	.74
21	You really understand your Super.	.57
40	Your Super lets you participate in planning your work.	.47
	Factor II: Two-Way Organizational Trust and Influence	
22	People in Co. say what they mean & mean what they say.	.59
23	People in Co. encouraged to be open and candid.	.75
24	People in Co. can freely exchange info. & opinions.	.61
26	Your Co. rewards and praises good performance.	.60
30	Top Management says what it means & means what it says.	.60
31	You get advance notice of changes that affect your job.	.41
32	You are sat. with Top Mgt. explan. why things are done.	.75
35	You believe co-workers are frank & candid with you.	.32
39	Your opinions matter in daily decisions about your job.	.52
41	Members of your work group estab. their own goals & objs.	.39
42	Your views have a real influence in your organization.	.78
43	Your recommendations are seriously heard & considered.	.71
	Factor III: Information Satisfaction	
25	You're kept informed on how Co. goals & objs. are met.	.84
27	Top Mgt. provides you information you really need.	.77
28	You receive information from preferred sources.	.41
29	You're pleased Mgr. keeps employees informed on welfare.	.80
33	Your job requirements are specified in clear language.	.51

(continued)

TABLE 7.4   (Continued)

No.	Title	Loading
	Factor IV: Supervisor Empathy with Subordinates	
34	You believe subordinates are frank and candid with you.	.42
36	Your subords. tell you what is bothering them.	.67
37	You really understand your subordinates' problems.	.67
38	Your subordinates *think* you understand their problems.	.78
	Factor V: Information Reliability	
44	Info. received from your subordinates is reliable.	.41
45	You think information from your co-workers is reliable.	.65
19	You believe your Supervisor *thinks* you understand him.	−.33

this question, studies with organizational members from different organizational levels are needed.

REFERENCES

Applebaum, R. L., & Anatol, K. W. E. (1979). The relationships among job satisfaction, organizational norms and communication climate. *Journal of Applied Communication Research, 2,* 83–90.

Barnard, C. I. (1938). *The functions of the executive.* London: Cambridge University Press.

Campbell, J., Dunnette, M., Lawler, E. E., & Weick, K. (1970). *Managerial performance and effectiveness.* New York: McGraw-Hill.

Carmines, E. G., & Zeller, R. A. (1979). *Reliability and validity assessment.* Beverly Hills, CA: Sage.

Cawsey, T. (1973, April). *The interaction of motivation and environment in the prediction of performance potential and satisfaction in the life insurance industry of Canada.* Paper presented to the Midwest Academy of Management, Chicago, IL.

Coan, R. T. (1984). *A field-experimental study of the relationship between opportunity for upward communication and facets of job satisfaction.* Unpublished doctoral dissertation, Ohio State University, Columbus, OH.

DeCharms, R. (1968). *Personal causation: The internal affective determinants of behavior.* New York: Academic Press.

Dennis, H. (1974). *A theoretical and empirical study of managerial communication climate in complex organizations.* Unpublished doctoral dissertation, Department of Communication, Purdue University, West Lafayette, IN.

Downs, C. W. (1979). The relationship between communication and job satisfaction. In R. Huseman, C. M. Logue, & D. L. Freshley (Eds.) *Readings in Interpersonal and Organizational Communication* (3rd ed., pp. 363–376). Boston: Allyn & Bacon.

Ewen, R. B., Smith, P. C., Hulin, C. L., & Locke, E. A. (1966). An empirical test of the Herzberg two-factor theory. *Journal of Applied Psychology, 50,* 544–550.

Falcione, R. L., Daly, J. A., & McCroskey, J. C. (1977). Job satisfaction as a function of employees' communication apprehension, self-esteem, and perceptions of their immediate supervisors. In B. D. Ruben (Ed.) *Communication Yearbook I* (pp. 363–375). New Brunswick, NJ: Transaction Books.

Falcione, R. L., & Werner, E. (1978, May). *Organizational climate and communication climate: A state of the art.* Paper presented to the International Communication Association, Chicago, IL.

Gibb, J. R. (1961). Defensive communication. *Journal of Communication, 11,* 141–48.

Green, P. E. (1978). *Analyzing multivariate data.* Hinsdale, IL: Dryden Press.

Grunig, J. E. (1973, May). *Information seeking in organizational communication: A case study of applied theory.* Paper presented to the International Communication Association, Montreal, Canada.

Hellriegel, D., & Slocum, J. W., Jr. (1974). Organizational climate: Measures of research and contingencies. *Academy of Management Journal, 17,* 244–280.

Herzberg, F., Mausner, B., & Snyderman, B. (1959). *The Motivation to work* (2nd ed.). New York: Wiley.

Ireland, R. D., Van Auken, P. M., & Lewis, P. V. (1978). An investigation of the relationships between organizational climate and communication climate. *Journal of Business Communication, 16,* 1, 3–10.

Ivancevich, J. M., & McMahon, J. T. (1982). The effects of goal setting, external feedback and self-generated feedback on outcome variables: A field experiment. *Academy of Management Journal, 25,* 359–372.

Jablin, F. M. (1977). *An experimental study of message-response in superior–subordinate communication.* Unpublished doctoral dissertation, Department of Communication, Purdue University, West Lafayette, IN.

Jablin, F. M. (1979). Superior–subordinate communication: The state of the art. *Psychological Bulletin, 86,* 1201–1222.

Johnson, B. M. (1977). *Communication: The process of organizing.* Boston: Allyn & Bacon.

Kaczka, E., & Kirk, R. (1968). Managerial climate, work groups and organizational performance. *Administrative Science Quarterly, 12,* 252–271.

Knipp, J. E. (1985). *The impact of communication climate perceptions on job satisfaction: A survey of Orange County commercial banks.* Unpublished master's thesis, California State University, Fullerton, CA.

Krivonos, P. D. (1978). Relationship of intrinsic-extrinsic motivation and communication climate in organizations. *Journal of Business Communication, 15,* 4, 53–65.

Kulhavy, R. W., & Schwartz, N. H. (1981). Tone of communication and climate perception. *Journal of Business Communication, 18*(1), 17–23.

Lawler, E. E., Hall, D. E., & Oldham, G. R. (1974). Organizational climate: Relationship to organizational structure, process and performance. *Organizational Behavior and Human Performance, 11,* 139–55.

Likert, R. (1967). *The human organization: Its management and value.* New York: McGraw-Hill.

Litwin, G. H., & Stringer, R. A. (1986). *Motivation and organizational climate.* Boston: Harvard University Press.

Miller, K. I., & Monge, P. R. (1986). Participation, satisfaction and productivity: A meta-analytic review. *Academy of Management Journal, 29,* 727–753.

Muchinsky, P. M. (1977). Organizational and communication relationship to organizational climate and job satisfaction. *Academy of Management Journal, 20,* 592–607.

Nadler, P. S. (1985). Deregulation: Coping in a new environment. *Bankers Monthly, 102* (1), 11–13.

Petelle, J. L., & Garthright-Petelle, K. (1985, May). *Task characteristics, structural characteristics, organizational relationships and communication processes: A contingency approach to job performance, phase III.* Paper presented to the International Communication Association, Honolulu, HI.

Pincus, J. D. (1984). *The impact of communication satisfaction on job satisfaction and job performance: A field study of hospital nurses.* Unpublished doctoral dissertation, University of Maryland, College Park, MD.

Pincus, J. D. (1986). Communication satisfaction, job satisfaction and job performance. *Human Communication Research, 12*(3), 395–419.

Pincus, J. D., & Rayfield, R. E. (1986, August). *The relationship between top management communication and organizational effectiveness.* Paper presented to the Association for Education in Journalism and Mass Communication, Norman, OK.

Pincus, J. D., & Rayfield, R. E. (1989). Organizational communication and job satisfaction: A meta research perspective. In B. Dervin & M. J. Voight (Eds.), *Progress in communication sciences* (Vol. 9, pp. 183–208). Norwood, NJ: Ablex.

Plunkett, E. A. (1982). *A study of the relationship between superior-subordinate communication and job satisfaction.* Unpublished doctoral dissertation, Georgia State University, Atlanta, GA.

Porter, L., & Lawler, E. (1965). Properties of organization structure in relation to job attitude and job behavior. *Psychological Bulletin, 41,* 23–51.

Pritchard, R., & Karasick, B. (1973). The effects of organizational climate on managerial job performance and job satisfaction. *Organizational Behavior and Human Performance, 9,* 110–119.

Redding, W. C. (1972). *Communication within the organization: An interpretive review of theory and research.* New York: Industrial Communication Council.

Redding, W. C. (1979). Organizational communication theory and ideology: An overview. In D. Nimmo (Ed.), *Communication Yearbook 3* pp. 309–334). New Brunswick, NJ: Transaction Books.

Richetto, G. M. (1977). Organizational communication theory and research: An overview. In B. D. Ruben (Ed.), *Communication Yearbook 1* (pp. 331–346). New Brunswick, NJ: Transaction Books.

Richmond, V. P., & McCroskey, J. C. (1979). Management, communication style, tolerance for disagreement and innovativeness as predictors of employee satisfaction: A comparison of single factor, two-factor and multiple factor approaches. In J. D. Nimmo (Ed.), *Communication Yearbook 3* (pp. 359–374). New Brunswick, NJ: Transaction Books.

Richmond, V. P., Wagner, J. P., & McCroskey, J. C. (1983). The impact of perceptions of leadership style, use of power and conflict management style on organizational outcomes. *Communication Quarterly, 31*(1), 27–36.

Roberts, K., & O'Reilly, C. (1974). Measuring organizational communication. *Journal of Applied Psychology, 59*, 321–326.

Ruch, R. S., & Goodman, R. (1983). *Image at the top.* New York: The Free Press.

Schneider, B., & Bartlett, C. (1970). Individual differences and organizational climate: Measurement of organizational climate by multi-trait matrix. *Personnel Psychology, 23*, 493–512.

Schneider, A. E., Donaghy, W. C., & Newman, P. J. (1976). Communication climate within organizations. *Management Controls, 23*, 159–162.

Schuler, R. S. (1979). A role perception transactional process model for organizational communication-outcome relationships. *Organizational Behavior and Human Performance, 23*, 168–191.

Smith, P. C., Kendall, L. M., & Hulin, C. L. (1969). *The measurement of job satisfaction in work and retirement.* Chicago: Rand McNally.

Sussman, L. (1974). The relationship between message distortion and job satisfaction: A field study. *Journal of Business Communication, 11*(4), 25–29.

Taylor, J. C., & Bowers, D. G. (1972). *Survey of organizations.* Ann Arbor, MI: Institute for Social Research, University of Michigan.

Vinson, B. F. (1978). Effective communication of corporate policies and objectives. In W. H. Baughn & C. E. Walker (Eds.), *Bankers handbook* (pp. 86–97). Homewood, IL: Dow Jones-Irwin.

Wanous, J. P., & Lawler, E. E. (1972). Measurement and meaning of job satisfaction. *Journal of Applied Psychology, 56*, 95–105.

Weatherford, S. W. (1982). *Communication, job satisfaction and organizational commitment in the hospital environment.* Unpublished doctoral dissertation, University of Georgia, Athens, GA.

Wheeless, L. R., Wheeless, V. E., & Howard, R. D. (1982, May). *The relationship of communication-related variables to employee satisfaction: Communication with supervisor vs. decision participation.* Paper presented to the International Communication Association, Boston, MA.

Chapter 8

Involvement: A Key Variable in People's Reaction to Public Policy Issues

Robert L. Heath
William Douglas
University of Houston

One widely researched aspect of communication focuses on how people receive and process information and evaluation to form opinion and become disposed to behavior. One explanation of this process features the concept of involvement, the extent to which personal interest serves as an incentive to receive new information and compare it to previously held information to form an opinion toward an object, situation, or issue (Cacioppo, Harkins, & Petty, 1981; Cialdini, Petty, & Cacioppo, 1981; Petty & Cacioppo, 1981, 1986a; Petty, Cacioppo, & Schumann, 1983; Petty, Kasmer, Haugtvedt, & Cacioppo, 1987; Sherif, Sherif, & Nebergall, 1965; Wright, 1980).

The theory defines *cognitive response* as "a unit of information pertaining to an object or issue that is the result of cognitive processing" (Cacioppo et al., 1981, p. 37). A central issue of involvement theory is whether people desire to learn more about topics in which they are personally involved. One line of analysis argues that involvement lessens the desire to receive new information on an involving issue (Sherif et al., 1965). In contrast, others have argued that as personal interest increases so does issue-relevant thought (Petty & Cacioppo, 1981, 1986a). People respond self-interestedly to situational factors (Grunig, 1987b) and use existing information to evaluate that advocated by advertisements (Wright, 1973, 1974).

Believing that involvement increases the incentive to learn new information, Grunig (1987a) advised public relations practitioners to target active and involved publics, even those that are critical of corporate actions. Active publics are more likely than their passive counterparts to seek and process information on public policy issues that companies address. Grunig focused his advice: "I advocate symmetrical dialogues with active publics engaged in the debate" (p. 32). This advice is reinforced by Winters (1988) who reported that a Chevron Corporation corporate advertising campaign affected the opinions and buying behavior of "unfavorables" more than "favorables." The campaign featured discussions of what Chevron does to solve environmental problems. The "unfavorables" were particularly sensitive ("involved") to this ad claim because of their environmental consciousness. The ads may have been influential because they specified the steps Chevron was taking rather than merely asserting its commitment to corporate social responsibility. Not only did the ads improve the "unfavorables'" attitudes toward Chevron, but they also increased buying preference of Chevron products.

People become activists as their involvement increases because they recognize that their personal interest is at stake and that only by acting collectively can they alleviate a problem (Grunig, 1987b). Willingness to be involved with environmental issues is predicted more by the personal interests people see in the issues than by their education level or socioeconomic status (Donohue, Tichenor, & Olien, 1975). Involvement is increased when problem recognition is high and constraints against activism are low. Examples of constraints that limit activism are loss of job or difficulty in getting information (Grunig & Hunt, 1984). High involvement motivates information seeking, for instance on a health-related topic. When situations produce little involvement, behavior is likely to be a product of situational constraints rather than attitude or knowledge. Perceived risk produces erratic relationships among knowledge, attitude, and belief and does not always lead to a desire for more knowledge (Chaffee & Roser, 1986).

Petty and Cacioppo (1986b) argued that attitude use follows a development model. It progresses from simple positive or negative associations to the point where "the formation and change of some attitudes become very thoughtful processes in which issue-relevant information is carefully scrutinized and evaluated in terms of existing knowledge" (p. 131). For this reason, involvement research has acknowledged that individuals use different cognitive processes depending on the extent of personal interest.

This line of inquiry led to the development of Petty and Cacioppo's Elaboration Likelihood Model (ELM) (Petty et al., 1983). As described by this model, information processing and attitude change can result either from *central* or *peripheral* cognitive processes. Central processes require diligent and careful analysis of information, whereas peripheral processes depend on positive or negative associations between the object and other stimuli (such as a soft drink ad associating the product with enjoyable scenes) or a high credibility source. Peripheral processes are not careful and diligent, and central processes are significantly less dependent on positive or negative associations or source credibility. When people lack knowledge they rely on peripheral cues (Wood, Kalgren, & Preisler, 1985).

As well as discussing the cognitive processes used to assess complex and simple arguments, Petty and Cacioppo (1986a) claimed that involvement theory explains (a) attitude discrepant behavior; (b) comprehensive learning, retention, and recall of issue relevant messages; (c) idiosyncratic responses to attitudes; and (d) information integration and evaluation. Attitude change via the central route is relatively enduring and predictive of behavior. Peripheral processes occur when individuals have not personally studied the information and draw upon positive or negative associations with the object, the situation in which they learned about it, or about the source of information. ELM, its supporters have reasoned, can account for situations where individuals have or seek substantial amounts of information to make decisions (central route) or are willing to make decisions with very little information (peripheral route). Messages that create high involvement do so because they show the relevance of the product/service/issue to the receiver's personal interests. In such circumstances, message or issue relevant thought will likely occur; people are likely to devote effort to detailed understanding of an issue when it is relevant to their interests.

Supporters of the ELM have reasoned that people want to form correct attitudes that can be used to make decisions and adapt to their environment (Petty et al., 1987). The extent to which persons are involved with an object or topic will affect how they elaborate about the object or topic. Message impact depends on the extent or direction of argument elaboration. During persuasion, elaboration occurs when people engage in issue-relevant thinking and focus on message content by comparing it against thoughts stored in memory; in this condition, elaboration likelihood is high. Personal relevance motivates people to obtain and process more information in an effort to hold correct attitudes.

Creating Involvement During Research

Noting that the concept of involvement is used in different ways, Salmon (1986) conceptualized four levels of involvement: (a) a personality trait, (b) the product of ego involvement, (c) salience based on future consequences of a stimulus, and (d) the characteristics of an issue or product. The last dimension is the one most likely to account for the information seeking and processing typical of public policy issues.

In conducting involvement research, typical protocols either involve exposing subjects to a message and manipulating the degree of involvement by demonstrating how a product or topic affects subjects' personal interests or by examining persons who are involved with a cause, such as Sierra Club members. In the first case, involvement may be artificially produced and in the second instance high-involved persons may be incorrectly assumed to differ in crucial ways from those who are not involved. Studies that draw data only from involved people can provide useful insights, but comparisons and conclusions must be tempered if low-involved persons are not also included.

In the first research protocol, subjects are told that a new product is soon going to be available in their test market area (high involvement) or informed that the test markets are in other locations (low involvement). Researchers using such tactics

attempt to hold message content the same for all test groups, except for manipulation of levels of personal interest and involvement. Such studies use measures, such
as self-reported interest in the product, to compare levels of involvement. This
manipulation does not account for the level of involvement subjects bring to the
study. Research findings that depend on the manipulation of involvement may lack
ecological validity. For example, product or service advertisements are placed only
when products are available and must be couched in ways that elicit cognitive
processing that stems from the level of involvement each person has prior to
encountering the ad.

Relying on research findings generated by these research procedures may pose
problems for persons interested in public policy advertising. Public policy issues,
such as solutions to the prevalence of illegal drugs or the ramifications of nuclear
arms reduction, may require different cognitive processes than does response to
product or service advertising. High-involved people may have more arguments
with which to evaluate messages or they may merely be prone to use those they
have. Issue ads may be targeted to involved audiences in an effort to enhance
involvement by showing how the issue is related to audience self-interest (such as
the need for nuclear energy to lessen dependence on foreign oil) or by explaining
that grass roots involvement is needed to solve some problem. To understand how
people receive and process public policy information, researchers need more insight into the arguments people hold on policy issues and to determine how they
are affected by involvement. For these reasons, issue advertising and other forms of
public policy advocacy are prime candidates for involvement studies. Involved
groups can be targeted for reinforcement, change, or actuation. Levels of involvement may be increased by demonstrating to audiences how their personal interest
is affected by some policy issue.

Effects of Involvement

Although plagued by mixed results, involvement research has produced findings
that partially support the ELM and provide insight into attitude formation, resistance, and behavioral intention. High-involvement subjects rely extensively on
the content of advocacy messages, whereas low-involved subjects use sources to
form judgments (Petty et al., 1983). Demonstrating that low-involved subjects pay
more attention to sources than messages, Wright (1973, 1974) discovered that
low-involved subjects produce more source derogations than do high-involved
subjects, and that high-involved subjects generate more supporting and more
counterarguments than do low-involved subjects. High-involved subjects are more
critical of advocacy arguments than are low involved. High-involved subjects rate
strong, cogent arguments more favorably than low-involved subjects do, and they
are more critical of weak arguments than are their low-involved counterparts (Petty
& Cacioppo, 1984; Petty et al., 1983). The number of arguments present in a

message is more likely to influence the judgment of low-involved than high-involved subjects. In contrast, the quality of the message is more likely to influence the judgment of high- than low-involved subjects (Petty & Cacioppo, 1984).

Despite the influence involvement has on the formation of opinions, it does not always generate behavior intention, but does increase behavioral intention, persistence of opinions, and resistance to counterpersuasion (Petty & Cacioppo, 1986b). High-involved subjects who receive cogent arguments are more likely to express a desire to purchase the test product than are high-involved subjects who receive weak arguments or low-involved subjects. Content × involvement × behavioral intention interaction exists, but source credibility × involvement × behavioral intention interaction does not (Petty et al., 1983; Wright, 1973, 1974). Wright (1974) found that high-involved women who read the test ad rather than heard it were more likely than men to state behavior intention toward the product. Wright reasoned that the failure to always show that involvement leads to attitude change and behavioral intention occurs because of the counterargument, proargument, or source derogation that may be unique to each study. A curvilinear relationship exists between the degree to which a persuadee is involved in the persuasive topic and the effects source credibility has on that person's attitudes. As involvement increases so does the impact of source credibility to a point after which further involvement can actually reduce attitude change (Stiff, 1986).

Recall often is treated as a major component in persuasion studies. It is reasonable to assume that if people remember more of a message its impact will increase. But involvement is not found to enhance subject's ability to recall claims made in messages. High-involved subjects are more likely to recall the product brand name than are the low-involved subjects who received messages attributed to a peer; low-involved subjects who received a message attributed to high credibility sources are as likely to recall the product brand name as are their involved counterparts. Neither high nor low involvement promotes recall of arguments used in advocacy messages (Petty et al., 1983; Wright, 1973, 1974).

Agreement is also influenced by involvement. Cacioppo and Petty (1979) discovered that when subjects hear repeated messages, at first they agree with the messages, but agreement falls after repeated exposure. Agreement is unrelated to recall of message arguments. Frequency of exposure leads at first to decreased counterargument that is followed by increased counterargument. Subjects thought more about the topic as messages were repeated, and topic-related thinking was related to agreement. Message repetition affects agreement, counterargument, and topic-related thinking.

Grunig (1987a) discovered that high-involved individuals are more likely to become activists than are low-involved persons. And high-involved members of activist groups are more likely to participate in information seeking (sending for free materials) and information processing (watching all of a TV program discovered to address the issue related to the activism).

According to Grunig (1987b), people who are actively involved with public policy issues have better formed cognitions about those issues and should be willing to engage in individual actions related to them. This may result because people seek information in order to reduce uncertainty regarding corporate activities that have consequences for their well-being and when no major constraints stand in the way of information seeking and active participation. Laying out this equation, Grunig (1987b) concluded: "Publics with high problem recognition and level of involvement and weak constraint recognition are more likely to communicate actively about situational issues, to construct organized cognitions about those issues, and to engage in individual behaviors related to those issues" (p. 30).

To advance the understanding of involvement, particularly in regard to public policy issues, a study was conducted to explore several factors: (a) whether self-reported levels of involvement relate to the number of arguments that individuals hold in regard to policy issues; (b) whether involved individuals have more arguments to support their position; (c) whether the communication patterns of involved individuals are different; and (d) whether involvement is associated with extremity of opinion position. This research assumed that asking subjects to verbalize thoughts is a viable means for determining how receivers take in and process advocacy messages (Wright, 1980). If a comparison model is to be a viable explanation of the cognitive processes involved in reacting to public policy issues, then research is needed to explain this comparison process.

METHODOLOGY

Overview

The first step in this study was to identify policy issues about which some persons were highly involved and others were low involved. Sixteen public policy issues were submitted to 68 undergraduate students randomly drawn from communication classes at the University of Houston. Each subject was asked to indicate the degree to which each issue was personally important (7-point Likert scale—"very important" to "very unimportant"). These responses were analyzed to determine which issues should generate an even proportion of high- and low-involved subjects. Three issues met these criteria best and were selected for the study: (a) making English the national language, (b) creating a Palestinian homeland, and (c) divestiture of US companies in South Africa.

Participants

Eighty-nine students enrolled in undergraduate communication courses participated in the study. The students were randomly assigned to one of the three issue conditions. Each group received identical questionnaires except for the public policy issue. No time limit was placed upon how long persons had to complete the form, but most finished in 10–15 minutes.

Procedures

Each of the three issues identified in the preliminary stage of the inquiry (i.e., English as the national language, etc.) was used in a separate questionnaire that asked subjects to indicate how important the issue was to them, how often they talk about the issue, read about it, watch a television program about it, and whether they support or oppose the policy objective. Participants were asked to respond to each of these items by marking a 7-point Likert scale ("very important"–"very unimportant", "very often"–"not at all," or "support"–"oppose") and to argue in support of their position. Responses to this final item were coded in two ways. Two independent judges counted, first, the total number of arguments made by each participant (interjudge agreement = .83) and, second, the number of those arguments explicitly supporting the participant's policy position (interjudge agreement = .88). The judges were instructed to view as an argument those comments that (a) stated or implied why an idea was good or bad; (b) contained or implied the presence of "because," or "should be" reasoning; (c) expressed values; or (d) contained information relevant to the merits of a position. The judges were instructed to not code as an argument any statement that expressed only personal commitment ("I strongly believe in this issue") or that merely voiced agreement or disagreement with the issue.

Results

Although the objective of this study was to determine the effects of involvement on the number and type of arguments presented by participants, there was clearly some likelihood that those variables would be systematically affected by "issue" and/or the interaction between issue and involvement. In order to explore this possibility, the seven dependent variables (frequency with which a person *talked, read,* and/or *watched* a television program about the issue, the *support/opposition,* the *extremity* of the opinion, the *total number of arguments* presented, and the *proportion* of those arguments supporting the policy position) were entered into a MANOVA in which the independent variables were "issue" (English as the national language, a Palestinian homeland, and South African divestiture) and "involvement" (high, moderate, low). Levels of the involvement variable were created by treating as "high involved" those participants who scored a 6 or 7 on the importance item, "moderate involved" those who scored a 4 or 5, and "low involved" those who scored 3 or lower. This procedure generated 34 highly involved participants, 33 moderately involved, and 22 low involved.

The MANOVA revealed no evidence of an "issue by involvement" interaction (Pillai's $F < 1$) although the multivariate main effects of the issue variable were

TABLE 8.1
Means and Standard Deviations Across Levels of Involvement

	High	Moderate	Low
Frequency talk about	3.88 (1.61)[a]	2.15 (1.25)[ab]	1.04 (0.21)[ab]
Frequency read about	4.38 (1.72)[a]	3.15 (1.91)[ab]	1.50 (0.91)[ab]
Frequency watch tv about	3.12 (2.03)[ab]	2.06 (1.56)[a]	1.18 (0.50)[b]
Support/Opposition	5.74 (1.86)[ab]	4.39 (1.56)[a]	3.68 (1.13)[b]
Extremity of opinion	2.38 (0.85)[ab]	1.12 (1.14))[a]	0.59 (1.01)[b]
Number of arguments*	1.72 (1.08)[ab]	1.14 (0.81)[a]	0.80 (1.08)[b]
Proportion support agts	0.74 (0.40)[a]	0.52 (0.49)[b]	0.15 (0.27)[ab]

*indicates that, in univariate F tests, $p < .02$; in all other cases, $p < .001$.
Within row, means with the same letter differ significantly ($p < .05$).

marginally significant [Pillai's F (14, 150) $= 1.61, p < .09$]. These effects accrued from significant between-group differences in regard to support/opposition [F (2,80) $= 3.14, p < .05$] and the total number of arguments generated [$F(2,80) = 5.09, p < .01$]. Separate Newman-Keuls multiple comparison tests showed that significantly more support was shown for English as the national language than for creation of a Palestinian homeland; similarly, significantly more arguments were generated concerning the issue of English as the national language than in regard to an independent Palestinian state.

Examination of the main effects of involvement showed significant multivariate effects due to that variable [Pillai's F (14, 150) $= 6.05, p < .001$]. As is shown in Table 8.1, all of the associated univariate tests revealed significant between-group differences. Newman-Keuls tests indicated further that, compared to persons lower in involvement, high-involved participants (a) reported seeking out issue-associated information more frequently and talking more frequently about the issues with others, (b) expressed more extreme and more supportive opinions on the issues, and (c) generated more total arguments and a greater proportion of arguments supporting their opinion position. In contrast, persons low in involvement appear to (a) engage in low levels of information seeking so that particular issues do not become salient and leak into conversation with others, (b) adopt neutral opinion positions, and (c) construct few arguments about an issue.

Supplementary analyses were performed, both within and across issues, in which raw involvement scores were correlated with participants' scores on the other variables. The results of these analyses are displayed in Table 8.2.

Although the within-issue correlations are based upon comparatively few observations and, so, must be treated cautiously, the results are congruent with those of the MANOVA. In particular, involvement appears to be associated not only with the extent to which persons seek out and discuss topic-relevant information but also their ability to integrate that information into argument form. Such results are consistent with the proposition that one way in which persons fashion argument,

TABLE 8.2
Correlations Between Involvement and Other Variables

	Overall	English	Palestine	Divestiture
Frequency talk about	.67	.60	.67	.72
Frequency read about	.57	.57	.74	.44
Frequency watch tv about	.44	.38	.52	.44
Support/opposition	.67	.80	.22	.45
Extremity of opinion	.58	.64	.62	.45
Number of arguments	.35	.09	.72	.25
Proportion support agts	.49	.47	.52	.51
n =	89	30	32	27

especially arguments that buttress their own opinions, is through conversation with others. Because issues should be comparatively more salient to persons high in involvement, so that the issues more frequently leak into conversation, such per-sons should also have considerably more opportunity to develop and rehearse appropriate arguments.

DISCUSSION

As predicted, levels of involvement seem to limit and regulate the number and kind of arguments people hold on issues, as well as their communication behavior in regard to those issues. Involved individuals have more arguments to use when receiving and processing information about issues but appear to be easier commu-nication targets to reach because they seek out more topic-relevant information. Compared to other participants, those classified as high involved reported higher levels of issue related reading and televiewing. In this regard, it is worth noting that mean "reading" scores were consistently higher than mean "televiewing" scores, suggesting that television is a less useful information source than print. These results are consistent with those reported by both Wright (1974, 1981) and Heath and Douglas (1986).

Similarly, involvement appears to affect the extent to which persons talk about issues. This is consistent with the general model presented in this paper. As persons become more involved in an issue, they seek out additional information and, so, develop more complex communication repertoires (e.g., more arguments and more arguments in support of their own policy position). This process is likely to not only increase the salience of an issue but also persons' ability to communi-cate competently about the issue.

It is worth noting that, in this study, even highly involved individuals generated both supporting and disconfirming arguments on issues. Because of the presence of positive and negative arguments, any model of persuasion used to discuss public policy issues should acknowledge that individuals integrate both supportive and disconfirming information into opinions (Ajzen & Fishbein, 1980; Fishbein & Ajzen, 1975, 1981). In this regard, future research should examine the extent to which persons resist disconfirming arguments and the cognitive strategies they use to manage resistance.

As demonstrated in Table 8.2, the correlations between level of involvement and measures of both communication behavior and extremity of opinion were consistent across topics. In contrast, the correlations between the involvement variable and amount of support/opposition and number of arguments varied substantially. As inspection of Table 8.2 shows, the inconsistency occurred between the "English as the national language" issue and that concerning "creation of a Palestinian home-land." In regard to the first of these, involvement was associated with support of English as the national language. However, involvement was not predictive of the number of arguments participants generated. This pattern of findings suggests that, on this issue, a "standard set" of arguments is publicly available so that involvement has minimal effect. On the Palestinian homeland issue, there appeared to be high-involved persons at both ends of the support/opposition continuum, both able to generate a high number of arguments. Such a pattern may be common of extremely divisive issues such as that concerning Palestine. Such a claim is speculative, however, and, again, deserves further research attention.

ACKNOWLEDGMENTS

The authors acknowledge the assistance of Kohava Simhi and Robert Lecates.

REFERENCES

Ajzen, I., & Fishbein, M. (1980). *Understanding attitudes and predicting social behavior.* Englewood Cliffs, NJ: Prentice-Hall.

Cacioppo, J. T., Harkins, S. G., & Petty, R. E. (1981). The nature of attitudes and cognitive responses and their relationships to behavior. In R. Petty, T. Ostrom, & T. Brock (Eds.), *Cognitive responses in persuasion* (pp. 31–54). Hillsdale, NJ: Lawrence Erlbaum Associates.

Cacioppo, J. T., & Petty, R. E. (1979). Effects of message repetition and position on cognitive responses, recall, and persuasion. *Journal of Personality and Social Psychology, 37,* 97–109.

Chaffee, S. H., & Roser, C. (1986). Involvement and the consistency of knowledge, attitudes, and behaviors. *Communication Research, 13,* 373–399.

Cialdini, R. B., Petty, R. E., & Cacioppo, J. T. (1981). Attitude and attitude change. *Annual Review of Psychology, 32,* 357–404.

Donohue, G. A., Tichenor, P. J., & Olien, C. N. (1975). Mass media and the knowledge gap: A hypothesis reconsidered. *Communication Research, 2,* 3–23.

Fishbein, M., & Ajzen, I. (1975). *Belief, attitude, intention, and behavior*. Reading, MA: Addison-Wesley.

Fishbein, M., & Ajzen, I. (1981). Acceptance, yielding, and impact: Cognitive processes in persuasion. In R. E. Petty, T. M. Ostrom, & T. C. Brock (Eds.), *Cognitive responses in persuasion* (pp. 339–359). Hillsdale, NJ: Lawrence Erlbaum Associates.

Grunig, J. E. (1987a). Research in the strategic management of public relations. *International Public Relations Review, 11*(2), 28–32.

Grunig, J. E. (1987b, May). *When active publics become activists: Extending a situational theory of publics*. Paper presented at International Communication Association, Montreal, Canada.

Grunig, J. E., & Hunt, T. (1984). *Managing public relations*. New York: Holt, Rinehart & Winston.

Heath, R. L., & Douglas, W. (1986). Issues advertising and its effect on public opinion recall. *Public Relations Review, 12*(2), 47–56.

Petty, R. E., & Cacioppo, J. T. (1981). *Attitudes and persuasion: Classic and contemporary approaches*. Dubuque: Wm. C. Brown.

Petty, R. E., & Cacioppo, J. T. (1984). The effects of involvement on responses to argument quantity and quality: Central and peripheral routes to persuasion. *Journal of Personality and Social Psychology, 46*, 69–81.

Petty, R. E., & Cacioppo, J. T. (1986a). *Communication and persuasion: Central and peripheral routes to attitude change*. New York: Springer-Verlag.

Petty, R. E., & Cacioppo, J. T. (1986b). The elaboration likelihood model of persuasion. In L. Berkowitz (Ed.), *Advances in experimental social psychology* (Vol. 19, pp. 123–205). New York: Academic Press.

Petty, R. E., Cacioppo, J. T., & Schumann, D. (1983). Central and peripheral routes to advertising effectiveness: The moderating role of involvement. *Journal of Consumer Research, 10*, 135–146.

Petty, R. E., Kasmer, J. A., Haugtvedt, C. P. & Cacioppo, J. T. (1987). Source and message factors in persuasion: A reply to Stiff's critique of the elaboration likelihood model. *Communication Monographs, 54*, 233–249.

Salmon, C. T. (1986). Perspectives on involvement in consumer and communication research. In B. Dervin & M. J. Voigt (Eds.). *Progress in communication sciences* (Vol. 7, pp. 243–268). Norwood, NJ: Ablex.

Sherif, M., Sherif, C., & Nebergall, R. (1965). *Attitude and attitude change: The social judgment-involvement approach*. Philadelphia: W. B. Saunders.

Stiff, J. B. (1986). Cognitive processing of persuasive message cues: A meta-analytic review of the effects of supporting information on attitudes. *Communication Monographs, 53*, 123–133.

Winters, L. C. (1988). Does it pay to advertise to hostile audiences with corporate advertising? *Journal of Advertising Research, 28*(3), 11–18.

Wood, W., Kalgren, C., & Preisler, R. (1985). Access to attitude relevant information in memory as a determinant of persuasion: The role of message attributes. *Journal of Experimental Social Psychology, 21*, 73–85.

Wright, P. L. (1973). The cognitive processes mediating acceptance of advertising. *Journal of Marketing Research, 10*, 53–62.

Wright, P. L. (1974, Summer). Analyzing media effects on advertising responses. *Public Opinion Quarterly, 38*, 192–205.

Wright, P. L. (1980, January). Message-evoked thoughts: Persuasion research using thought verbalizations. *Journal of Consumer Research, 7,* 86–94.

Wright, P. L. (1981). Cognitive responses to mass media advocacy. In R. E. Petty, T. M. Ostrom, & T. C. Brock (Eds.). *Cognitive responses in persuasion* (pp. 263–282). Hillsdale, NJ: Lawrence Erlbaum Associates.

Chapter 9

First Amendment Protection for Public Relations Expression: The Applicability and Limitations of the Commercial and Corporate Speech Models

Catherine A. Pratt
The Ohio State University

Public relations practitioners recognize the central importance of communication to their occupation and the logical importance of legal protection for public relations expression. But aside from several articles in the profession's trade publication, *PR Journal* ("The Issue of Issue Ads," 1986; Walsh, 1986),[1] on the nexus between commercial and corporate speech cases and public relations, there has not been a great deal of substantive analysis or on-going dialogue in publications or at professional conferences about the connection between the limitations placed on commercial and corporate speech by the Supreme Court and the applicability of these limitations to public relations expression. The focus of law-related articles, textbook coverage, and conference sessions is aimed at the ramifications of specific laws and regulations to the practice of public relations (e.g., SEC disclosure mandates, postal rules, FCC requirements, lobbying regulations, etc.). The broader implications of First Amendment decisions in commercial and corporate law for public relations practitioners have been left largely unexplored.[2] This is a signifi-

---

[1]Walsh posited a connection between commercial speech "activity" and public relations "activities" (p. 9). He cautioned public relations practitioners to maintain awareness of the Court's attitudes toward and ruling on commercial and corporate speech: "It's a small step from banning all advertising on a product to all of the other kinds of promotion for a product" (p. 10).

[2]For example, the Public Relations "Body of Knowledge" (*PR Review*, Spring, 1988, pp. 3–40) lists no primary sources (case law and regulation) among its entries under "Legal." The "Fundamental Readings" section lists two mass communication law books (Gillmor & Barron, *Mass Communication*, 3rd ed., and Nelson & Teeter, *Law of Mass Communications*, 4th ed.) and Simon's 1969 *Public Relations Law*. It also includes references to the legal chapters in five of the more widely-used introduc-

cant omission because although the Supreme Court has not yet specifically mentioned public relations in its First Amendment rulings, it is likely to rule eventually on a case that includes the terms *public relations*. Given the judicial system's reliance on precedent and analogy (Statsky, 1974, p. 363) and the tendency of the Court to "extend" rather than "create" law when deciding cases perceived as "related" (p. 421) it is logical to assume that the Court will use already formulated doctrines as "templates" in deciding the appropriate level of First Amendment protection for public relations expression.[3]

Following traditional legal methodology, this chapter documents the omission of public relations references in legal sources, identifies and analyzes the areas of law the Court is likely to view as the equivalent of public relations, and predicts the level of First Amendment protection most likely for public relations communication.

---

tory texts in public relations; Cutlip, Center, and Broom, *Effective Public Relations*, 6th ed.; Grunig and Hunt, *Managing Public Relations*; Moore and Kalupa, *Public Relations: Principles, Cases, and Problems*, 9th ed.; Newsom and Scott, *This is PR*, 3rd ed.; and Wilcox, Ault, and Agee, *Public Relations Strategies and Tactics*. Modifying that list by substituting the recently released second edition of Wilcox et al. and adding the recently released second edition of Baskin and Aronoff, *Public Relations: The Profession and the Practice* (which includes a new legal chapter), results in a grouping of fundamental references that have been presented as containing the significant aspects of law pertinent to public relations practice. But none of the sources listed provides a current, thorough overview of the First Amendment as it might affect public relations practitioners. The two law texts are not written from a public relations perspective, the public relations law book is 20 years old, and the remaining references are either content specific or chapters in introductory texts. Of the introductory tests included, only Cutlip et al. include more than a passing reference to the cases involved in determining First Amendment protection for commercial and corporate speech. It is the only text among those included in "Body of Knowledge" "Fundamental Readings" legal section that directly cites cases in the endnotes of the legal chapter. The other books (including Baskin et al.) rely on secondary sources such as articles from *PR Journal* and Simon's 1969 law book. Baskin et al.; Cutlip, et al.; and Moore et al. include subsections on the First Amendment, although Cutlip et al. cover the issues more thoroughly with sections that address both commercial and corporate speech. Baskin et al. mention commercial and corporate speech cases in passing under a subhead "Commercial Speech" and Moore et al. mention corporate and commercial cases under the subheading "Corporate Free Speech." Wilcox et al. provide a "Corporate Free Speech" subhead but do not include commercial speech cases. The remaining two texts focus on specific regulations without addressing corporate and commercial speech doctrines directly.

The "First Amendment Applications" section of the legal listing is also void of any nontrade First Amendment overviews.

Frank Walsh's (1988) recent publication from the Foundation for Public Relations Research and Education, Inc. includes a section on "Advertising and Corporate Speech" (pp. 65–74). But Walsh focuses more on warning public relations practitioners about First Amendment limitations they will encounter as they turn to advertising. His only real extension of the limitations on commercial/corporate speech to traditional public relations activities is in the later part of the section where he reiterates the connection he made in his September 1986 *PR Journal* article between restricting cigarette advertising and the potential for restrictions on cigarette promotion (see footnote 1).

[3]Statsky (1974), in his *Legal Research Writing and Analysis: Some Starting Points*, emphasized the inclination of courts to follow already chartered waters: "Our judicial system is greatly dependent on precedent. Judges are not inclined to upset the status quo. They seldom want to make new law. The cardinal rule is: follow a precedent" (p. 421).

The study concludes that when the Court finally addresses the First Amendment's applicability to public relations communication, it is likely to look at commercial and corporate speech cases for guidance in determining the appropriate level of protection. It is further suggested here, that the Court's use of these two categories in patterning the protection for public relations communication will result in less complete protection than would be awarded speech removed from the commercial or corporate penumbra.

PUBLIC RELATIONS AND THE FIRST AMENDMENT

The Supreme Court has never decided a First Amendment case specifically referred to as a *public relations* case. At present *public relations* is not considered a term with "legal meaning," as evidenced by its omission from *Black's Law Dictionary, 5th ed.*, and *Words and Phrases* (Vol. 35 Proxy-Public System). *Words and Phrases* does list *commercial speech, advertising, advertisement,* and even *advertising agencies,* as concepts defined in the process of legal adjudication. *Corpus Juris Secundum* (General Index M–Q), a legal encyclopedia, lists *advertising* and *commercial speech* as areas of law, but the closest it gets to public relations is a listing of *publicity,* and that listing is generated by fair trial/free press cases, not public relations cases.[4]

This omission in legal reference works is important because the judicial system in this country functions by precedent, the system of "'stare decisis et non quieta movere,' to adhere to precedent and not to unsettle things which are settled" (Price, Bitner, & Bysiewicz, 1979, p. 144). This means that the courts try to follow "already established" law whenever possible, "taking the present case, finding past cases which are similar, and then applying the rules from those past cases"

---

[4]Readers unfamiliar with the methods employed in legal research or the reference materials mentioned in this analysis are directed to Price, Bitner, and Bysiewicz (1979), *Effective Legal Research, 4th ed.,* for a detailed discussion of the various reference tools available to the legal scholar. The book explains the relative merits of dictionaries, encyclopedias, law books, etc., as they relate to the construction of legal authority.

For an analysis of the traditional research process (including its biases and limitations) see the "Legal Research in Mass Communication" chapter in *Research Methods in Mass Communication* by Stempel and Westley. Readers interested in adopting more empirical or behavioral legal research methods are directed to Gillmor and Dennis, "Legal Research and Judicial Communication," in Chaffee's *Political Communication: Issues and Strategies for Research.* This article argues for legal research guidelines that embrace social science methodology and depart from the normative, adversarial approach associated with traditional legal research. (The Stempel and Westley chapter reiterates these arguments as well.)

There is no single "correct" way to approach legal research. The complex nature of our legal system suggests that multiple approaches are likely to provide the most insight into the past, present, and future course of First Amendment law. As Gillmor and Dennis suggest: "[T]he communication researcher should use the methodology most appropriate to the problem at hand" (Chaffee, p. 291).

(Wasby, 1978, p. 17).[5] The fact that legal reference materials do not list *public relations* as a legal concept makes it likely that Supreme Court Justices, as the arbiters of First Amendment questions, will rely on what they consider related areas for guidance in reaching a decision when they first encounter a case specifically designated as a public relations case. An analysis of commercial and corporate speech cases suggests that these areas will provide the Court with a related "template" for determining the appropriate level of protection.

THE COURT'S EARLY COMMERCIAL SPEECH APPROACH

The Supreme Court has never declared the First Amendment an absolute (Bosmajian, 1980; Dennis, Gillmor, & Grey, 1978). Throughout the history of free speech and press adjudication, the Court has said that certain expression, such as obscenity, is completely outside the protection of the First Amendment (*Roth v. U.S.*, 1957), and that other expression, such as broadcast speech, should receive only limited protection (*National Broadcasting Company v. U.S.*, 1943).

The Court's earliest decision on the question of whether commercial speech should be afforded First Amendment protection came in 1942 in *Valentine v. Chrestensen*, a case involving the distribution of handbills advertising an old Navy submarine on exhibition for an admission fee. The case resulted in the pronouncement that regulations restricting speech in this category would not be scrutinized in the same manner as regulations restricting non-commercial speech: "the Constitution imposes no such restraint on governments as respects purely commercial advertising" (p. 54). *Chrestensen* is generally read as eliminating First Amendment protection for commercial speech, although it can be argued that the case laid the groundwork for consideration of commercial speech as a category with limited protection in a two-tiered theory application (Barron & Diens, 1979). This definition of advertising as "different" from protected speech because of its economic self-interest remained the controlling attitude toward commercial speech as a category of expression for several decades. Although the Court did not fully define the category at issue, the opinion represents a classic categorical approach to regulation of expression. (The categorical approach is discussed here).

The Court did allow that some commercial expression transcended the limitations of total exclusion from First Amendment protection in *New York Times Co. v. Sullivan* (1964). According to the Court, this case was different from *Chrestensen* because the advertisement of *Sullivan* "communicated information, expressed

---

[5]Karl Llewellyn has suggested that the doctrine of precedent is followed for reasons ranging from "laziness . . . the time and energy saved by routine . . . the values of routine as a curb on arbitrariness and as a prop of weakness, inexperience and instability; the social values of predictability; the power of whatever exists to produce expectations and the power of expectations to become normative. . ." (cited in Cohen, *Legal Research*, 4th ed., 1985, p. 11). Regardless of rationale, however, the fact remains that our legal system is dependent on the doctrine.

opinion, recited grievances, protested claimed abuses, and sought financial support on behalf of a movement whose existence and objectives are matters of the highest public interest and concern" (*New York Times*, pp. 263–264).[6] This deviation from *Chrestensen* (a deviation that would not be substantially repeated until more than a decade later) can probably best be explained by noting that the case dealt with expression concerning civil rights and that the Court considered it a landmark libel, not commercial, speech case.

LIMITED PROTECTION FOR COMMERCIAL SPEECH

The Court began modifying its general approach to the "value" of commercial speech in a 1975 case, *Bigelow v. Virginia*. The case involved a published adver-tisement that concerned legal New York abortion services but violated a Virginia law that made it illegal to advertise abortion information. Although the Virginia Supreme Court upheld Bigelow's conviction—noting that the message in question was of a "purely commercial nature"—the U.S. Supreme Court rejected the view that advertising was completely outside the protective shield of the First Amend-ment, echoing the assertion in *Sullivan* that commercial speech may contain factual matters of public interest (*Bigelow v. Virginia*). The Court did not define which commercial speech was inside and which was outside the protective limits of the First Amendment, beyond the reference to the public interest value of some com-mercial speech (*Bigelow v. Virginia*, pp. 825). This foreshadowed the Court's later emphasis on the potential audience's right to receive expression as more important than the speaker's right of expression (*Virginia Pharmacy*, 1976). *Bigelow* did question the validity of using a reasonableness standard of review for commercial speech regulation. The reasonableness standard offers very limited protection be-cause it merely requires that the government show a restriction on speech is "reasonable" (Berger, 1980). Reasonableness has been described as a "nip-it-in-the-bud" approach to free speech because it may allow restrictions on speech with even a "remote" tendency to create danger (Tedford, 1985).[7]

The *Bigelow* Court reached its conclusion by balancing—specifically, the in-terests of the public in hearing the message with the interests of the state in regulating it. The general criticisms of balancing as a method of defining protection for expression center on the subjectivity of the balancing process. Laurent Frantz (1983) posed the dilemma of balancing as a succinct question: "How is the judge

---

[6]Prior to *Sullivan*, commercial speech was dismissed as a category based on the origin of the speech (economic self-interest of the speaker). Post-*Sullivan* cases routinely considered the content of the commercial speech to be one of the deciding factors in determining First Amendment protection.

[7]The classic description of the rationale for using the test is found in Justice Sanford's majority opinion in *Gitlow v. New York*, (268 U.S. 652, 1925). The reasonableness standard of review says that if a law can be construed as reasonable or if an expression could potentially have a bad tendency, the restriction is likely to be judged constitutional.

to convert balancing into something that does not merely give him back whatever answer he feeds into it?" (p. 748)[8] Thomas Emerson (1980) argued that in recent cases involving freedom of expression, the Court's balancing test could have struck the balance in favor of either side (p. 451).[9] A strict scrutiny standard of review— requiring that the regulation in question serve a compelling state interest and is narrowly drawn—would require more than a showing of just "legitimate" or "valid" interests on the part of the state. In a sense, even strict scrutiny is a form of balancing, but it "stacks the deck" in favor of expression.

Although the idea of protection for commercial speech was inherent in both *New York Times v. Sullivan* and *Bigelow*, the Court explicitly established limited commercial speech protection in *Virginia State Board of Pharmacy v. Virginia Citizens Consumer Council* (1976). *Virginia Pharmacy* declared a state ban on the advertising of prescription drug prices unconstitutional. The Court emphasized both consumer and societal interests in granting this limited First Amendment protection to a previously "unprotected category." *Bates v. State Bar of Arizona* (1977) struck down a state ban on newspaper advertising of legal services using much the same consumer-oriented rationale.

The establishment of limited protection for commercial speech was structured within the categorical approach used by the Court in areas like obscenity (no protection, *Miller v. California*, 1973; *Roth v. U.S.*, 1957) and "speech-plus" or action as expression (limited protection, Bogen, 1984, p. 95; *U.S. v. O'Brien*, 1968; *Tinker v. Des Moines*, 1969). The criticisms of any sort of categorical approach to First Amendment protection center around the difficulty of defining the excluded categories and the subjectivity involved in balancing interests weighted by categories into two different tiers of protection. Peter Schlag (1983) argued that when judicially applied, categorical approaches present the courts with pre-packaged justifications for particular outcomes that do not necessarily mesh with either the facts in the case at hand or with any comprehensive theory of First Amendment protection (pp. 733–734). Others have argued that categorical approaches are manageable if judicial consideration of the purpose and value of the speech at issue is factored into the review process, although a value-based approach inherently means a balancing of values by the judges involved (Barnes, 1985, p. 651; "Commercial Speech: A Proposed Definition," 1984, p. 1023; Schauer, 1982, p. 160).[10]

---

[8]For arguments supporting balancing as an approach to First Amendment adjudication, see Mendelson, "On the Meaning of the First Amendment: Absolutes in the Balance," *California Law Review* 50:821 (1962), pp. 825–826. Mendelson argued that balancing compels judicial responsibility and promotes "more particularized and more rational" decisions.

[9]Emerson admonished the Burger Court for failing to refine the balancing test by "delineating the weight to be given to specific factors" (p. 451). He argued that the Burger Court has simply applied a number of variations erratically.

[10]Schauer (1982) has suggested the value of speech is a key in understanding the parameters of free speech protection, but his interpretation of value would tend to help some commercial speech and leave some unprotected: "In dealing with free speech problems it is especially important that we look to the value of the product more than we look to the motives of the producer" (p. 160).

COURT EFFORTS TO DEFINE COMMERCIAL SPEECH PROTECTION

Throughout the early cases delineating First Amendment protection for commercial speech, the Court did not offer much help in defining when commercial speech would and would not be protected. *Bigelow* suggested that protected commercial speech was speech that did more than simply propose a commercial transaction; speech that conveyed information of potential interest and value to a diverse audience (p. 822). *Virginia Pharmacy* continued the focus on the receiver rather than the speaker of the commercial expression in question (p. 748). But in *Central Hudson Gas v. Public Service Commission* (1980) the Court offered a four-part test to determine whether a particular regulation of commercial speech violates the First Amendment. After defining commercial speech as "expression related solely to the economic interests of the speaker and its audience" (p. 561), the Court noted that "[c]ommercial expression not only serves the economic interest of the speaker, but also assists consumers and furthers the societal interest in the fullest possible dissemination of information" (pp. 561–562). Again focusing on the audience's right to receive rather than the speaker's right to talk, the Court said the decision on whether or not the commercial speech in question was protected speech would depend on determining its eligibility for protection independent of categorical determination. First, false or misleading speech or speech which concerns unlawful activity would be ineligible for protection. Second, the governmental interest in question had to be "substantial." Third, the governmental interest had to be "directly advanced" by the regulation. Fourth, the Court said it must be determined whether the regulation was "more extensive than necessary" to achieve the ends (p. 566).

The case concerned advertising by the Central Hudson Gas and Electric Corporation to promote the use of electricity. The advertising was opposed by a New York regulatory commission because it ran contrary to the commission's emphasis on energy conservation. The commission's ban specifically excluded "institutional and information" advertisements, the kind of advertisements traditionally associated with public relations activity. However, the term *promotional*, which was used to describe the advertisements directly affected by the ban, is a term often used in describing certain kinds of public relations activities or models.[11] The overlapping

---

[11]Grunig and Hunt (1988) used "promotion" as a descriptive word in their press agentry/publicity model of public relations (p. 25). An argument could also be made that the Cutlip et al. list of 10 major categories summarizing the activities typical of public relations assignments contains several designations that could include the concept of "promotion," notably "Writing," "Media Relations and Placement," "Special Events" (p. 64). While the Public Relations Society of America, among others, has worked to standardize the definition of public relations and establish an accepted code of ethics/professional standards, definitions of public relations vary widely depending on the context and the source. The lack of specificity in definition and the blurred lines between advertising/marketing and public relations (acknowledged by most introductory texts) would allow a legal argument to be made that the term "commercial speech" should include public relations as well as traditional advertising efforts.

of definitional terms and activities provides support for the assertion that the Supreme Court is likely to use the parameters of commercial speech protection as one of the guidelines for determining the protection to be afforded public relations speech.

That commercial speech protection is less than robust is evidenced by the Court's 1986 holding in *Posadas de Puerto Rico Associates v. Tourism Company of Puerto Rico*. In this case the Court ruled that it was constitutionally permissible for Puerto Rico to forbid gambling casino advertising directed at local residents be-cause the government had a substantial interest in reducing the demand for casino gambling among Commonwealth residents and the restriction directly advanced those interests. The advertised gambling was legal, the commercial speech was not misleading or fraudulent, and similar speech directed at nonresidents was not restricted, but those arguments did not sway the Court, although Justice Brennan's dissent argued that Puerto Rico could not constitutionally suppress truthful com-mercial speech in order to discourage lawful activity (pp. 285–292).

The *Posadas* decision would seem to support the contention that the four-part "balancing" test in *Central Hudson* provides no greater protection than balancing approaches in general. Thus, current law suggests that courts will award some protection to commercial speech, but will allow regulation/suppression not permit-ted when directed at noncommercial speech. The Supreme Court's inability to fully define what it considers to be commercial speech also leaves this area open for further interpretation.[12] Although decisions after *Virginia Pharmacy* began to so-lidify protection for commercial speech, it can be argued that *Posadas*, at best, casts doubt on the extent of commercial speech protection. Although it seems unlikely that the Court would eliminate protection entirely, predicting which commercial speech will be protected and which will not would seem to be more difficult now. If public relations speech is determined to fall under the rubric of commercial speech, this unpredictability could negatively affect the communication of public relations practitioners.

CORPORATE SPEECH PROTECTION

A parallel area of legal reasoning has given limited First Amendment protection to corporate speech. The two cases that illustrate this concept are *First National Bank of Boston v. Bellotti* (1978) and *Consolidated Edison Co. v. Public Service Com-mission* (1980). *Bellotti* involved the constitutionality of a state statute prohibiting

---

[12]Some scholars have done a more thorough job of defining commercial speech than has the Court. Farber, *Northwestern University Law Review* 372:387 (1979), posited that the direct functional rela-tionship between the message and a later commercial transaction is the correct method for defining commercial expression. His enumeration of specifics to guide the defining process goes much further than most Court-fashioned definitions. His approach, however, would likely place a great deal of public relations expression within the commercial speech parameters.

corporations from spending money to influence the vote on state referendum proposals not "materially affecting" the corporation. The Court, noting that the speech in question was political speech—speech "at the heart of First Amendment protection" (p. 776), declared the statute unconstitutional. The Court focused on the content of the communication and noted that similar political speech by individuals could not have been restricted in that manner: "The inherent worth of the speech in terms of its capacity for informing the public does not depend upon the identity of its source, whether corporation, association, union, or individual" (p. 777). The protection awarded corporate speech in *Bellotti* was not complete, however, in part because the Court followed its own commercial speech doctrine emphasis on the rights of the listener to receive the information rather than the rights of the speaker. Both the listener's-rights approach and the Court's focus on the political nature of the speech in question limit the parameters of freedom awarded corporate speech under the current model of protection (Rehnquist, *Bellotti* dissent, 1978, pp. 822–828; Prentice, 1981; Schneider, 1986; Sherrill, 1988).[13]

Special or enhanced protection for political speech offers a categorical approach that seems to provide more, not less, protection for the category in question. Problems arise, however, in defining what is encompassed by the term *political*. Alexander Meiklejohn (1961), the seminal proponent of this approach, eventually argued for a very broad definition that included any speech from which voters derive "knowledge, intelligence, sensitivity to human values; the capacity for sane and objective judgment which, so far as possible, a ballot should express" (p. 256). Robert Bork (1971), however, has offered a far more restrictive definition that limits First Amendment protection to speech that is "explicitly" political.[14] The distance between these two interpretations underlines the difficulties with an approach of this kind.

In *Consolidated*, the Court struck down a New York regulatory commission's order prohibiting the mailing by public utilities of bill inserts discussing controversial issues of public policy, in this instance, nuclear energy. The Court positioned the case as a corporate speech case, citing *Bellotti* and again emphasizing the public's right to receive (pp. 533–534). The case established a three-part test for determining the constitutionality of restrictions on corporate speech: (a) Was the

---

[13]Sherrill (1988) admitted "there's nothing wrong with self-interest, after all . . . it might help stir up a useful debate." But he bemoans First Amendment protection for corporations, arguing that "who" talks really matters. "If corporate speech gets protection, let it come from the commerce clause or the due process clause or some other part of the Constitution. The First Amendment belongs to human beings and the press, and it should be secured for their use only, before this nonsense becomes any more dangerously rooted" (pp. 20–24).

[14]Bork (1971) excluded speech indirectly affecting or influencing political attitudes and thus eliminates First Amendment protection for novels or films about politics. His argument is that freedom for nonpolitical speech "rests, as does freedom for other valuable forms of behavior, upon the enlightenment of a society and its elected representatives."

restriction a reasonable time, place, or manner restriction? (b) Was it a permissible subject-matter regulation? (c) Was it a narrowly tailored means of serving a compelling state interest? (p. 535).

Both *Bellotti* and *Consolidated* gave corporate speech limited First Amendment protection,[15] but the important variables seem to be the nature of the speech and the listener's interest, need, or right to receive the information. These corporate speech cases—like the commercial speech cases post-*Sullivan*—focus on the content of the expression as essential in determining First Amendment protection. Regulation aimed at speech content has traditionally been limited to time, place, and manner restrictions, but, as *Posadas* illustrates, differences in the Court's interpretation of what constitutes acceptable categories of "time," "place," and "manner" can be substantial ("Time, Place, or Manner Restrictions on Commercial Speech," 1983). The level of content regulation validated by the Court in commercial and corporate speech cases suggests that both areas are mired in a "second-class status" (Jackson & Jeffries, 1979).

CONCLUSION: LIMITED PROTECTION
FOR PUBLIC RELATIONS EXPRESSION

The approaches used by the Court in commercial and corporate speech cases should be of real concern to public relations communicators. Although it can be argued that commercial speech cases, at least post-*Virginia Pharmacy* and pre-*Posadas*, expanded protection for commercial speech, it must be remembered that the speech under scrutiny in these cases was speech that would not have been restricted had it been noncommercial speech. And while the corporate speech cases have been described as establishing or expanding speech protection for corporations, the same caveat applies: protection for the speech at issue would not have been in doubt had the cases not been cast as corporate speech cases. Thus, suggesting that these areas of law provide *some* protection for commercial and corporate speech misses an essential point: were these categories not applied to the speech at issue, protection would likely be more certain and more inclusive.

The activities addressed in the corporate speech cases certainly fit comfortably under the rubric of contemporary public relations activity (e.g., brochure and pamphlet preparation, issue advertising; Cutlip Center, & Broom, 1985). The

---

[15]Even before *Bellotti*, the Court had addressed the "rights" of corporations: "Publishing corporations are 'persons' entitled to the protections of the First Amendment" (*Grossjean v. American Press*, 297 U.S. 233, 1935). However, the rights connected with First Amendment protection seem to have been primarily meant for media corporations. Ithiel de Sola Pool (1983) sees this distinction as one between "commerce for commerce's sake . . . and . . . production of materials for public discussion, wherein the mere fact that profit is being made would not deprive the producer of protection" (pp. 20–24). This distinction might be a good conceptual differentiation between protected and nonprotected corporate speech, but its operational value is limited.

corporate speech model is probably the most likely to be applied if a public relations expression case were to develop in a corporate public relations setting. However, the nature of the economic relationship between a public relations firm and its clients more closely parallels the advertising agency/client relationship. Given the uncertainty of the Court's approach in determining the nature of commercial speech and the parameters of its protection, a public relations expression case emanating from an agency setting might be declared a commercial speech case. Although there are differences between the Court's approaches in commercial and corporate speech cases, the two areas of case law share a common trait: both offer less protection to speech than would be presumed in a non-commercial or noncorporate context.

Based on the various threads of analysis used by the Court in deciding protection for commercial and corporate speech, the public relations practitioner ought to consider the following when questions about First Amendment protection for expression arise: (a) Expression that is not true or is misleading is likely to be judged not protected by the First Amendment—even if that expression would be protected were it outside the commercial/corporate area. (b) Expression that can be classified as political or that addresses issues of public importance and interest is more likely to be protected. (c) Determining what expression will or will not receive protection is likely to remain difficult because the Court has never really operationalized "commercial," "corporate," "political speech," and "listener's rights."

The Court's approaches to commercial and corporate speech have focused on the expression's link to a specific business entity, the economic motivation of the producer of the expression, and what the Court calls the "hearty nature" of the expression at issue. A great deal of public relations communication fits within the current guidelines for commercial and corporate speech. Should the Court address First Amendment protection for public relations expression it would most likely look to these similar models for direction in determining the level of appropriate protection.

REFERENCES

Barnes, R. L. (1985). A Call for a Value-Based Test of Commercial Speech. *Washington University Law Quarterly, 63,* 649–706.

Barron, J., & Diens, C. T. (1979). *Handbook of free speech and free press.* Boston, MA: Little, Brown.

Baskin, O., & Aronoff, C. (1988). *Public relations: The profession and the practice* (2nd ed.). Dubuque, IO: Wm. C. Brown.

Bates v. State Bar of Arizona, 433 U.S. 350. (1977).

Berger, F. R. (1980). *Freedom of expression.* Belmont, CA: Wadsworth.

Bigelow v. Virginia, 421 U.S. 809. (1975).

Bogen, D. S. (1984). *Bulwark of liberty: The court and the first amendment.* Port Washington, NY: National University Publications, Associated Faculty Press.

Bork, R. (1971). Neutral Principles and Some First Amendment Problems. *Indiana Law Journal, 47,* 1–35.

Bosmajian, H. A. (1980). *Justice Douglas and freedom of speech.* Methuchen, NJ: The Scarecrow Press.

Central Hudson v. Public Service Commission, 447 U.S. 557. (1980).

Cohen, M. (1985). *Legal research in a nutshell* (4th ed.). St. Paul, MN: West Publishing.

Commercial speech: A proposed definition. (1984). *Howard Law Journal, 27,* 1015–1030.

Consolidated Edison Co. v. Public Service Commission, 447 U.S. 530. (1980).

Cutlip, S. M., Center A. H., & Broom, G. M. (1985). *Effective public relations* (6th ed.). Englewood Cliffs, NJ: Prentice-Hall.

Dennis, E., Gillmor, D., & Grey, D. (Eds.). (1978). *Justice Hugo Black and the first amendment.* Ames, IA: Iowa State University Press.

de Sola Pool, I. (1983). *Technologies of freedom.* Cambridge, MA: The Belknap Press of Harvard University Press.

Emerson, T. (1980). First Amendment Doctrine and the Burger Court. *California Law Review, 68,* 422–481.

Farber, D. (1979). Commercial Speech and First Amendment Theory. *Northwestern Law Review, 74,* 372–408.

First National Bank of Boston v. Bellotti, 435 U.S. 765. (1978).

Frantz, L. B. (1983). Is the First Amendment Law?—A reply to Professor Mendelson. *California Law Review, 51,* 729–754.

Gillmor D., & Dennis, E. (1975). Legal research and judicial communication. In S. Chaffee (Ed.), *Political communication: Issues and strategies for research* (pp. 283–305). Beverly Hills, CA: Sage.

Gillmor, D., & Dennis, E. (1981). Legal research in mass communication. In G. Stemple & B. Westley (Eds.), (1981). *Research methods in mass communication* (pp. 320–341). Englewood Cliffs, NJ: Prentice-Hall.

Gitlow v. New York, 268 U.S. 652. (1925).

Grossjean v. American Press, 297 U.S. 233. (1935).

Grunig, J., & Hunt, T. (1984). *Managing public relations.* New York: Holt, Rinehart & Winston.

The issue of issue ads. (1986, October). *PR Journal,* pp. 30–33, 42–43.

Jackson, T. H., & Jeffries, J. C. (1979). Commercial speech: Economic due process and the First Amendment. *Virginia Law Review, 65,* 1–41.

Legal research in a nutshell. (1985). St. Paul, MN: West Publishing.

Meiklejohn, A. (1961). The First Amendment is an absolute. *Supreme Court Review,* 245–266.

Mendelson, W. (1962). On the meaning of the First Amendment: Absolutes in the balance. *California Law Review, 50,* 821–828.

Miller v. California, 413 U.S. 15. (1973).

Moore, H. F., & Kalupa, F. (1985). *Public relations: Principles, cases, and problems* (9th ed.). Homewood, IL: Richard D. Irwin.

National Broadcasting Company v. U.S., 319 U.S. 190. (1943).

New York Times v. Sullivan, 376 U.S. 254. (1964).

Newsom, D., & Scott, A. (1985). *This is PR: The realities of public relations* (3rd ed.). Belmont, CA: Wadsworth.

Posadas de Puerto Rico Associates v. Tourism Company of Puerto Rico, 92 L. Ed. 2d 266. (1986).

Prentice, R. A. (1981). Consolidated Edison and Bellotti: First Amendment Protection of Corporate Political Speech. *Tulsa Law Journal, 16*, 599–657.

Price, M., Bitner, H., & Bysiewicz, S. (1979). *Effective legal research* (4th ed.). Boston, MA: Little, Brown.

Public relations body of knowledge. (1988, Spring). *PR Review*, pp. 3–40.

Roth v. U.S., 354 U.S. 476. (1957).

Schauer, F. (1982). *Free speech: A philosophical inquiry*. Cambridge, MA: Cambridge University Press.

Schlag, P. (1983). An attack on categorical approaches to freedom of speech. *UCLA Law Review, 30*, 671–739.

Schneider, C. E. (1986). Free speech and corporate freedom: A Comment on First National Bank of Boston v. Bellotti. *Southern California Law Review, 59*, 1227–1291.

Sherrill. (1988, January). Big business takes the first. *Harper's Magazine*, pp. 20–24.

Statsky, W. (1974). *Legal research writing and analysis: Some starting points*. St. Paul, MN: West Publishing.

Tedford, T. L. (1985). *Freedom of speech in the United States*. New York: Random House.

Time, place, or manner restrictions on commercial speech. (1983). *George Washington Law Review, 52*, 127–145.

Tinker v. Des Moines Independent Community School District, 393 U.S. 503. (1969).

United States v. O'Brien, 391 U.S. 367. (1968).

Valentine v. Chrestensen, 316 U.S. 52. (1942).

Virginia State Board of Pharmacy v. Virginia Citizens Consumer Council, 425 U.S. 478. (1976).

Walsh, F. (1986, September). Commercial speech. *PR Journal*, pp. 9–10.

Walsh, F. (1988). *Public relations & the law*. New York: Foundation for Public Relations Research and Education.

Wasby, S. (1978). *The Supreme Court in the federal judicial system*. New York: Holt, Rinehart & Winston.

Wilcox, D., Ault, P., & Agee, W. (1989). *Public relations: Strategies and tactics* (2nd ed.). New York: Harper & Row.

Chapter 10

Ethical Values or Strategic Values? The Two Faces of Systems Theory in Public Relations

Ron Pearson
Mount Saint Vincent University

It has been argued on a number of occasions that public relations is in a sorry state with respect to discipline-specific theory development (Ehling, 1984; Grunig & Hickson, 1976; Grunig & Hunt, 1984; Pavlik & Salmon, 1984). Although notable exceptions exist, many of the theories identified by public relations scholars and practitioners as relevant for public relations were developed in other disciplines including psychology, social psychology, sociology, and mass communication (Terry, 1987). This situation is changing and will continue to change as scholars investigate theories and test hypotheses about variables that are of particular interest to public relations. But more revealing about a discipline are the broader meta-theoretical perspectives or paradigms according to which a discipline carries out this research. For these can reveal tacit assumptions that are part of a discipline's self-knowledge.

Communication scholars generally have wondered what perspective—covering law (Berger, 1977), rules (Cushman, 1977), or systems (Monge, 1977)—is most appropriate for the study of communication and much discussion has taken place on this issue. This issue has not been debated by public relations scholars however, perhaps because of an apparent consensus about which paradigm is appropriate. Much public relations research, where it is not merely anecdotal, has been carried out under the covering law model. Little would seem to fit under a rules perspective, although Culbertson (1983) is a possible exception. Recently, however, a number of texts and journal articles have suggested that a systems perspective is, or should be, important in public relations, although this perspective is not argued for as an alternative to covering laws or rules, nor is an effort always made to clarify precisely what is meant by a systems approach. Pavlik (1987), using the language of Kuhn (1970), suggested that a systems perspective is an emerging paradigm in public relations. In a chapter entitled "An Emerging Paradigm: General System Theory," Pavlik wrote that "During the past decade, a number of scholars have conducted research to build a theoretical understanding of public relations. . . . Emerging from this systematic research is a public relations paradigm based on general system theory" (p. 126). Similarly, Long and Hazleton (1987) concluded that "General Systems Theory portends promise as meta-theoretical approach for organizing public relations" (p. 4).

Public relations textbooks are beginning to pick up systems theory themes, although many are not, which indicates as yet no monolithic move to embrace this perspective. Among recent texts that do not mention systems theory are Crable and Vibbert (1986), Dunn (1986), Reilly (1987), and Seital (1987). Yet the latest edition of the public relations text with the longest history—its first edition was published in 1952—has added a completely new chapter, called "Adjustment and Adaptation: A Theoretical Model for Public Relations," which employs systems theory (Cutlip, Center, & Broom, 1985). The new edition of Aronoff and Baskin (1988) also devotes a considerable amount of space to a discussion of systems theory. Similarly, Grunig and Hunt (1984) and Nager and Allen (1984) used a systems perspective in their public relations texts. In summary, although it is clear that not all discussions of public relations do not use systems theory, it is equally plain that systems theory has become an important meta-theoretical position within public relations.

This chapter examines the implications of public relations' interest in systems theory as a meta-theoretical perspective or paradigm. The chapter's thesis is that it is not at all clear what the adoption of systems theory and its language will mean for public relations. More specifically, it argues that systems theory can lead public relations in two different directions and that a profound choice confronts the profession about which direction is appropriate.

Having shown that systems theory is beginning to play an important role in public relations, the chapter raises four central questions suggested by this phenomenon, each of which is addressed in a separate section. For instance, by adopting the language and assumptions of systems theory, does public relations link itself to an outmoded idealism and a philosophical doctrine of internal relations that is difficult to defend? Does adoption of core systems theory concepts such as interdependence and interconnectedness have ethical implications for public relations? What does the adoption of a systems perspective imply for the discipline's relationship to functionalism? And finally, what might it mean for systems theory to go beyond functionalism? As these questions are addressed, the chapter endeavors to show why they are important for public relations and why public relations faces a profound choice about how systems theory will affect the disciplines's self-understanding and its vision for the future.

PUBLIC RELATIONS AND THE IDEA OF HOLISM

Katz and Kahn (1966) and Buckley (1967) were among the first to show how systems concepts could be made relevant to organizational management. Katz and Kahn emphasized systems theory's concern with problems of relationships, struc- ture, and interdependence. In the public relations literature, Bell and Bell (1976) introduced the language and ideas of systems theory, distinguishing between a functional approach to public relations that took into account that an organization and its environment were mutually dependent, and a functionary approach that did not.

Wolter and Miles (1983), echoing others, suggested that confusion and misun- derstanding about the profession of public relations is related to the fact that it has no unifying core of theory. They suggested that the focus of what they called the modern age has been the individual, the "I." But they argued this atomistic, individualistic focus is not appropriate in what they called the post-modern age and needs to be replaced with a "We" or "We-force" perspective.

> Managing public relationships of all living organisms is at issue—the other sex, other races, other countries, flora and fauna, lakes, rivers, air, planets, and even stars are interdependent concerns. For postmodern public relations, the we-force issues are marketing, social responsibility, conservation, international business, global politics, and most other forms of human interdependencies. Problems and opportunities are so multidimensional and interrelated that managing them requires a new postmodern public relations. (p. 15)

Wolter and Miles continued by linking their "ecological" view to the idea of a holistic system in which there is only "we" and no "I" and in which public relations replace private relations. Pavlik (1987) also picked up this theme of interconnectedness. "systems are by definition *whole*. They are not merely a collec- tion of unrelated parts, but rather an integrated whole . . . every part is to a degree *interdependent*. Thus a change in part causes change throughout the system" (p. 127).

Some of he earliest statements of the holistic thinking associated with system theory are found in idealist philosophies of Hegel and neo-Hegelians such as F. H. Bradley. Phillips (1976) suggested the main tenets of this thinking are based on the doctrine of internal relations that holds (a) that all entities are part of a whole that contains them, (b) that an entity's relations with other entities are part of what is essential to it, and (c) that the entities determine or qualify the whole of which they are a part while at the same time they are determined or qualified by the whole. Phillips suggested that the second tenet is the all important doctrine for it maintains that when an Entity A is related to Entity B it gains some property p as a result of the relationship such that outside of the relationship it does not have p and is therefore not −A. If all system parts are related to all other system parts, it follows that any change in one of the parts necessarily entails that all other parts of the system will also change. A consequence of this, it is argued, is that it is fruitless to isolate one part or variable in the whole for study because the entity isolated is not the entity that is part of the whole. This consequence, of course, was not lost on proponents of this doctrine for it was part and parcel of a belief that the reductionist, analytic approach of the sciences was inappropriate for the study of biological and social systems.

More dramatically than the other writers commenting on public relations, Wolter and Miles couched their theorizing about the "we-force" in a rhetoric that highlights the view of holism previously described. For they argued that no entity exists except in relationship with other individuals as part of a whole. Few public relations researchers, however, seem to want to accept the logical consequences of such a view, for it undermines the new philosophy of quantification and management by objectives techniques that are becoming important in public relations. A world view that says communication effects cannot be isolated and measured is not congenial to a profession that has only recently appropriated scientific evaluation procedures.

For the purpose of clarification, it is possible to identify at least three senses in which public relations scholars speak of systems theory. The strongest view includes the doctrine of internal relations. Wolter and Miles quite explicitly seemed to place themselves in this camp. A second view represents the adoption of a useful heuristic tool and a language for talking about public relations that can be applied in all public relations situations. This language emphasizes process and uses terms like *input, throughput,* and *output* that can all be given specific public relations content. It also recognizes the strategic and sometimes ethical importance of being attentive to interdependencies. Gollner (1983), for instance, without invoking the concept of holism, talked about the way institutions are crowding in on one another, about increasing complexity and institutional interdependence, and even about the idea that decision *outputs* of one organization are increasingly becoming the decision *inputs* of another. Moreover, this second view of systems theory often emphasizes a management by objectives (MBO) approach that stresses precisely the kind of analysis early proponents of the doctrine of internal relations attacked. Last, it is possible to identify a third approach, which uses none of the language of systems theory but merely advocates proceeding in a systematic manner. Ehling and Hesse (1983) suggested that Chase's (1977) discussion of issues management be interpreted in this way.

It is fair to say, that for most public relations scholars, the adoption of a systems perspective includes the ideas associated with the second position stated earlier. The ideas of interdependence and interconnectedness are emphasized along with MBO principles. These ideas are not seen to be incompatible as they are in position one. Yet this does not mean that there is a complete lack of ambiguity in this middle position. For as the next section attempts to show, adoption of the language of interdependence and interconnectedness can be given two interpretations. One interpretation emphasizes ethical considerations, the other emphasizes strategic considerations.

TYPES OF NECESSITY AND ETHICAL IMPLICATIONS

It might be concluded that the emerging system perspective is useful for public relations because of its heuristic value and the emphasis it places on relationships, interconnectedness, and the idea of interdependence. But relationships can be characterized in a number of ways. Historically, systems perspectives have emphasized logical relations among variables, terms, parts, systems, and subsystems, arguing that a change in one part of the system logically must have an impact on other parts of the system because of the interconnectedness of these parts. If public relations seems not to be advocating a philosophical doctrine of internal relations, however, it seems unlikely that public relations practitioners and scholars are advocating logical necessity. For it is plain that a crisis in an organization's environment does not press a public relations department to dust off its crisis communication plan according to any logical necessity. Some public relations scholars would argue that it is still an open question whether there is any nomic necessity of the type covering laws theorists appeal to that would help explain how organizations respond to their environments. But few would deny that it is of great strategic or ethical import whether the organization responds to a crisis or remains silent. Thus, a kind of practical necessity of the kind appealed to by rules theorists, may be of greater value in theoretical explanations relevant to public relations than either nomic or logical necessity.

That a prudently managed organization takes into account its environment—other organizations, groups and individuals who have a stake in how the organization behaves—is thus arguably not a matter of logical or nomic necessity. Rather, it can be argued that it is a strategic imperative linked to organizational survival and associated with a number of historical forces—social, political, and technological. For instance, one result of technological advancement in communication is that organizations, to use Gollner's (1983) metaphor, are crowding in on each other. Schon (in Gollner, 1983) wrote that "The new electronic technologies of communications have, in particular, evolved as though they were going to produce . . . instantaneous confrontations of every part of society with every other part" (p. 33). It is strategically imperative that organizations be prepared to make the appropriate communication responses in this new environment; organizational survival depends on it. At this stage of the discussion, however, it remains an open question whether strategic necessity, a necessity connected to survival of an organization, is to be understood as the practical necessity to which social rules theorists appeal. Indeed, it may be helpful conceptually to distinguish strategic necessity from practical necessity, where the latter, unlike the former, incorporates moral consideration. The distinction between strategic and practical or ethical necessity is a useful one. Indeed, it has already been suggested in the public relations literature by Sullivan (1965). Sullivan argued that strategic values were a subset of technical values, those concerned with effective and efficient goal achievement. These could be considered amoral because they do not take into account whether goals are morally right or wrong. Questions of morality, according to Sullivan, were a separate set of questions. To continue this line of thought, some of Apel's ideas are introduced here, for he argued that system interdependence and interconnectedness have profound ethical implications.

Like Gollner, the philosopher Apel (1980) also argued that scientific and technological advances have drawn parts of the world closer together to create a globally uniform civilization in which human action and inaction have potentially universal effects. The result, he believed, is paradoxical in a way that raises ethical concerns. To make his point, Apel distinguished three realms of human endeavor: (a) a micro-domain that includes such institutions as family, marriage, and neighborhood; (b) a meso-domain at the level of national politics; and (c) a macro-domain at the level of all of mankind. Part of the paradox, Apel suggested, is that although scientific advancement has meant that human action has effects in the macro-domain, there has been no concomitant advance in the area of ethics.

Ethics, said Apel, are still at the level of the micro-domain even as the need for a universal ethics becomes ever more pressing. "Today the technological consequences of science have secured for human actions and inactions such a range and scope that it is no longer possible to be content with moral norms which regulate human life in small groups" (p. 226). Apel is thinking specifically of the technological consequences associated with the invention of the atomic bomb (the total destruction of life) and with effects and side effects of industrial technology (pollution). He concluded that "the results of science present a moral challenge for mankind. Scientific-technical civilization has confronted all nations, races and cultures, regardless of their group-specific, culturally relative morals traditions, with a common ethical problem" (p. 228).

In summary, Apel's analysis suggests the apparent adoption of systems theory by public relations can be interpreted in a specific way. Systems theory, with its doctrines of interconnectedness and interdependence, makes it unavoidable that one focus on interorganizational or intergroup (i.e., intersystem) relationships. It has been suggested that these relationships are not fruitfully conceptualized as either logical or nomic, but might better be thought of as either strategic or ethical. Apel's analysis stresses the ethical side of these relationships. If organizational actions have consequences for more and more subsystems, then it would follow that the ethical obligations or organizations are similarly extending further and further.

But the fact of interdependence might also mean for organizations that they must take more inputs into account when they plan the strategies intended to secure organizational security and growth. Such considerations of strategy do not necessarily take into account moral issues but often emphasize organizational goals and objectives. By distinguishing the strategic and the ethical, the outline of two sides or faces of systems theory begins to appear. One side emphasizes the moral implications of a systems view. The other emphasizes the question of what strategies are functional for achieving organizational objectives. Will public relations theorists who adopt a systems perspective privilege the ethical or the strategic implications of system interdependence? To being exploring this idea further, it is necessary to inquire into the relationship between systems theory and functionalism.

SYSTEMS THEORY AND FUNCTIONALISM

Although the adoption of a systems perspective seems to make arguments like Apel's relevant for the public relations profession, it also links public relations theory with approaches to anthropological and sociological analysis and explanation known as functionalism. Sztompka (1974) suggested this connection is unavoidable in that the two approaches are much the same. He said that "Functional analysis may be regarded as a branch of what is widely known as 'system approach,' 'systemic analysis,' or 'general systems theory'" (p. 56). Others, Hage (1972) for instance, suggest there are important differences between systems theory and functionalism.

In attempting to describe and explain other cultures, anthropologists began by asking what function a particular social role or ritual had for the overall system of culture. A strict functionalist approach would assume that every aspect of a culture—its rituals, ideas, philosophies, material objects, and so on—was an indispensable part of the whole culture and contributed in some fashion to the whole. It can be seen that this view reflects the assumptions similar to those described in connection with the doctrine of internal relations. Thus, for functionalism, the central question is what function a particular aspect of a culture plays with respect to the overall structure of that culture, and in what ways particular structural arrangements are functional. A structural role can be functional whether a social actor intends or is aware of the function an action fulfills (i.e., whether the function is latent or manifest, Merton, 1948).

A functionalist approach also emphasizes a focus on outcomes; in communication it redirects attention to the consequences of communication and away from the communication process (Dance & Larson, 1976). Keeping this in mind, it can be seen why, in the approaches of those public relations theorists who invoke the language of systems theory, management by objectives systems are often chosen as the preferred decision-making model. For MBO routinely emphasizes the importance of effects and results of activities over the importance of the activities themselves to ask how a particular set of message effects is functional for an organization.

Functionalism is susceptible to a number of criticisms. Although the theory's assumptions seem to make sense when applied to small-scale primitive social groupings, they are more difficult to justify for modern, complex, and dynamic communities and societies. According to Sztompka (1974), three main charges have been brought against functionalism, although all three are in a sense related. These are the charges of teleological bias, a static bias, and an ahistorical bias.

The first of these charges claims, essentially, that functionalism is a form of disguised metaphysics that must appeal to final causality as a form of explanation. Scientific theories, in contrast, appeal to efficient causality where the cause is temporally prior to the effect. In functionalism, functions are explained in terms of their contribution to the achievement of cultural or system goals where these goals are taken for granted, or argued for, as part of a theory of history. In various theories, social forms are functional because they promote the will of God, the ends of some evolutionary process, the imperatives of nature, or the economic goals of Marxism or capitalism. In all these cases, a particular interpretation of history and a particular set of values is taken as the correct empirical description of social reality. It is then in terms of this theory that cultural or system goals are posited. Even when the goals are stated in seemingly more neutral language (i.e., in terms of system maintenance, achievement of homeostatic balance, or defense against system entropy) the same kinds of questions about what are the appropriate interpretations of history and social values are usually begged. When assumptions like these are made, functionalism is also vulnerable to the charges that it is static and ahistorical, that it cannot easily explain change. For by definition, a social form cannot be functional from the point of view of the preferred interpretation when, in the name of structural change, it threatens system balance or is functional vis-à-vis the social goals of a radical subsystem.

One of the most current discussions of the strengths and weaknesses of systems approaches and functionalism is the debate between Habermas and Luhmann where an important issue is the question of how the social subject is to be integrated into a society that functions as a self-regulating system (McCarthy, 1982). Habermas argued that the teleological assumptions implicit in any system perspective must always be open to rational, unconstrained discussion and critique. There would be no "natural" systems imperatives immune from such discussion. Luhmann, on the other hand, said this view is naive in the face of the complexity of modern social systems where system administrators need autonomy. For systems theorists, the aim is not the reflective enlightenment of members of a social system but the continued existence of the system; indeed, such enlightenment and system transparency could be dysfunctional for the system. Habermas' (1973/1975) own argument on this point is that current "legitimation crises" of advanced capitalism are partly a result of the opacity of decision-making processes.

A discussion of the relationship between functionalism and systems theory raises a number of questions for public relations. An almost incomprehensible number of messages flows daily back and forth between organizations and their publics. But how do organizations and their publics see this flow of information?

What manifest functions do they think it serves? What latent functions might it serve? Are public relations departments, departments that conceive of themselves as performing a management function, "administering" their publics on a model that sees system imperatives as best served when publics are shielded from some of the complexities of policy decisions? Or can public relations be a communication process that facilitates genuine discussion and critique of policy questions? When public relations managers enter public relations situations with pre-established objectives, do they make the same kind of teleological assumptions that a functionalist makes? Can these assumptions be opened up for discussion? These choices can be viewed as choices about the type of necessity that a public relations person incorporates into his or her approach to a systems-oriented public relations management. Emphasizing strategic necessity justifies administering publics to achieve system survival objectives; emphasizing practical or ethical necessity justifies the raising of moral questions and involving publics in discussions of them.

The call for an increasingly sophisticated social scientific orientation on the part of public relations practitioners needs to be balanced by a recognition that some practitioners may interpret this as an invitation to find more sophisticated techniques for managing and administering publics rather than for improving understanding. It is useful to recall that Bernays (1952), who was among the first to recommend the application of social scientific techniques in public relations, was also in favor of social planning because he did not think the general public was capable of participating in the decision-making processes of the modern organization (Olasky, 1987).

The key question for public relations is whether the emergence of a systems paradigm will also reinforce a narrow functionalist perspective that ultimately will restrict the range of discussion on public issues because such discussion is seen to be dysfunctional. The concern can be expressed another way as a tension between strategic and practical or ethical necessity. Finally, the tension might also be described as a tension between two possible tendencies in system theoretic approaches—one that emphasizes functionalism and one that emphasizes the ethical or humanist implications of global interdependencies. These two approaches can be schematized as follows

Emphasis on Functionalism
- favors language of management by objectives and implied possibility of reductionism and analytic methods
- strategic necessity; perhaps nomic necessity
- emphasis on system maintenance and environmental control
- emphasis on monologue, unbalanced communication effect and persuasion

Emphasis on Idea of Interdependence
- favors language of holism, though without accepting a doctrine of internal relations

- antireductionist
- practical or ethical necessity
- emphasis on interrelationships and their practical and moral implications; admits possibility of system change and adaption
- emphasis on dialogue, mutual understanding and balanced communication effects

WHEN IS SYSTEMS THEORY NOT FUNCTIONALISM?

It is important to be clear on the question whether a systems approach to public relations necessarily takes up the biases and weakness of functionalism. For if there are two faces to systems theory, as was previously suggested, it is vitally important to see how they are related. Is there an internal logic to systems analyses that privileges functional ways of thinking? Or can systems theory be conceptualized to privilege the second, more humanist, mode of thinking outlined above? Hage (1972) discussed this point and noted that functionalism and systems approaches are similar in that they both incorporate many of the same elements and variables. But an important difference also exists—functionalism emphasizes structure, out-put, and performance whereas systems theory emphasizes input, throughput, and output. Thus, it is argued that the addition of *input* to the model clearly dis-tinguishes systems theory from functionalism.

But input can be of more than one kind. To see these differences, it is worth examining a typology of system regulatory processes suggested by Hage (1972) and linking these to different kinds of feedback. Hage listed control, adjustment, and adaptation as three system-regulatory processes. For an organization to control its environment, input need not be anything more than the thinnest, quantitative feedback about the overt behavioral responses of social actors in the organization's environment. If these social actors are demonstrating violently against the cost of medical facilities, coercion, or perhaps persuasive messages, can be used to main-tain these behaviors within acceptable limits. To give another example: child abuse can be controlled by law enforcement and punishment. For an organization to adjust to its environment, on the other hand, could include responses like the reallocation of system resources to make available more doctors and hospitals and thereby lower the cost of these services. In the case of child abuse, adjustment might mean creation of drop-in centers and educational programs for parents in high-risk categories. But to make these adjustments, an organization needs more *understanding* than is afforded by quantitative feedback. Further, for organizational adaptation, an organization needs rich and thick accounts of its environment in order reach valid understandings and interpretations of it. For Hage, adaptation involves actual changes in system structure. Thus, reallocation of medical resources might not be enough. Instead, more radical system changes in terms of the production of nourishment and leisure, for instance, might be considered as a way of lessening the need for increased medical resources. Similarly, structural changes that reduce poverty and other social conditions associated with child abuse might be considered as adaptive measures to deal with child abuse. But to understand what are the real needs of social actors in the environment so that these kinds of changes can be made requires a specific kind of input, input that is qualitatively different from that needed for environmental control.

To summarize, a system approach that thinks in terms of control, and perhaps even adjustment, may not escape a functionalist perspective that begs questions about system needs and about the needs of environmental subsystems. On the other hand, an organization that can adapt structure after seeking and interpreting input to understand (and not just measure) its environment, employs a systems approach that does seem to go beyond a narrow functionalism. But if it goes beyond functionalism, it does so not simply by virtue of the fact that there is input, but because there is input of a certain kind. The addition of input to functional ways of thinking, therefore, does not necessarily get beyond functionalism.

Burrell and Morgan (1979) also developed a particularly useful discussion of functionalism and systems theory and argued that systems theorists can be victims of the metaphors, often mechanistic or organismic, they choose for systems analy-sis. Burrell and Morgan argued that social and organizational analysis takes place within four broad paradigms determined by theoretical assumptions along two dimensions. These dimensions are a subjective–objective dimension and a regula-tion–radical change dimension. Essentially, the first dimension is characterized by the debate between phenomenological and positivistic approaches to social or organizational analysis and, according to Burrell and Morgan, this debate has obscured in recent years issues connected with the second dimension. This second dimension is a continuum from sociologies of regulation concerned with the status quo, social order, consensus, social integration and cohesion, solidarity, need satisfaction, and actuality, to sociologies of radical change concerned with radical change, conflict, modes of domination, contradiction, emancipation, deprivation, and potentiality.

Burrell and Morgan argued that the functionalist paradigm has been dominant for academic sociology and organizational studies. It is safe to say that they would include public relations studies within this paradigm, as Trujillo and Toth (1986) have noted. According to Burrell and Morgan (1979)

> The functionalist paradigm generates regulative sociology in its most fully developed form. In its overall approach it seeks to provide essentially rational explanations of social affairs. It is a perspective which is highly pragmatic in orientation, concerned to understand society in a way which generates knowledge which can be put to use. . . . It is usually committed to a philosophy of social engineering as a basis of social change and emphasizes the importance of understanding order, equilibrium and stability in society and the way in which these are maintained. It is concerned with the effective 'regulation' and control of social affairs. (p. 26)

Burrell and Morgan included systems theory within this broad, functionalist, sociology of regulation. But they did this, not because the two are necessarily just different versions of the same approach, but because most appropriations of systems theory for social and organizational analysis merely dress up functional analysis in new clothes.

> [T]he full implications of an open systems approach have not been pursued in any great real depth. The concept has been adopted in a very partial and often misleading way. For many theorists, the adoption of an open system perspective has been a very limited venture, confined to recognizing and emphasizing the environment as an influence . . . and reformulating traditional models in terms of systems concepts. More than anything, the call to adopt an open systems approach has been interpreted as a call to take heed of the environment and little else. (p. 60)

Taking the environment into account requires only the adoption of input variables and, as previously noted, adopting the concept of input is a necessary but not sufficient condition for escaping functionalism. According to Burrell and Morgan, only a sophisticated and thoughtfully applied systems theory will go beyond functionalism. They suggested that part of the difficulty is in discovering appropriate metaphors; too often social systems theory makes use of inappropriate mechanistic and organismic analogies. Among other things, these analogies bring with them the idea of *system needs* and the intellectual baggage of structural functionalism. They said that "of particular importance as far as the organismic analogy is concerned are those (principles) which imply that the system has needs; that these are necessarily geared to survival or homeostasis; and that the subsystems contribute to the well-being of the system as a whole" (p. 63). One can see that this concern with needs results partly from the impact of objectivism and the attendant belief that there are real and abiding system imperatives that are unchanging and ineluctable. If an organismic metaphor penetrates public relations thinking, system organizational needs will come first; they will be taken for granted as natural. A most important question for public relations is what it will make of its apparent choice of systems theory as a meta-theoretic perspective. The following paragraphs sketch out another alternative for what systems theory might mean for public relations.

Burrell and Morgan suggested Buckley's (1967) approach starts to get beyond a systems theory that is really functionalism in disguise by using a morphogenic analogy for system processes. According to Buckley: "Morphostatic processes . . . (include) equilibrium, homeostasis, and negative feedback. These conserving, deviation-counterbalancing processes have come to be emphasized in the literature at the expense of structure-elaborating, deviation-promoting processes that are central to an understanding of higher level systems such as the sociocultural" (p. 59). Buckley also said that "The modern [morphogenic] systems perspective provides a theoretical framework for the sociocultural system that is significantly more appropriate and adequate than the mechanical-equilibrium or organismic-functional models dominating much of current social science thinking" (p. 81).

But it is important to become clearer about precisely what kind of meaning Buckley wanted to give his morphogenic analogy to see how it goes beyond mechanistic and organismic analogies. The important step for Buckley is accomplished by jettisoning the theory of final causality (teleological explanation) often associated with organismic analogies and replacing it with some kind of efficient causal explanation. Yet the kind of "cause" Buckley seemed to have in mind is motive or desire, the kind of cause one usually associates with purposeful, human action, and not the kind of cause one associates with inorganic bodies. His thinking becomes clear in this passage:

> [T]he ground work has been laid for elucidating the conditions making for self-regulation, development, or disintegration—instead of assuming automatic regulations or 'mechanisms of control'—for any system we are dealing with. And *the decision-making of learning, thinking, groups of individuals is given an important place as a psycho-social process* that brings into conjunction previously unrelated events or conditions, by way of social action and transaction, to produce the current sociocultural structure. Thus, *decision-making is seen as the exemplar, in the sociocultural system, of the general selective process* occurring in every adaptive system. (p. 79; italics added)

This is a crucial passage in Buckley. A social system is not analogous to an organism with its taken for granted, natural, and indomitable needs. Rather it is analogous to a group of human decision makers, a meeting for instance, or a speech community, which can examine the needs it often takes for granted and discover that they are not always natural or inevitable. McCarthy (1985), in commenting on Habermas, also discussed the differences between a functionalism that must assume and take for granted some system imperatives with one that endeavors to funnel these imperatives, and the rationales that sustain them, through a rational decision-making process where they might become discursively transparent. Habermas (cited in McCarthy, 1985) called this an hermeneutically enlightened functionalism, although he might equally well have talked about an hermeneutically enlightened systems theory. The goals of social systems are not interpreted simply in terms of system self-preservation but are based on rational discussion among system members, the kind of discussion that perhaps Buckley had in mind when he suggested human decision making was the exemplar in sociocultural systems of the general selective processes that take place in all systems. According to Habermas, "the meaning in relation to which the functionality of social processes is measured is now linked to the idea of a communication free from domination. . . . In place of the goal state of a self-regulating system we would like the anticipated end state of a formative process" (cited in McCarthy, 1985, p. 52).

This formative process for Habermas is, of course, a communication process, and one in and through which what Habermas called "autonomous publics" establish relations with institutions such that "the self-steering mechanisms" of these institutions are made "sufficiently sensitive to the goal-oriented result of radically democratic will formation" (cited McCarthy, 1985, p. 50). It follows that, if a systems approach to public relations takes a human decision-making community as an appropriate analogy for a social system, a number of important questions are raised for both practitioners and scholars. What makes this decision-making process rational? Under what conditions can one say it is a decision-making process free of domination and constraint? When is it truly democratic? For a public relations practice that adopts a systems perspective, yet seeks a way of going beyond a narrow and strategic functionalism, these kinds of questions become central.

CONCLUSION

In summary, it is not clear what the adoption of systems theory will mean for public relations. It may simply provide the profession with a highly technical, and sometimes obfuscating and mystifying language, with which to talk about organizational goals and objectives without subjecting these to critical analysis. It may simply be a way of entrenching narrow organizational self-interest as the inevitable and natural motives for organizational action. In other words, systems theory may simply make a narrow functionalism look new and respectable. This use of systems theory would emphasize the idea of strategic necessity.

But systems theory could also provide the language and the concepts for reconstructing public relations as a particular kind of collaborative decision-making process. It could provide the language and the concepts for an approach to public relations that emphasizes practical necessity and ethical considerations based on the kinds of conclusions Apel drew when he examined the implications of the increasing interdependency of modern social systems. The focus for public relations theory and practice would then shift to the structure of this communicative and collaborative decision-making processes and the role it might play in mediating the tensions among interdependent social systems.

REFERENCES

Apel, K.-O. (1980). *Toward a transformation of philosophy* (G. Adey & D. Frisby, Trans.). London: Routledge & Kegan Paul.

Aronoff, C., & Baskin, O. (1988). *Public relations: The profession and the practice*. St. Paul, MN: West Publishing.

Bell, S. H., & Bell, E. C. (1976). Public relations: Functional or functionary? *Public Relations Review, 2*(2), 47–57.

Berger, C. R. (1977). The covering law perspective as a theoretical basis for the study of human communication. *Communication Quarterly, 25*, 7–18.

Bernays, E. L. (1952). *Public relations*. Norman, OK: University of Oklahoma Press.

Buckley, W. (1967). *Sociology and modern systems theory.* Englewood Cliffs, NJ: Prentice-Hall.

Burrell, G., & Morgan, G. (1979) .*Sociological paradigms and organisational analysis.* London: Heinemann.

Chase, W. H. (1977, October). Public issue management: The new science. *Public Relations Journal, 33,* 25–26.

Crable, R. E., & Vibbert, S. L. (1986). *Public relations as communications management.* Edina MN: Bellwether Press.

Culbertson, H. M. (1983). Three perspectives on American journalism. *Journalism Monographs, 83.*

Cushman, D. P. (1977). The rules perspective as a theoretical basis for the study of human communication. *Communication Quarterly, 25,* 30–45.

Cutlip, S. M., Center, A. H., & Broom, G. M. (1985). *Effective public relations* (6th ed.). Englewood Cliffs, NJ: Prentice-Hall.

Dance, F. E., & Larson, C. E. (1976). *Functions of human communication.* New York: Holt, Rinehart & Winston.

Dunn, S. W. (1986). *Public relations.* Homewood IL: Irwin.

Ehling, W. P. (1984). Application of decision theory in the construction of a theory of public relations I. *Public Relations Research and Education, 1*(2), 25–39.

Ehling, W. P., & Hesse, M. B. (1983). Use of 'issue management' in public relations. *Public Relations Review, 9,* 18–35.

Gollner, A. B. (1983). *Social change and corporate strategy: The expanding role of public affairs.* Stamford: Issue Action Press.

Grunig, J. E. (1988). Review of "Public relations: What research tells us". *Journalism Quarterly, 65,* 216.

Grunig, J. E., & Hickson, R. H. (1976). An evaluation of academic research in public relations. *Public Relations Review, 2*(1), 31–43.

Grunig, J. E., & Hunt, T. (1984). *Managing public relations.* New York: Holt, Rinehart & Winston.

Habermas, J. (1975). *Legitimation crisis* (T. McCarthy, Trans.). Boston: Beacon Press. (Original work published 1973)

Hage, J. (1972). *Techniques and problems of theory construction in sociology.* New York: Wiley.

Katz, D., & Khan, R. L. (1966). *The social psychology of organizations.* New York: Wiley.

Kuhn, T. (1970). *The structure of scientific revolutions.* Chicago: University of Chicago Press.

Long, L. W., & Hazleton, V., Jr. (1987). Public relations: A theoretical and practical response. *Public Relations Review, 13*(2), 3–13.

McCarthy, T. (1982). *The critical theory of Jürgen Habermas.* Cambridge, MA: MIT Press.

McCarthy, T. (1985). Complexity and democracy, or the seducements of systems theory. *New German Critique, 35,* 27–53.

Merton, R. K. (1948). *Social theory and social structure.* New York: The Free Press.

Monge, P. R. (1977). Theory construction in the study of communication: The systems paradigm. *Journal of Communication, 23,* 5–16.

Nager, N. R., & Allen, T. H. (1984). *Public relations management by objectives.* New York: Longman.

Olasky, M. N. (1987). *Corporate public relations and American private enterprise: A new historical perspective.* Hillsdale, NJ: Lawrence Erlbaum Associates.

Pavlik, J. V. (1987). *Public relations: What research tells us.* Beverly Hills: Sage.

Pavlik, J. V., & Salmon, C. T. (1984). Theoretic approaches in public relations research. *Public Relations Research and Education, 1*(2), 39–49.

Phillips, D. C. (1976). *Holistic thought in social science.* Stanford, CA: University of California Press.

Reilly, R. T. (1987). *Public relations in action.* Englewood Cliffs, NJ: Prentice-Hall.

Seital, F. P. (1987). *The practice of public relations* (2nd ed.). Columbus, OH: Charles E. Merrill.

Sullivan, A. J. (1965). Values in pubic relations. In O. Lerbinger & A. J. Sullivan (Eds.), *Information, influence and communication: A reader in public relations* (pp. 412–439). New York: Basic Books.

Sztompka, P. (1974). *System and function: Toward a theory of society.* New York: Academic Press.

Terry, K. E. (1987, May). *An empirical investigation of the applications of public relations theory and education to public relations practice.* Paper presented to the conference on Communication Theory and Public Relations, Normal, IL.

Trujillo, N., & Toth, E. L. (1986, August). *Organizational paradigms for public relations research and practice.* Paper presented to the Public Relations Division, Association for Education in Journalism and Mass Communication, Norman, OK.

Wolter, L. J., & Miles, S. B. (1983). Toward public relations theory. *Public Relations Journal, 39*(9), 13–16.

Chapter 11

Organizational Culture and Ethnoecology in Public Relations Theory and Practice

James L. Everett
University of Wisconsin—Madison

Contemporary models of public relations theory and practice are built from the perspective that public relations is the management function that helps organizations adapt to environmental requirements through the establishment of mutually beneficial relationships. These models are characterized as ecological because they base the role and significance of organizational public relations in the organization/environment relationship. Within the terms of these models, successful public relations is predicated on the ability of the practitioner to describe and manage change requirements within the organization as well as the environment. In public relations theory, organizational adaptation results from developing strategies in the form of organizational and environmental change programs that produce and maintain stability in the organization/environment relationship. The outcome of successfully mediating organization/environment relationships through internal and external change programs is an adapted organization.

In this chapter I argue that when these ecologically based models of public relations are linked to the perspective that organizations are evolving, sociocultural systems (Weick, 1969, 1979), a distinct set of implications emerge for public relations theory and practice. In public relations theory, a sociocultural perspective on organizations links cultural, behavioral, and environmental factors in a framework informed by the principles of sociocultural and ecological anthropology, organizational communication, and organizational sociology. I argue for a view of organizational culture as a cognitive system based in the historical experience of the group and shared among group members. When this culture concept is linked with Weick's sociocultural perspective on organizations and ecological models of public relations, then an understanding of the interplay between organizational ecology and organizational culture (the domain of ethnographic ecology or eth-noecology) become crucial to the development of public relations theory and refinement of practice. The implications of such a framework for the practice of public relations center on the need to systematically describe and manage the relationship between the organizational culture and organizational ecology.

I begin by examining the ecological models that frame contemporary discus-sions of the role and significance of public relations to organizations. I link this ecological context to the literature of organizational culture and ethnography in organizational theory. I describe the enterprise of organizational ethnography that provides descriptions of organizational cultures. I integrate organizational eth-nography with ecological public relations models in order to detail the implications of ethnoecology in public relations research and theory. Finally, I illustrate how ethnoecology can inform public relations through a case study that describes the relationship between culture and adaptive strategy in a nonprofit organization.

ECOLOGICAL MODELS IN PUBLIC RELATIONS

Public relations focuses on what Scott (1987) described as the "reciprocal ties that bind and relate the organization with those elements that surround and penetrate it" (p. 117). This view of the functional significance of public relations is part of the standard "contingency perspective" that according to Duncan and Weiss (1979) dominates the literatures of organizational theory and management. Dun-can and Weiss asserted that this approach holds that "organizations are treated as open systems which engage in exchanges with their environments" (p. 76).

Most contemporary conceptualizations of the discipline stress that public rela-tions theory and practice is derived from the overtly ecological context of the organization/environment relationship. Cutlip, Center, and Broom (1985) for-malized this approach in the prototype model for defining and describing the organizational role and functional significance of public relations—the Adjustment and Adaptation Model.

Cutlip, Center, and Broom argued that within the Adjustment and Adaptation Model, "The ecological approach . . . sees public relations as one way the organi-zation adapts to its environment" (p. 102). They contend that "ecology is used to introduce the interaction of organizations and their social environments" (p. 184). Cutlip et al. claim that:

> organizations must continually adjust their relationships with publics in response to everchanging social milieu. Because organization-publics systems exist in changing environments, they must be capable of adapting their goals and relationships to accommodate change pressures from their complex and dynamic settings. (p. 185)

In a similar ecologically based model, Long and Hazelton (1987) argued that pubic relations is the function "through which organizations adapt to, alter, or maintain their environment for the purpose of achieving organizational goals" (p. 6).

Although historically public relations has focused on producing change in the environment, contemporary models of practice posit "reciprocal change" as the key to adequate practice of public relations. For example, Grunig and Hunt's (1984) "two-way symmetric" model of public relations emphasizes the potential for *reciprocal change* and effects between an organization and its publics. Crable and Vibbert (1986) argued that "public relations is a process aimed at adjusting organizations to their environments, and at adjusting environments to the organization" (p. 6). They claim that "the value or worth of public relations communication for any given organization ultimately resides in the ability of public relations to adjust relationships" (p. 394). The concept of reciprocal change present in public relations models requires that practitioners systematically identify factors of the external environment as well as the perceptions of organizational members concerning the organization and its environment in order to meet the change requirements inherent to ecological processes. The theoretical significance of the concept of reciprocal change is the recognition that organizational adaptation (the goal of pubic relations practice) is predicated on environmental change as well as the capacity of the organization to change to meet environmental requirements. This component of reciprocal change provides the drive for the study of ethnographic ecology (i.e., ethnoecology) in public relations. Ethnoecology is the description and analysis of culturally based perceptions of organizational ecology shared among organizational members. These perceptions mediate the potential for organizational change related to organizational adaptation. As Scott (1987) noted, such perspectives on organizations are built from the view that "to survive is to adapt; and to adapt is to change" (p. 91).

ORGANIZATIONAL CULTURE THEORY

One of the most active areas of recent organizational research and theory is the study of organizational culture. There are a diverse set of conceptualizations of the culture concept in organizations. Work in the area includes views of culture as shared meanings (Gregory, 1983; Pettigrew, 1979), shared values and norms (Schwartz & Davis, 1981; Tichy, 1982), shared behavior (Baker, 1980; Tunstall, 1983), and shared symbols (Barley, 1983; Pfeffer, 1981). One of the most explicit discussions of the significance of organizational culture is provided by Schein (1985). Schein argued that organizational culture is essential to understanding organizations and organizing processes. He asserted that "the examination of cultural issues at the organizational level is absolutely essential to a basic understanding of what goes on in organizations, how to run them, and how to improve them" (p. 30). Schein argued that with respect to organizational/environment relationships, "once culture is present in the sense of shared assumptions, those assumptions, in turn, influence what will be perceived and defined as the environ-ment" (p. 51).

In the literature of organizational communication, the concept of organizational culture is largely developed under the terms of an interpretive perspective that bundles several related approaches (e.g., Deetz, 1982; Pacanowsky & O'Donnell-Trujillo, 1982; Smircich, 1981). Within this interpretive perspective, the concept of culture is used as a "root metaphor" for the organization. In other words, the organization is viewed as if it were a culture. This view of organizations as cultures has been contrasted with "functionalist" perspectives on organizations (e.g., Put-nam, 1983). Functionalist studies view organizations as instruments of production or mechanisms to capture certain goals. Organizational culture is treated as an independent variable that manipulates behavior and beliefs (e.g., Baker, 1980). These two conceptualizations of organization are responsible for the development of distinctive research programs (Smircich, 1983). They are both contingent on a conceptualization of organization from which the concept of culture is derived. Thus, the significance of the concept of culture of organizational studies is delim-ited within a conception of organization.

Current concepts of culture in the anthropological literature suggests that view-ing organizations as equivalent to cultures is inadequate as an approach to the study of organizations. The conceptual inadequacy stems from the failure to dis-tinguish between cultural and behavioral features of organizational life. The need to keep the cultural distinct from the social is a prominent concern among culture theorists in anthropology (e.g., Garbarino, 1977). According to Keesing (1974), major modern culture theorists including Geertz, Goodenough, Levi-Strauss, and Schnieder have recognized "the dangers of swallowing the social into the cultural or the cultural into the social" and:

> share the premise that the cultural and social realms are distinct though interrelated:
> neither is a mere reflection of the other- each must be considered in its own right.
> Such a conceptual untangling is basic to the refinements of theory and narrowing of
> the "culture" concept of the last twenty years. (p. 84)   .

Interpretive perspectives on organizational culture represent the culture concept as "everything that constitutes organizational life" (Pacanowsky & O'Donnell-Trujillo, 1982, p. 122). In public relations theory, use of culture concept needs to be refined to refer to a more specific set of phenomena. Such a refinement is in keeping with the effort to narrow the referent for culture in other disciplines. According to Keesing (1974):

> The challenge in recent years has been to narrow the concept of 'culture' so that it
> includes less and reveals more. As Geertz argues, 'cutting the culture concept down

to size . . . [into] a narrow, specialized, and . . . theoretically more powerful concept' has been a major theme in modern anthropological theorizing. (p. 73)

Given this argument for a more focused definition of culture, we can examine a view of organizations as sociocultural systems, and explore the significance of such a perspective to public relations theory and practice.

ORGANIZATIONS AS SOCIOCULTURAL SYSTEMS

Systems concepts of organizations are a common perspective in public relations theory that treats organizations (e.g., Cutlip, Center, & Broom, 1985; Grunig & Hunt, 1984). As Grunig (1984) noted, "Systems theory seems especially useful for managing either a two-way asymmetric or two way symmetric public relations department, both of which are designed to help the organization deal with its environment" (p. 93). A significant refinement to standard treatments of organizations as systems is Weick's (1969, 1979) proposal that organizations are best conceptualized as sociocultural systems. Given the distinction between behavior and culture detailed earlier, and in keeping with ecological models of public relations, within such a perspective the organization represents "the social realizations or enactments of ideational designs-for-living in particular environments" (Keesing, 1974, p. 82). As a sociocultural system, the organization has two essential properties: a cultural component and a social component. The social component includes recurrent patterns of behavior of organizational members over time. A sociocultural perspective suggest a concept of culture derived from the tradition of cognitive anthropology. Within this tradition, Keesing (1976) argued that culture refers to:

> systems of shared ideas, to the conceptual designs, the shared systems of meanings, that underlie the ways in which a people live. Culture so defined refers to what human learn, not what they do. Goodenough [asserts] that knowledge provides "standards for deciding what can be done, for deciding what to do about it, for deciding how to go about it." (p. 139)

Thus, the sociocultural perspective is built from the view of culture as a cognitive system of historically shaped and socially acquired beliefs and values (Keesing, 1974; Quinn & Holland, 1987). Culture as a shared cognitive system transforms individual cognition into a set of collective understandings among organizational members. Keesing (1976) argued that the culture concept should be used:

> to refer to systems of shared ideas, to the conceptual designs, the shared systems of meanings that underlie the ways in which a people live. Culture, so defined, refers to what humans learn, not what they do and make. (p. 139)

In keeping with the emphasis on organizational/environmental relationships in public relations theory, the significance (as well as the challenge) of a sociocultural perspective on organizations for public relations theory is that it links cognitive aspects of organizations ("culture") to social (behavioral) components within specific environmental backgrounds. Treating the organization as a sociocultural system facilitates analysis of the "extent and conditions of linkage between symbolic and substantive outcomes in organizations" (Pfeffer, 1981, p. 8). Research that proceeds from a sociocultural perspective in public relations examines the relationship between ideational aspects of the organization and the actions of the organization (collective behavior) within the context of organizational adaptation.

In organizational theory, the antecedents of a sociocultural approach are formulated by Weick (1969, 1979) in his "sociocultural evolution model" of organizing. Following Campbell's (1965) discussion of biological evolution, Weick proposed that the processes of sociocultural evolution can explicate the processes of human organizing. He developed a model based on three essential elements identified in evolutionary processes—variation, selection, and retention. Weick argued for several "amendments" to biological evolutionary theory to make it applicable to organizational theory. The most important of these amendments is the substitution of the concept of enactment for the process of variation in biological evolution. Weick argued that enactment (i.e., the process by which the environment is constituted by organizational members) should be used instead of variation when referring to human organizing. In Weick's view, variation is introduced into organizing processes within the enactment process. Retention of the variation is mediated by the selection process in Weick's model. Not all variations are adopted and stored in the retention system. Not all retained variations are adaptive.

Weick's sociocultural evolution model of organizing is the first formal effort to adapt the concepts and propositions of evolution and ecology to human organizing. Although there exists a history of anthropological approaches that utilize similar models to study cultures (e.g., Steward's, 1955, cultural ecology, and Sahlins and Service's, 1960, account of general and specific evolution of social systems), Weick's work is the first to call for such an approach within organizational theory. It is important to note that the concepts of social evolution and ecology are *not* intended as metaphors by Weick or the sociocultural perspective presented in this chapter. Following the analytical traditions of ethology, archaeology, ecological anthropology, and particularly organizational ecology in sociology, the concepts of evolution and ecology are central devices for exploring organizations. In organizational ecology this argument is articulated by Hannan and Freeman (1977). They argued that:

> we make a strong continuity-of-nature hypothesis. We propose that, whenever the stated conditions hold, the models lead to valuable insights regardless of whether the populations under study are composed of protozoans or organizations. We do not argue "metaphorically." (p. 962)

Perhaps one of the most succinct arguments for the significance of evolutionary concepts in the analysis of sociocultural systems is provided by Alland (1967). He contended that:

> Evolution is a process through which systems are developed and are modified in relation to specific environmental backgrounds. All the [Darwinian] theory requires is that there be mechanisms of variation (producing new variables) and mechanisms of continuity (preserving maximization) present in these systems and that these systems be subject to environmental selection. There is no requirement that these systems be specifically biological in nature. (p. 196)

Conceptualization of organizations as sociocultural systems that evolve (i.e., develop and change) in response to environmental change carries several important implications for public relations theory. First, it distinguishes between thought and action within the organization and separates each into analytically distinct realms. Second, such a conceptualization provides that if organizations are evolving sociocultural systems, then questions of variation, selection, and retention within the cultural component of the organization are fundamental analytical issues in the analysis of organizational ecology. Finally, following the theoretical implications of ecological models in public relations, a sociocultural perspective on organizations implies that the relationship between the organizational environment and the sociocultural system is, over time, a primary agent in shaping organizational culture as well as many features of organizational life. The consequence of this relationship to the organizational culture is culture change. The consequence of the relationship to the sociocultural system (i.e., the organization) is adaptation—the "fit" of the organization to environmental features. Thus, understanding the cultural features of organizational life is framed within the interaction between the organization and the environment of the organization. It is this concept of reciprocal change in ecological models of public relations that establishes the foundation for ethnographic ecology (ethnoecology) in public relations. As soon as organizations are taken to be sociocultural systems, reciprocal change is predicated on how the cultural aspect of an organization influences the organization/environment relationship. The imperative for this approach is given by the proposition that "environmental factors interact with social and cultural ones, and neither operates independently" (Orlove, 1980, p. 253). Anderson (1973) argued a similar proposition. He asserted that "the culture and the environment are seen as constituting a functionally inseparable unity that may be analyzed but cannot be divided" (p. 209). In organizational studies, Ansoff and Baker (1986) contended that cultural models of requirements for organizational success held by managers must be matched to "external realities of the environment" (p. 84). The authors argued that "continued perception of external reality through the eyes of historical culture creates a strategic myopia which will delay the firm's response to new challenges and can have a major impact on its success" (p. 84).

The implications to public relations theory and practice of the view that culture mediates adaptive strategy, and, ultimately, organizational adaptation, has been identified by Grunig (1987). He observed that "we are increasingly finding that public relations policy is a product of organizational culture" (p. 70). Although the public relations literature has been slow to explicitly recognize the significance of culture studies to describing and managing organizations, there do exist arguments in which the concept of organizational culture operates implicitly. In an acknowledgment of the significance of the culture concept to public relations theory and practice, Crable and Vibbert (1986) argued for the need to conduct "organizational appraisal" in order to assist in producing an adapted organization. They argued that the goal of appraisal is to "make some sense of the organization and its problems—from the point of view of the organization" (p. 13). Two central areas for appraisal concern the "self-perceptions" of the organization and perceptions about the environment held by organizational members. Crable and Vibbert argued that this information is essential to understanding organizational "policies, programs, and relationships" (p. 288). When organizations are viewed as sociocultural systems, such concepts as "organizational appraisal" and "organizational self-concept" are the province of organizational ethnography.

ORGANIZATIONAL ETHNOGRAPHY

Ethnographic research was the foundation for the development of the discipline of cultural anthropology. In this field, ethnography attempts to provide "the general description and overview of the culture, the effort to construct what it means to live in that particular community, to believe as they do, to work as they do, to live as they do" (Goldschmidt, 1977, p. 25). According to Goodenough (1964) the aim of ethnography is to "depict the system for perceiving, believing, evaluating and acting" used by a group (p. 14).

The large and growing literature on organizational culture has established the need and general outlines of organizational ethnography (Gregory, 1983; Morey & Luthans, 1984; Sanday, 1979; Van Maanen, 1979). Work in the area of organizational ethnography has a lengthy intellectual history dating back to human relations studies in the 1920s (Gregory, 1983). Organizational ethnography holds promise for theory building and public relations practice given models of reciprocal change and effects in organization/environment relationships. Morey and Luthans (1984) argued that ethnographic methods "offer insider, subjective data of immediate practical utility for practicing managers and researchers" (p. 28). Ethnographic methods include participant observation, interviews of key informants, and document analysis. Ethnography is a systematic and comprehensive way to achieve an empirically based description of individual member perceptions about the organization and its environment, and to link those perceptions to the larger context in which they operate collectively—the organizational culture.

Grunig (1987) argued that it is essential for public relations practitioners to understand how the culture of an organization shapes and constrains strategy toward the environment and environmental relationships. Crable and Vibbert (1986) also argued that understanding "perceptions or images of the environment" is essential to public relations practice (p. 301). When organizations are viewed as sociocultural systems, it is necessary to establish this charge within the domain of the organizational culture. It is at the cultural level of analysis that the collective set of perceptions of environment become accessible to public relations managers. This specific need frames and refines the role and nature of ethnography in public relations. Organizational ethnography in the context of public relations research and theory must focus on the cultural regulation of organizational ecology. Thus, the specific domain of organizational ethnography with significance to public relations is ethnographic ecology or ethnoecology.

ETHNOECOLOGY

Ethnoecology examines the "way in which cognitive organization of recognized environmental phenomena affects (consciously or unconsciously) ecological relations" (Ellen, 1982, p. 210). Ellen argued that "a proper understanding of indigenous knowledge and cognitive structures is theoretically crucial to the analysis of ecological relations" (p. 206). This argument is the central rationale for the adoption of ethnoecological theory and analysis in public relations. Ellen (1982) argued for the theoretical significance of ethnoecology in cultural studies of human ecology. He asserted that "It is because we see nature in terms of cultural images, and because it is to these we respond, that a proper understanding of indigenous knowledge and cognitive structures is theoretically crucial to the analysis of ecological relations" (p. 206).

Research focusing on environmental and ecological models held by group members is an important trend in human ecological and behavioral studies (Ellen, 1982; Orlove, 1980; Ortner, 1984). Orlove (1980) argued that descriptions of the ecological models held by group members (actor-based models) permits examination of "the proximate factors which influence the behavior of individual and aggregates" (p. 248).

Ethnoecology has a lengthy history in the literature of anthropological ecology. In an early overview of the task of ethnoecology, Frake (1961) asserted that "The aim of ethnoecological research is to provide a better understanding of how people perceive their environment and how they organize these perceptions" (p. 281). According to Vayda and Rappaport (1968), the aim of ethnoecology is to:

> present a people's view of the environmental setting itself and their view of the behavior appropriate to that setting . . . it is reasonable to regard a people's cognition with respect to environmental phenomena as part of the mechanism producing the

actual physical behavior through which people directly effect alterations in their environment. (p. 490)

The significance of ethnoecology to public relations theory and practice is found in the view that organizational culture mediates the organization/environment relationship. The concept of reciprocal change predicates the efficacy of public relations on the capacity to produce change in the organization as well as the environment. When organizations are taken to be sociocultural systems, environmentally driven organizational change is bound to the more general problem of culture change. This view of the significance of culture to group adaptation has substantial theoretical and empirical precedent in the literature of anthropological ecology (e.g., Jochim, 1981; Orlove, 1080; Steward, 1977).

In the organizational literature, Kanter (1983) provided a strong-case argument for the mediation of adaptation by the knowledge structures of organizational members. She contended that the organizational culture in the form of perceptions of the environment and environmental change pressures stimulate organizational change rather than actual "pressures" from the environment. Schein's (1984) research indicates that the culture of an organization influences adaptation through the development of consensus around such problems as organizational strategy and goals, performance measures, and "remedial and repair strategies" necessary when goals are not acquired (p. 8). These problems are central to the project of ethnoecology in public relations. In order to address such problems it is necessary to identify the type of research data that ethnoecology provides to public relations practice.

The Data of Organizational Ethnoecology

There exists an important difference between cognitive material that operates at the individual level (e.g., the causal maps identified in Weick's, 1979, model of organizing), and cognitive material at the organizational (collective) level. As Gioia (1986) argued, "contrary to tradition, cognition in organizations should not be construed only as a phenomenon occurring at the level of the individual" (p. 350). It is this difference that defines the potential contribution of ethnoecology to public relations theory and practice. This contribution is based in the view that the organization/environment relationship focus of public relations is, in part, a culturally constructed system. A view of organizations as sociocultural systems necessarily shifts descriptive and explanatory efforts from the individual to the cultural level of analysis. Daft and Weick (1984) argued this view in their contention that:

> the organizational interpretive process is something more than what occurs by individuals. Organizations have cognitive systems and memories. . . . Individuals come and go, but organizations preserve knowledge, behaviors, mental maps, norms and values over time. The distinctive feature of organizational level information activity is sharing. (p. 285)

Public relations practitioners must be able to identify these shared organizational knowledge structures (the cultural component of the organization) because these features shape and constrain environmental interpretation and, consequently, organizational ecology and adaptation.

At the organizational level of analysis, ethnoecology provides cultural data in the form of two types of cognitive structures: cultural propositions and cultural frames. Cultural propositions are beliefs and values shared among organizational members concerning the organization and its operating environment. Spiro (1984) offered an extensive discussion of cultural propositions. He identified two primary attributes for propositions: (a) they are "developed in the historical experience of the group," and (b) they are "acquired through various processes of social transmission" (p. 324).

Cultural frames are the second type of cognitive material important to ethnoecology in public relations. Cultural frames are significant in that they operate as a fundamental core around which cultural propositions are organized and elaborated into a coherent system of knowledge. The frames are conceptually equivalent to cultural "schemata" which give structure to other cultural propositions which, in turn, operate as the organization's system of beliefs and values. Hutchins (1980) described schema as "a form or template from which an arbitrarily large number of propositions can be constructed" (p. 51). According to Rice (1980). "a schema can be thought of as an abstracted pattern into or onto which information can be organized" (p. 153). Weick's (1979) discussion of schemata in cognitive processes in organizations provides a description of the fundamental importance of these materials to organizational processes. He asserted that a "schema is an abridged, generalized, corrigible organization of experience that serves as an external frame of reference for action and perception. A schema is the belief in the phrase, I'll see it when I believe it. Schemata constrain seeing" (p. 50). Cultural frames give meaning and coherence to all the cultural propositions which collectively operate within the organization. Cultural frames are collected by thematic analysis (Spradley, 1979) that entails identifying recurrent themes from the cultural propositions confirmed at the group level.

A CASE STUDY IN ETHNOECOLOGY

The following illustration of ethnoecological research provides insight into the cultural mediation of organizational adaptive strategy. The illustration is drawn from the author's study of a nonprofit cultural institution (Everett, 1985), and documents the significance of cultural frames to operational policy and adaptive strategy.

The study organization—a large, urban public library—was founded in the early 1900s. During the period of study, the organization employed over 400 people and operated 21 branches throughout the city. In 1985, the library had an annual operating budget of $12 million. Approximately 95% of this budget was provided by allocations from city government. The organization grew rapidly through the 1970s until 1975 when the operating budget provided by the city began to be reduced or held at no increase. The researcher was employed by the organization for a period of 4 years. This employment provided an ideal means of establishing a participant–observer relationship with the organization. Pelto (1970) defined this relationship as permitting the observation of "details of daily life and activity enacted by people who have become relatively indifferent to, and unabashed by, the presence of a 'foreigner'" (p. 91).

Cultural propositions were developed from a series of interviews with "key informants"—the eight members of the senior management committee of the organization. This is the "interpretive system" identified by Daft and Weick (1984) in their work on cognitive processes in organizations. Interview data was discussed and assessed at the organizational level by conducting group interviews (each group had approximately 8 to 10 members from various levels throughout the organization). Informant interviews were conducted over a period of 4 weeks. Group interviews were then held over another 4-week period of time. Thematic analysis of 58 cultural propositions led to identification of nine cultural frames that organized an array of central organizational values and norms.

This discussion focuses on the nature and influence of two interrelated cultural frames that significantly influence operational and strategic directions of the organization. The frames are:

- City funding provides an operational imperative for free and open access for the public.
- This organization serves two types of users: those who need access to general information as well as the sophisticated, high-technology oriented user with specialized information needs.

These two cultural frames organize cultural propositions in the form of norms and values that influence or constitute the strategy that shapes organizational ecology, and, consequently, influences organizational adaptation. Thus, through the use of ethnoecological methods (participant observation, key informant interviews, and document analysis), it is possible to detail some of the cultural constraints to organizational adaptation.

As in any publicly supported organization, the users of the facility and its services are a central component of the organizational environment. The cultural frames link two primary sets of propositions related to organizational ecology. One set of propositions relate values about organizational mission (the concept of free and open access in the first frame) to values about organizational funding (free and open access as an imperative given by public funding in the second frame).

The second set of cultural propositions link values about organizational products and services to organizational perceptions about the nature of the customer public. These perceptions are built from a perceived distinction in the user public between generalized and specialized users. Nowhere is this distinction more evident than in the organization's 5-year strategic plan (FYSP). This document was the culmination of months of planning activities throughout the organization and almost $120,000 in planning-related expenses. The strategic plan is thus a crucial document for identifying organizational perceptions of environmental contingencies and adaptive strategies to meet those contingencies. The dichotomization of users into general and specialized categories is reflected in the long-range plan as the *need* to isolate "basic" services "equally available to all" as well as "specialized" services to "meet the specific needs of particular segments of the population and go beyond the definition of basic Library service" (FYSP, p. 7). The influence of the cultural conception of a dichotomous population of users is very visibly at work in the development of strategic directions for the organization. The strategic plan maps out a strategy based on the assumption that:

> [the city] will have two major expectations of its library system: first that it continue to provide basic library services—circulation of materials . . . second, that it simultaneously provide an increasing amount of information-based [specialized] services. (FYSP, p. 15)

The dichotomization of users into two categories is strongly tied to the first frame by its linking of organizational mission to public access and use. This linking results in a dominant organizational value to serve both the public with generalized information needs as well as the more sophisticated public with highly specialized information needs. The contradiction inherent to such an organizational value is recognized by organizational members who served in several different group meetings that "The library find itself saying we cannot survive with the [organizational] charter of being all things to all people." The operational dilemma given by the interplay of the values driven by the two cultural frames is that high-technology access and delivery systems for specialized users require costs that reduce the levels and efficiency of service to more general users. Thus, although the frames provide a fundamental set of organizational values that link mission, funding, services, and publics, they also provide inherent operational contradictions.

The cultural frames and related propositions described here are part of a larger, ever-changing system of knowledge within the organization that constitutes the organizational culture. This system has been assembled over time and transmitted among organizational members. The portion of the knowledge system represented by the frames has particular pertinence to public relations because of its significance to organizational ecology. The frames are significant to understanding that ecology since they organize an assortment of values that drive understandings of and adaptive strategies toward the organizational environment.

IMPLICATIONS OF ETHNOECOLOGY TO
PUBLIC RELATIONS THEORY AND PRACTICE

I have argued that organizations are best understood as sociocultural systems that develop and change in response to specific environmental backgrounds. This perspective is derived from an assortment of disciplinary perspectives including public relations, organizational communication, organizational sociology and cultural anthropology, and human ecology. The value of convergent theoretical perspectives is anticipated by Orlove (1980). He suggested that as work in culture/environment interaction proceeds it is likely to produce an important benefit:

> materialist and idealist approaches [roughly equivalent to the functionalist and interpretive approaches in organizational theory] . . . are likely to find more common ground through interpretation of culture and ideology as systems which mediate between actors and environments through the construction of behavioral alternatives. (p. 262)

By virtue of the central models of its role and significance, public relation's theorists and practitioners are uniquely situated to explore this cultural mediation of actors and environments in organizational contexts.

I have argued that contemporary models of public relations place its functional role and theoretical significance within an ecological perspective. This perspective holds that public relations contributes to organizational adaptation through the development of mutually beneficial relationships between the organization and its environment. Such relationships are predicated on the capacity for change in both the organization as well as the environment.

Given this ecological perspective on public relations, when one adopts Weick's view of organizations as sociocultural systems, there arise several specific implications for public relations theory and practice. Perhaps the most important implication is the significance of public relations to understanding and formalizing organizational self-concepts. The view of organizations as sociocultural systems places such concepts squarely in the domain of organizational ethnography. Within this ethnographic context, public relations focuses on the relationship of the organizational culture to organizational ecology. I have argued that it is this relationship that is best explored using the theoretical features and methodological tools of ethnoecology. This focus is driven by the view that organizing processes and the environment are in a continuous dynamic interaction. This suggests that an adequate understanding of organizational adaptation necessarily requires an account of interactions of the organizational culture and the organizational environment.

A second important set of implications to the linking of a sociocultural perspective with ecological models of public relations is that ethnoecology provides a means of contextualizing *individual* perceptions held by organizational members within the organizational culture. For practitioners, such a context is essential to adequately manage organizational action toward the environment or develop organizational change programs to meet problems of external adaptation. As soon as organizations are taken to be dominated by or equivalent to cultural systems, then the identification and analysis of individual perceptions necessarily becomes secondary to understanding and describing how these perceptions are linked into *collective* representations and action. I have argued that this linking takes place within the historically based, socially transmitted cultural framework of the organization. This is the analytical and theoretical domain of organizational ethnoecology. Therefore, when public relations defines its organizational role and significance withinan ecological perspective, and given a view of organizations as sociocultural systems, ethnoecology is a fundamental aspect of public relations theory and practice.

REFERENCES

Alland, A. (1967). *Cultural adaptation in cultural evolution: An approach to medical anthropology*. New York: Columbia University Press.

Anderson, J. W. (1973). Ecological anthropology and anthropological ecology. In J. J. Honigmann (Ed.), *Handbook of social and cultural anthropology*. Chicago: Rand McNally.

Ansoff, H. I., & Baker, T. E. (1986). Is corporate culture the answer? *Advances in Strategic Management, 4,* 81–93.

Baker, E. L. (1980, July). Managing organizational culture. *Management Review,* 8–13.

Barley, S. R. (1983). Semiotics and the study of occupational and organizational cultures. *Administrative Science Quarterly, 28,* 393–413.

Campbell, D. T. (1965). Variation and selective retention in socio-cultural evolution. In H. R. Barringer, G. J. Blanksten, & R. W. Mack (Eds.), *Social change in developing areas* (pp. 19–49). Cambridge, MA: Schenkman.

Crable, R. E., & Vibbert, S. L. (1986). *Public relations as communication management*. Edina, MN: Bellwether Press.

Cutlip, S. M., Center, A. H., & Broom, B. M. (1985). *Effective public relations* (6th ed.). Englewood Cliffs, NJ: Prentice-Hall.

Daft, R., & Weick, K. E. (1984). Toward a model of organizations as interpretation systems. *Academy of Management Review, 9,* 284–295.

Deetz, S. (1982). Critical interpretive research in organizational communication. *Western Journal of Speech Communication, 46,* 114–118.

Duncan, R., & Weiss, A. (1979). Organizational learning: Implications for organizational design. *Research in Organizational Behavior, 1,* 75–123.

Ellen, R. (1982). *Environment, subsistence and system*. Cambridge: Cambridge University Press.

Everett, J. L. (1985). *Culture and ecology in the analysis of organizations*. Unpublished doctoral dissertation, University of Colorado, Boulder, CO.

Frake, C. (1961). Cultural ecology and ethnoecology. *American Anthropologist, 64,* 53–59.

Garbarino, M. S. (1977). *Sociocultural theory in anthropology: A short history.* New York: Holt, Rinehart & Winston.

Gioia, D. A. (1986). Symbols, scripts, and sensemaking: Creating meaning in the organizational experience. In H. P. Sims, Jr. & D. A. Gioia (Eds.). *The thinking organization* (pp. 49–75). San Francisco: Jossey-Bass.

Goldschmidt, W. (1977). Should the cultural anthropologist be placed on the endangered species list. *Bucknell Review, 12,* 15–29.

Goodenough, W. (1964). Introduction. In W. Goodenough (Ed.), *Explorations in cultural anthropology* (pp. 1–24). New York: McGraw Hill.

Gregory, K. (1983). Native-view paradigms: Multiple cultures and culture conflicts in organizations. *Administrative Science Quarterly, 28,* 359–376.

Grunig, J. E. (1987). Review of "Strategic organizational communication: Cultures, situations, and Adaptation; Organizational communication; Organizational communication: Traditional themes and new directions"; and "Communication and organizations: An interpretive approach." *Public Relations Review, 13,* 68–70.

Grunig, J. E., & Hunt, T. (1984). *Managing public relations.* New York: Holt, Rinehart.

Hannan, M. T., & Freeman, J. (1977). The population ecology of organizations. *American Journal of Sociology, 82,* 929–964.

Hutchins, E. (1980). *Culture and inference.* Cambridge, MA: Harvard University Press.

Jochim, M. A. (1981). *Strategies for survival: Cultural behavior in an ecological context.* New York: Academic Press.

Kanter, R. M. (1983). *The change master.* New York: Simon & Schuster.

Keesing, R. (1974). Theories of culture. *Annual Review of Anthropology, 3,* 73–97.

Keesing, R. (1976). *Cultural anthropology: A contemporary perspective.* New York: Holt, Rinehart & Winston.

Long, L. W., & Hazelton, V. (1987). Public relations: A theoretical and practical response. *Public Relations Review, 13,* 3–13.

Ortner, S. B. (1984). Theory in anthropology since the sixties. *Comparative Studies in Society and History, 26,* 126–166.

Morey, N. C., & Luthans, F. (1984). An emic perspective and ethnoscience methods for organizational research. *Academy of Management Review, 9,* 27–36.

Orlove, B. S. (1980). Ecological anthropology. *Annual Review of Anthropology, 9,* 235–273.

Pacanowsky, M. E., & O'Donnell-Trujillo, N. (1982). Communication and organizational cultures. *Western Journal of Speech Communication, 46,* 115–130.

Pelto, P. J. (1970). *Anthropological research: The structure of inquiry.* New York: Harper & Row.

Pettigrew, A. M. (1979). On studying organizational Cultures. *Administrative Science Quarterly, 24,* 570–581.

Pfeffer, J. (1981). Management as symbolic action. *Research in Organizational Behavior, 3,* 1–52.

Putnam, L. L. (1983). The interpretive perspective: An alternative to functionalism. In L. L. Putnam & M. E. Packanowsky (Eds.), *Communication and organizations* (pp. 31–54). Beverly Hills, CA: Sage.

Quinn, N., & Holland, D., (1987). Culture and cognition. In D. Holland & N. Quinn (Eds.), *Cultural models in language and thought* (pp. 3–40). Cambridge: Cambridge University Press.

Rice, G. E. (1980). On cultural schemata. *American Ethnologist, 7,* 152–171.

Sahlins, M., & Service, E. (Eds.). (1960). *Evolution and culture.* Ann Arbor, MI: University of Michigan Press.

Sanday, P. R. (1979). The ethnographic paradigms(s). *Administrative Science Quarterly, 24,* 527–538.

Schein, E. (1984). Coming to a new awareness of organizational culture. *Sloan Management Review, 25,* 3–16.

Schein, E. (1985). *Organizational culture and leadership.* San Francisco: Jossey-Bass.

Schwartz, H., & Davis, S. M. (1981). Matching corporate culture and business strategy. *Organizational Dynamics, 10,* 30–37.

Scott, W. R. (1987). *Organizations: Rational, natural and open systems* (2nd ed.). Englewood Cliffs, NJ: Prentice-Hall.

Smircich, L. (1981, June). *The concept of culture and organizational analysis.* Paper presented at the Speech Communication Association/International Communication Association Conference in Interpretive Approaches to Organizational Communication.

Smircich, L. (1983). Concepts of culture and organizational analysis. *Administrative Science Quarterly, 28,* 339–358.

Spiro, M. E. (1984). Some reflections on cultural determinism and relativism with special reference to emotion and reason. In R. A. Shewder & R. L. Levine (Eds.), *Culture theory: Essays on mind, self, and emotion* (pp. 323–346). New York: Cambridge University Press.

Spradley, J. P. (1979). *The ethnographic interview.* New York: Holt, Rinehart & Winston.

Steward, J. H. (1955). *Theory of culture change.* Urbana, IL: University of Illinois.

Steward, J. S. (1977). The concept and method of cultural ecology. In J. C. Steward & R. F. Murphy (Eds.), *Ecology and evolution* (pp. 43–57). Urbana, IL: University of Illinois Press.

Tichy, N. M. (1982, Autumn). Managing change strategically: The technical, political, and cultural keys. *Organizational Dynamics,* 59–80.

Tunstall, W. B. (1983). Cultural transition at AT&T *Sloan Management Review, 24,* 15–26.

Van Maanen, J. (1979). The fact of fiction in organizational ethnography. *Administrative Science Quarterly, 24,* 539–549.

Vayda, A. P., & Rappaport, R. A. (1968). Ecology, cultural and noncultural. In J. A. Cliffton (Ed.), *Introduction of cultural anthropology* (pp. 477–497). Boston: Houghton Mifflin.

Weick, K. E. (1969). *The social psychology of organizing.* Reading, MA: Addison-Wesley.

Weick, K. E. (1979). *The social psychology of organizing* (2nd ed.). New York: Random House.

Author Index

Subject Index